1

Distinguish

Without

(re[

The Ante-Room, London: Heinemann, 1934
(reprinted by Arlen House, Dublin, 1980).

Mary Lavelle, London: Heinemann, 1936
(reprinted by Virago, London, 1984).

Farewell Spain, London: Heinemann, 1937.

Pray for the Wanderer, London: Heinemann, 1938.

The Land of Spices, London: Heinemann, 1941
(reprinted by Virago, London, 1988).

The Last of Summer, London: Heinemann, 1943
(reprinted by Arlen House, Dublin, 1982).

That Lady, London: Heinemann, 1946
(reprinted by Virago, London, 1985).

Introduction to *The Provincial Lady*, 1947.

That Lady: A Romantic Drama, New York: Harper & Brothers,
1949.

Teresa of Avila, London: Max Parrish, 1951.

The Flower of May, London: Heinemann, 1953.

As Music and Splendour, London: Heinemann, 1958, reprinted
Penguin Ireland, 2005.

Dublin and Cork (photographs by R.S. McGowan and text by
Kate O'Brien), London: Spring Books, 1961.

My Ireland, London: Batsford, 1962.

Presentation Parlour, London: Heinemann, 1963, reprinted
Poolbeg, Dublin, 1994.

'Constancy', in Kevin Casey (ed.), *Winter's Tales from Ireland*,
Dublin: Gill & Macmillan, 1972.

Portrait by Mary O'Neill, 1936

KATE O'BRIEN
A Writing Life

EIBHEAR WALSHE

University College, Cork

IRISH ACADEMIC PRESS
DUBLIN • PORTLAND, OR

First published in 2006 by
IRISH ACADEMIC PRESS
44, Northumberland Road, Dublin 4, Ireland

and in the United States of America by
IRISH ACADEMIC PRESS
c/o ISBS, Suite 300, 920 NE 58th Avenue
Portland, Oregon 97213-3644

Website: www.iap.ie

British Library Cataloguing in Publication Data
An entry can be found on request

ISBN 0-7165-3398-7 (cloth)
ISBN 0-7165-3399-5 (paper)

Library of Congress Cataloging-in-Publication Data
An entry can be found on request

Typeset in 11pt on 13pt Sabon
by FiSH Books, Enfield, Middx.
Printed by MPG Books Ltd., Bodmin, Cornwall

FOR DONALD

Contents

List of Illustrations   viii

Acknowledgements   ix

1   Limerick, 'My dear native place': 1897–1916   1

2   Earning a living: 1916–26   21

3   Writing Mellick: 1926–34   41

4   Banned: 1934–41   60

5   Resistance writing: 1941–50   92

6   Lotus Land: 1950–60   113

7   Long distance: 1960–74   132

Notes   150

Bibliography   161

Index   191

List of Illustrations

Frontispiece: Portrait by Mary O'Neill, 1936

1. Kate O'Brien, her mother Katty, centre, and her brother Michael, 1902
2. Boru House, Limerick, Kate's birthplace
3. Kate O'Brien and her brothers Michael, Eric and Gerard, 1903/04
4. Kate with her brother Tom, 1910
5. Laurel Hill, Limerick, in the early twentieth century
6. The chapel in Laurel Hill
7. The dormitories in Laurel Hill
8. Kate with her sisters Nance and May, early 1920s
9. Kate and her husband Gustaaf Renier, 1923/24
10. Stephie, Margaret Stephie Stephens
11. Mary O'Neill 1930s
12. Gustaaf Renier 1920s
13. May O'Brien at Ashurst Bank, 1929
14. Kate, Stephie and Veronica Turleigh, 1928
15. Kate and Stephie, 1929
16. Kate in the late 1920s, at Ashurst
17. Portrait by Lafayette, 1926
18. Kate with Ruth Stephens and Veronica Turleigh
19. Mary O'Neill in Connemara, 1950s
20. Kate with her godson, Austin Hall, early 1940s
21. Kate at work in England, 1940s
22. Three portraits of Kate by Howard Coster, 1950s
23. Kate and Joyce Grenfell, Connemara, 1953
24. Kate in the early 1970s
25. Kate's last home, 'Boughton' in Kent mid-1960s

Acknowledgements

Writing this life of Kate O'Brien has been a rewarding and exciting project for me over the last eight years and not least because of the people I have met in the course of my research; I would like to express my gratitude for all the generous help and support during this time. In particular, I would like to thank Kate O'Brien's family, her sister-in-law, Rosemary, and her nephews, John and Donough O'Brien, and Nance O'Mara's daughter-in-law, Mary O'Mara, and granddaughter, Clare Hannigan, for their assistance with this book and for permission to use family letters. The photographs were given to me by Orlaith Kelly, Mary Steward, Elizabeth Hall, Adrian Cantillon of Laurel Hill School, Limerick, the O'Brien family, Ken Bergin, University of Limerick, Caroline Whitehead and the National Portrait Gallery, London and I thank them all, and Anne Fitzgerald, Paul Sheehan, Teresa Murphy, Elaine Hurley and Jennifer Crowley for all the technical help with them.

Firstly thanks to research leave from the Department of English, University College, Cork and, with the aid of grants from the Arts Faculty Research Fund, UCC and from the then President of UCC, Dr Michael Mortell, I was able to work at various institutions and archives in Ireland, Britain and the US and I want to acknowledge the support of UCC and of these librarians and archivists. The two most important Kate O'Brien archives are at the McCormack Library of Special Collections at Northwestern University Library, Evanston, Illinois, and at the University of Limerick in Ireland and I would like to thank Ken Bergin and John Lancaster in Limerick and R. Russell Maylone and Sigrid Perry at Northwestern. I would like to acknowledge the assistance of an NUI publications grant towards the production of this book.

I would like to thank the following who shared with me their memories of Kate O'Brien: the late Shivawn Lynam, Elizabeth Hall,

Christopher Fitzsimon, the late Professor Lorna Reynolds, the late Paul Smith, Jim and Kate Hughes, the late Dick Walsh, Frank Richardson, Lady Violet Powell, Mrs Jennifer Lyons, Mary Steward, Rosamund Dashwood, Professor Dermot Keogh, the late Gus Martin, the late Sir John Gielgud, Benedict Kiely, Ruth and Caroline Whitehead, Ignatius Demsey, James Liddy and John McGahern. In particular, I want to express my great thanks to Orlaith Kelly for all her help, support and encouragement. Mary O'Neill's nephew, Austin Hall, deserves special mention for all his patience and help with my work.

I was fortunate to be assisted in my search for materials on Kate O'Brien by the late Michael O'Toole, who generously allowed me use his considerable archive of Kate O'Brien bibliographical material and who was always encouraging to me in my work and I regret not being able to show him this finished work. Also of great practical help were Joan Murphy, Dr Tina O'Toole, Elizabeth Kirwan, Tom McCarthy, Gerard Dineen, Dr Ian Flanagan, Mary Leland, Dr Sinead Mooney, Dr Jim Byrne, Nicole O'Connor, Eileen Murphy, Eileen O'Carroll, Dr Judith Priestman, Bill Fagelson, Anne Moynihan, Kay Glynn, Ania Corless, Dr Lance Pettitt, Mari McKay, Carmel Calil, Dr Jane Dunn, Peter Carson, Dr Katherine O'Donnell, Maria Donovan, Barra O' Seaghdha, Catherine Phil McCarthy, Nuala Ni Dhomhnaill, Brian Doherty, Seamus Hosey, Charles Foran, Mary Ladky, Alec Scott, Fergus McGarvey, Professor Michael Cronin, Dr Dolores McKenna, Juliette Pechenart, Professor Roy Foster, Professor Declan Kiberd, Aintzane Legarreta Mentxaka, Louise C. Callaghan, Des Fitzgerald, Elizabeth Murphy, Adrian Cantillon, Peter Gahan, Dr Anne Walsh, Professor Terence O'Reilly, Dr Damien Bracken, Professor Catherine O'Brien. Steve Bartholomew, Dr Jools Gilsen Ellis, Dr Silvia Diaz Fabre, Professor Inez Praga Terente, Ana Gomez, Pilar Vilar, Dr Fiorenzo Fantaccini, Dr Emma Donoghue, Gloria Greenwood, Dr Anne Fogarty, Dr Tony Roche, Dr Peadar Sioniod and Dr Aoife Leahy.

Other sources were located at the Boole Library, UCC, the British Library, London, the National Library of Ireland, the library of Trinity College, Dublin, the English National Portrait Gallery, London, the British Library periodicals at Colindale, London, BBC Archive, Reading, England, RTE sound and stills library, Dublin, *The Spectator* archives, London, *The Irish Times* library, Dublin, the Department of Western Manuscripts, the Bodleian Library, Oxford, the University of Bristol Library, the University of Reading Library, the Harry Ransom Humanities Research Center, University of Texas at Austin, Random

House UK, Penguin UK.

On a personal level, I want to thank all my friends in the Department of English, University College, Cork for being so supportive all through this project, particularly Mary Breen and Anne Fitzgerald and also I owe so much to dear friends like Michael Dillon, Pat Ruane, Garry Grimes, John Calnan, John Bergin, Stephen Vaughan, Len Hayes, Walt Kilroy and Dominic Whyte. I would like to acknowledge my family, especially my parents, John and Celine Walshe, for all the loyal support and a special thanks to my brother, Sheamus Walshe, my sisters, Ria White and Oonagh Cooney, and my aunts, Jacinta Morrissey and Miriam Keegan, and to their families. In Madrid Sheila Quinn was a great friend and a guide to Spain and I want to thank her and Enrique for all their hospitality. Barry Stokes in New York was a support and a dear friend and, in Dublin, Ciaran Wallace saw me through every stage of this process with his habitual good sense, clear thinking and unending kindness and consideration. I am very lucky in our friendship.

This manuscript benefited from several close readings and I would like to thank Roz Cowman for her insights into Kate O'Brien's writing, for editing each draft, for all the books that she lent me and for her friendship, for which I am most grateful. John McGahern was kind enough to read a draft of the book and to give me a detailed and most welcome series of recommendations and the biography has benefited hugely from his comments. Jonathan Williams also gave the manuscript a great deal of care and attention and I thank him for his clear-sightedness. Finally I was lucky enough to have two wonderful readers at every stage of composition, Dr Carmel Quinlan, whose scholarship and wit made our work together such a pleasure; her support and dear friendship is invaluable to me. I would like to dedicate this book to Donald O'Driscoll, with my love and gratitude for his companionship all this time.

I would like to acknowledge all the excellent work and support of Cáit ní Cheallacháin and the Kate O'Brien Weekend, Limerick. I also wish to say thank you for the publication grant from the Arts Faculty, University College, Cork and to Dr Attracta Halpin of the National University of Ireland. I would like to thank Peter Feeney and John Glennon of RTE and acknowledge the kind permission of RTE Libraries and archives to quote from Kate O'Brien's broadcasts. I would like also to thank Hugh McFadden, literary executor of the John Jordan estate, Georgia Glover, of David Higham, literary agents of the Kate O'Brien estate, Emma Butterfield of the National Portrait Gallery and Gerard Lyne and the Board of the National Library of Ireland for all other permissions. I would also like to thank Winifrid Power and Lisa Hyde for all the excellent help.

Eibhear Walshe
Cork, January 2006

Photographic Credits

Limerick, 'My dear native place': 1897–1916

One of the most popular English films of the 1940s was David Lean's *Brief Encounter*, released in 1946, with a script by Noel Coward. The heroine, Laura (Celia Johnson), a conventional middle-class wife and mother, is tempted to have a love affair, which threatens her happy marriage. At one point in the film, Laura is shown making her way to Boots' Lending Library, because, as she tells us, 'the librarian promised to save me the latest Kate O'Brien'. Such was Kate O'Brien's popularity at the time that her novels could be referred to with familiarity in the mainstream cinema. Nor is this reference to Kate O'Brien accidental. Noel Coward knew her professionally and had been involved in producing a stage version of one of her novels.

Kate O'Brien was, in her own time, a widely read, accessible novelist in Britain, Ireland and the United States. She wrote for such respected literary journals as *The Spectator*, *The Bell* and *The Irish Times*; she broadcast regularly for the BBC and adapted her best-selling novels for the stage in London and on Broadway. One novel, *That Lady*, even became a Hollywood movie. She was a regular Book Club and Book Society choice, and her appearance at the 'Tea with an Author' afternoon at Harrods in London is proof of her fame with the general reading public.

In the course of a hugely productive writing life, Kate O'Brien travelled, lectured, wrote literary essays, reviewed novels and was broadcast on the radio and on television. In her personal life, she maintained a wide circle of friends, a number of life-long relationships with other women and close contact with her family. Living most of her adult life in England, she moved about constantly, with many changes of address, little financial security and erratic earnings from freelance journalism and fluctuating royalties from her novels. She worked hard and made money, but spent most of it on continuous travel and on maintaining high standards of hospitality. In the last fourteen years of her life, she was poor, her books were mostly out of print and she was living in a small house in Kent, paid for by her sister.

In her fiction, Kate O'Brien was a subversive. She created novels that were deceptively traditional in form but radical in content – each novel a Trojan horse smuggling in forbidden topics, such as adultery, lesbianism and venereal disease through the medium of her civilised, graceful narratives. When her novel *Mary Lavelle* was banned in 1936, she wrote to her brother-in-law, Stephen O'Mara, defending her aesthetic position: 'I had undertaken the examination of violent feeling, violent courage, violent youth, and used a violent music.'[1] As a result of this 'violent music', her books were banned in her native Ireland, mainly because of her representation of lesbian and gay characters. She invented a literary identity for her own Irish bourgeois class and a successfully realised fictive independence and viability for her young Irish female protagonists. There was a melancholy within Kate O'Brien's literary sensibility, the melancholy of the lapsed Catholic, at odds with the sexual codes of her religious education, yet still enraptured with the beauty of its ceremonies and its liturgy. Proud of her Irish middle-class origins, she was, nevertheless, antagonistic to the insular moral codes and the censorship laws of the newly emergent Irish state. Out of these contradictions her fictions were created.

In *My Ireland*, dedicated to her 'dear native place', Kate O'Brien wrote: 'It was there indeed that I learnt the world and I know that wherever I am, it is still from Limerick that I look out and make my surmises.'

Kate O'Brien was born Kathleen Mary Louie O'Brien on 3 December 1897 in Limerick, the principal city in the south-west of Ireland. She was the seventh child and fourth daughter of Tom O'Brien and his wife Katty, born Katherine Thornhill. Kate O'Brien was called Katty in early childhood, then Kitty by her siblings, her schoolfriend and her husband, but, when it came to the publication of her first piece of journalism, she reverted to her baptismal name of Kathleen. However, with the success of her first play, she became 'Kate' – the name Kitty O'Brien being, in Britain, a little too stage Irish. She once remarked that, in recollecting her past, she could see herself very clearly as a child but not at all clearly as a young adult. In her memories of the past, it is clear that Limerick shaped her literary imagination profoundly. Indeed, her novels can be read as elegies for the lost world of her comfortable Limerick bourgeois home. The most influential elements from this childhood – her home, Boru House, the early loss of her mother, the overbearing presence of her beloved father and the nuns at her Limerick convent school, Laurel Hill – all find their way into the fiction. As she once wrote in an essay called 'Memories of a Catholic education': 'In childhood, we assemble ourselves. At the childhood, we are the armoured or the wounded or the enlightened.'[2] Kate saw herself as both armoured and enlightened by her Limerick influences. It is clear, however, that Limerick also wounded her.

Her father, Thomas Frazer O'Brien, born in 1853, was the youngest son of a dispossessed tenant farmer from Kilfinane, a village in County Limerick. Her paternal grandfather, also called Thomas O'Brien, was evicted in 1852 and made his way into Limerick city, where he began trading as a horse dealer. At the time of Kate's birth, the O'Briens were making a great deal of money supplying horses to the army and to the gentry at home and abroad. Ireland was still part of the British empire and participating in the imperial economy. In her memories of Limerick, her father Tom was the key figure, a source of pride and authority for her adult self, and that pride was partly owing to the fact that his wealth was recent and hard won. In a television interview, she described her father as 'a wealthy man, we had a bourgeois and sheltered and happy childhood'[3] and she used the story of the O'Brien family's rise from eviction to wealth as the basis for her first novel, *Without My Cloak*.

Her grandfather and father made money from horses, educated their sons with the Jesuits in Limerick and moved class from evicted tenant farmer to solid bourgeoisie. As Kate recounted in *Presentation Parlour*:

> This Tom O'Brien was, by Kilfinane standards; indeed by any, a man of the world. He was, in fact, the child of the post-Famine evictions, for his father had been turned out of his small holdings near by, in Bruree country – about 1850 and had made his way with wife, young daughter and two sons, and with a few household remnants on an ass-cart, as far as Limerick. Then, middle-aged and ill, he had sought about for a new way of living. He began to buy and sell horses.... During the first or second year of this new beginning his last child – twenty years younger than his only daughter – was born. By the time this boy Tom was leaving school, his father was an admired citizen of Limerick, and was building himself a brick villa to flank the paddock and stables where he had based his business of blood-stock breeding.

The career of this founding patriarch, her O'Brien grandfather, became a key element for Kate O'Brien's self-invention and for her sense of self. Given that many Irish middle-class families came into prosperity late in the nineteenth century, she was at pains to stress the innate nobility and civility of her own class and her people. In her novels, her Irish bourgeois families – the Considines, Mulqueens and Lavelles – are natural aristocrats, transcending peasant origins effortlessly in the space of one generation. Thus, her grandfather's eviction even became a matter of distinction. She records her paternal aunt, Aunt Hickey, saying: 'If ever there was a fortunate eviction, wasn't it my father's?'

Kate's father, Tom, inherited a flair for business, or so she believed: 'He was a horse dealer and horse breeder, they had a very large trade with Tattersalls and Tilling',[4] and this made him a good match. In November 1886, at the age of thirty-three, Tom O'Brien married twenty-two-year-old Katty Thornhill from Kilfinane, the east Limerick village where the O'Briens had lost their farm. Kate's mother was the eldest daughter of Patrick Thornhill, a prosperous shopkeeper and farmer and an old friend of the O'Brien family. Between 1887 and 1902, Tom O'Brien and Katty Thornhill had ten children, three daughters older than Kate, May, Clare and Nance, and six sons, Jack, Michael – who died as an infant, Tom, Eric, another Michael and Gerard. In *Presentation Parlour*, Kate was equally proud of her Thornhill ancestors:

> In the 1650s, a soldier of Cromwell's army named Thornhill, having fought at the sieges of Limerick and Clonmel, was garrisoned awhile at Kilmallock, and at the allocation of lands to the conquered decided to take his share and settle down on the western face of Ardpatrick. He married a girl of the neighbourhood and almost certainly, if to his surprise, became a papist. Or if he did not, his children, without doubt, were papists to a man. And three hundred years later to the very decade, my grandfather, Patrick Thornhill, then only a boy, was having to fight with guile and energy – in common with uncles, brothers, cousins – to hold on to the same lands which the original conquerer had given to their Plantation ancestor.

She endows her Thornhill forefathers (she does concentrate on her male ancestors) with the same spirit of hardiness and independence as her O'Brien forefather:

But in spirit and character, they were never serfs at all... throughout the crazily difficult and tragic nineteenth century, the Thornhills kept on farming and raising good cattle stock with intelligence and success; so that they were able to hold to their lands, meet the fantastic extortions of agent and absentee landlord, keep the trust and respect of their own class and kind, and put money in the bank. To have done all those things at one and the same time was to be at once spirited, quick-witted and honourable.

How did she know this? Her Thornhill mother and grandfather had both died when Kate was still a young child. She must have learnt of this proud myth of ancestry from her mother's younger sisters, Mary and Fan Thornhill, nuns at the Presentation Convent in Limerick city. Male forefathers dominate her celebration of her family's origins, but, on the touchy subject of inherited good looks, she does make one mention of a female ancestor, her maternal grandmother. Surviving photographs of her siblings attest to the outstanding good looks of the O'Brien family. In particular, her eldest sister May was tall and elegantly beautiful, in the style of the celebrated beauty Hazel Lavery, the wife of the painter Sir John Lavery whose portrait graced the Irish pound note for many years. Kate's unhappy sense of being the least beautiful in a good-looking family is evident in her description of a fault-line in female heredity:

> Grandfather Thornhill married – I surmise about 1862 – a handsome young women, well endowed, from Cork....I say she brought good looks, but they were of a Roman Emperor kind that blunted here and there in descent the sharp clean-edged beauty of Grandfather's line; and I think that certain descendants, Aunt Fan for one and I for another, can blame Grandmother Thornhill in some measure for our decline from good looks into a too heavy handsomeness.

This frankness about her own loss of good looks in middle age has a bleak sense of distaste common to all her references to her appearance. As a result of this sense of distaste, beauty fascinated her as a novelist and led to her insistence on physical distinction as a counterpart to moral fineness and exactitude. Her central characters are, without exception, physically perfect. As Ana de Mendoza expresses it in *That Lady*: 'Beauty, good aspect, in all things and people moved her very quickly: she was attracted or repelled decisively by physical attributes.'

Parallel with her celebration of her O'Brien and Thornhill heritage was Kate's pride in her native Limerick, a vital element within her self-construction as a writer. Described by Irish writer Frank O'Connor as 'architecturally one of the pleasantest spots in Ireland',[5] Limerick had a confident and wealthy Catholic middle class at the time of Kate's birth and her family had found a place within the culture of that bourgeois society. Boru House, the O'Brien family home, stood on Mulgrave Street, a main road on the outskirts of the city, and here Kate passed her childhood. The house had been built in 1880 by her grandfather, the evicted tenant farmer turned horse dealer. Its name reflected a pretentious insistence by the older Tom O'Brien that the family could claim direct descent from Brian Boru, a high king of Ireland and the hero of the Battle of Clontarf. All her references to Boru House are unflattering. In a fragment of autobiography called 'Recollections of childhood',[6] she describes it as 'an ugly-looking, big brick house'. However, she was clear about its material comforts:

> We lived just outside Limerick in a house built in our own grandfather's time, that is, in the very worst time of house building. It was a house of very ugly exterior, but inside it was roomy and comfortable and very well run with its shining mahogany and good fires and bright lights.[7]

Her grandfather chose to build Boru House on unfashionable Mulgrave Street because of its proximity to the Limerick horse fair and because of the extensive stables at the back of the house. Nevertheless, it was not a suitable house for a family of young children, and it never features in any of her novels. 'We had almost no garden but we had a large airy paddock. Father had a stud farm about two miles out in the country from our house. There was a big kitchen garden there with fruit trees and strawberry beds and a summerhouse. I remember summer days of gluttony in that garden.'[8] Irish historian John Logan points out, 'Boru House was one of only three houses of its size on Mulgrave Street and many of the neighbouring families were either working class or artisan class.'[9]

Extremes of poverty and of middle-class wealth stood side by side on Mulgrave Street. Significantly, Boru House was not situated in one of the fashionable bourgeois suburbs of Limerick and so the O'Brien children grew up economically distant from their immediate neighbours and geographically distant from their social peers. This left Kate unsure and defensive in the social and domestic details of her Irish middle-class narratives. As Irish literary critic Declan Kiberd has noted: 'The alert reader may register a suspicion that the author herself has some difficulty in rendering the details of upper-class Catholic life.'[10]

The single most important event of Kate O'Brien's childhood was the death of her mother, aged thirty-nine, from cancer in February 1903, when Kate was five. Not surprisingly, she had few surviving memories of her mother:

> I only remember her in flashes, vivid flashes, she was very beautiful, very gay, always laughing, I was rather suspicious of that laughing. I was a cautious, solemn sort of child. What was the joke Mother had about me? She was to have a short and exacting sort of life, with deep shadows in it here and there and passages of anxious disappointment, for she had married a gay and generous and an adoring man but not an easy or a disciplined man.[11]

Katty O'Brien's real importance in her youngest daughter's life was her absence. Both *The Ante-Room* and *The Flower of May* centre on the prolonged deaths of mothers and many of her other characters – Mary Lavelle, Helen Archer, Angele Kernahan and Claire Halvey – are motherless from an early age.

This early loss also meant that Kate came to see loneliness as essential, and even nurturing, for the creative process. As she put it:

> I lived this way or that but mainly alone. But my choice has always been to live alone. For a writer, it is almost essential to be alone. I can't imagine being badgered around by someone else who sort of half owned you when you are trying to write a novel.[12]

In a fragment of autobiography, she argued that the creative artist needed isolation:

> I have lived alone always – even when closely associated with other lives. I have always been split – as I imagine many intelligent people know themselves to be. Loneliness is a condition of human life, which one begins to understand, or rather to confront than understand, in adolescence.[13]

When asked in an interview in 1966 if she had had a hard upbringing, she was adamant: 'Oh, no. There was a certain amount of sadness in our household because my father, who was a gay, kind man, was left a widower when we were all very young and he became very sad because of that. But we were well looked after.'[14] On a practical level, her mother's early death meant that Kate was sent to boarding-school at the age of five. It also meant that her father, who was fifty at the time of his wife's death, was now her only source of parental affection and authority. In truth, many of her childhood memories centre on moments of anxiety created by her father's desire to control his children's lives. In Kate's own words, Tom O'Brien was short, stocky and Roman headed, with thick, close-cut dark hair, bright blue eyes and a clipped moustache.

A school friend at Laurel Hill convent school remembered him as a fond father to his four daughters, who was permitted to call every Sunday afternoon and bring them home to Boru House, a privilege accorded to few boarders. It was only at Christmas that he had complete control over his children, and Kate's memories of these festive occasions reflect an atmosphere of gaiety with some underlying tension. 'Useless to hope for a private message from anyone at Christmas. Father, in sheer pleasure, had to see and consider all that came into his house.'[15] Again and again in her memoirs, she returns to these incidents of tension. Each time, she attempts to offset the potential cruelty of the memory by evoking the comfort and grace of her middle-class home and her father's essential good nature. Writing for *The Spectator*, she recalls it as 'a day on which we seemed to be under field orders, on the very brink of battle . . . his method of waking you when he was feeling gay was an assault. On each bedroom door in the house, he played with his bare knuckles the longest, most accurate fortissimo that it was possible to imagine, let alone listen to.'[16]

In *Presentation Parlour*, these recollections appear again, with the same underlying atmosphere:

> Father would have no going to Midnight Mass. The riff-raff of the town were loose at that hour, he said, and he would not have his children meet it. And in the churches crowded by the poor and the dirty we might get fleas, or worse afflictions. Let him not be judged un-Christian for this – for he was not. He was only a clean-habited and affectionate man who wanted to keep us in good health and as long as possible unaware of violence and uproar in life.

However, the O'Brien children learnt all too soon about uproar, as this account of Christmas morning in *Presentation Parlour* shows: 'So, breakfast over, we younger ones were not given half enough time to brood over our presents; we had to be upstairs, changed into our newest and best and setting off hours too early.... This was Father's idea – and over such a matter this kindest of men was a tyrannical fusspot.'

Only once, in 'Recollections of childhood', does Kate permit herself some torturous speculation on her father's difficult emotional nature.

> I honestly don't think that it's an exaggeration to say that it would be difficult to find anywhere a more gracious or sensitive man than he was, or a more truly kind-hearted. Looking back now, I see that his temperament was light and quick and vulnerable and that he suffered more than most people from the inescapable grief of growing old. He was in fact the wrong man for loneliness, which my mother's death imposed on him – but his children could not see that, naturally, and we were often baffled and exasperated by the long periods of depression, not to say melancholia that overtook him. But his rallies from these moods were amazing and his gaiety when he was gay had naturalness, a generosity, which I think it takes some form of knowledge of life and character to appreciate.[17]

Kate never outgrew her childhood idealisation of her father, believing him to be unsuited to loneliness, as if any man or woman suited loss. Having lost one parent so early, she felt unable to question the memory of the one who remained. It was only in her fiction that she depicted cruel or deficient fatherhood. Her fictive fathers are either ineffectual, like Joey Morrow or Danny Mulqueen, or selfish and destructive, like Dr Lavelle or Harry Murphy. The only idealised father figure is Henry Archer, but he is English, intellectual and homosexual.

Apart from her father, Kate's sisters were her closest companions throughout her childhood and this closeness continued into adult life. The youngest of the four O'Brien girls – she was only five when her mother died – Kate was the focus of their care and attention all her life. They were some distance in age from her: May was ten years older, Clare five and Nance four, and Kate was herself the only girl in the middle of four brothers, Michael, Tom, Eric and Gerry.

Her eldest sister, May, born in 1887, became a surrogate mother

to Kate, taking over the running of the O'Brien household in 1903
when she was herself only fifteen. May O'Brien continued to
housekeep at Boru House until her father's death in 1916 and,
thereafter, whether living in London or Dublin, she was very much
part of Kate's adult life, as photographs and letters attest. May
provided Kate with a great deal of maternal affection, but at a cost.
In letters to May, Kate was careful to present herself as pious and
conservative. As her friend Lorna Reynolds wrote of Kate: 'I
remember when I first met her, famous, long removed from Ireland,
intellectually independent.... How surprised I was to find her still
so emotionally involved with her family, so anxious not to upset or
disturb her sisters, how determined, especially, to do them all credit
in Limerick.'[18]

Nance and Clare also remained close to Kate in her adult life and
Clare's London flat and Nance's prosperous Limerick home, Strand
House, were places of refuge for her during her endlessly vagrant
life. Nance's husband, Stephen O'Mara, a successful Limerick
businessman and politician, was also a firm friend and an avid
reader of her novels. His respectful but trenchant criticisms of her
writing sparked off many lively debates between the two. Kate's
brothers, although not as close to her as her sisters, nevertheless
played a part in her life and are glimpsed here and there in her
autobiographical writings. Her eldest brother Jack, remembered by
a school friend of Kate's as very handsome,[19] took over the family
firm after their father's death. The business itself failed two years
after Tom O'Brien's death and Jack moved to England and settled in
Shropshire. He was one of the few members of the family to marry
and have children and he lived on to survive most of his siblings,
including Kate. Tom, the brother closest to Kate in age, was a
beloved figure in her memoirs of childhood, sharing her passion for
reading and for music; she characterised him as 'strong and
original'.[20] Tom's death from fever in 1918, at the age of twenty-two
and far away in India, was a profound and painful blow to Kate.
Equally painful was the death, two years later, of her next youngest
brother, Eric, who also died in India. These deaths came at a time of
disruption for Kate, following the death of her father in 1916 and
the loss of Boru House in 1918, and her memoirs reflect this. Music
enabled her to recall her lost brothers with unalloyed sweetness:
'Eric, who was to die riding his horse to victory when he was twenty,
was always in love in those days that I remember... he sang as the

birds sing, as the happy boy that he was and always in tune. And he was always in love. So he died young.'[21]

Her next brother, Michael, moved to New York, where he worked on the stock exchange and was helpful to Kate when investing money from the Broadway production of *That Lady*, but he appears in few of her family writings. The youngest brother, Gerry, remained in Limerick, where he became a farmer and married and had children (Tom and Katty O'Brien had very few grandchildren). He and his wife Rosemary and their sons John and Donough remained close to Kate and her O'Brien nephews eventually became her literary heirs.

With this childhood in Boru House in mind, what does her fiction reveal about her conception of family life? From her first novel, *Without My Cloak* (1931), her Irish protagonists move away from family, from Ireland and from bourgeois conformity towards Europe, independence and sexual autonomy. Her final novel, *As Music and Splendour* (1958), imagines, among other things, a successful escape from constricting family ties for her characters. This leads on to the related question – how did her upbringing influence her depiction of emotional intimacy and of the erotic? In novels like *The Ante-Room* and *As Music and Splendour*, music is the primary mode of communication, the only means by which love or the erotic can be articulated. Indeed, for a novelist who was banned for obscenity, she rarely depicts the sexual in her fictions and the few episodes of sexual love are disruptive.

An unpublished short story called 'Manna', written in 1962 and sold with Kate O'Brien's literary archive in 1971, is highly revealing in this regard. Its setting is a fictive village called Kilhooly, where the six-year-old protagonist, Josie, is visiting her Aunt Maggie. (This is clearly drawn from Kate's own childhood visits to her Aunt Annie, her mother's youngest sister, who was married and living in Fermoy in County Cork.) Central to the story is Josie's fascination with a nearby medical hall or chemist shop: 'Mr Bandon's yard was really her cousin's favourite place in Davis Street but it wasn't Josie's. The medical hall was hers. That certainly smelt more interesting than any other place anywhere.'[22] (In *My Ireland*, an autobiographical reference to her Aunt Annie echoes this sensory recollection: 'How peculiar, how delicate the smell of a medical hall. There was one in Fermoy, I remember.') 'Manna' is the story of a sexual attack upon Josie by the young man who works in the medical hall, a young man whose only characteristic is his physical beauty: 'Josie turned attentively. She admired this young man, who almost never spoke to her. He had gold curly hair and a lovely smile . . . she did consider his beauty remarkable.'[23] As the story unfolds, Josie's innocent delight in the young man's good looks gradually disappears as his behaviour towards her becomes more and more unpleasantly sexual: 'She thought he was unhappy; he seemed to be pounding against her somehow and in the sunlight she thought that his beautiful face was even more beautiful than it had seemed upstairs.'[24] 'Manna' ends with the intervention of another adult and the rescue of the child Josie, who is left with a shocked realisation of the sexual nature of the attack. This late, unpublished short story is a disturbing and untypical piece of writing, with an intense physicality and sexual clarity that is absent from the rest of her work. It has the authenticity of a remembered incident.

Boru House was the primary place of emotional enlightenment for Kate, but her school, Laurel Hill, was the crucial source for her intellectual and aesthetic formation. The O'Brien children all went to school in Limerick, the boys to the Jesuit Crescent College and the girls to Laurel Hill, which was run by the Society of the Faithful Companions of Jesus. Kate was a pupil there from 1903 until 1916. Her older sisters, May, Clare and Nance, were already enrolled as boarding students at Laurel Hill in February 1903 when Katty O'Brien died and so it was decided that Kate would join her sisters there at the unusually early age of five.

Founded in 1820 by a pious French noblewoman, Victoire d'Houet, the Society of the Faithful Companions of Jesus had set up a convent in Limerick in 1844. By 1903, it was well established as the favoured school for daughters of the local merchant and professional classes.[25] Physically, the convent of Laurel Hill, which was less than a mile from Boru House, is a large, imposing building with high enclosing walls and a bleak, intimidating aspect. (It still operates very successfully as a school in Limerick.) In Kate O'Brien's time, there were fewer than forty students but over twenty nuns and a supporting domestic staff of twenty-three lay nuns, so Laurel Hill had more staff than pupils.[26] It was known locally as the 'French Convent' and, in her novels, Kate is at pains to stress the ease with which the Mellick (her fictional name for Limerick, borrowed from the name of a nearby village) school used French as an everyday language, but in fact there was only one French-born nun working there during these years before World War I.

In remembering her past, Kate gave approval of her father's decision: 'I had, as it happens, a great deal of school. Father wisely decided to send me to boarding school with my sisters before I was six, as Mother was dead, rather than leaving me at home in the nursery with little baby brothers and an old nurse.'[27] However, she never acknowledged in any of her autobiographical writings any sense of hurt at this loss of home and the loss of her surviving parent, coming so soon after her mother's death. In her fiction, a glimpse of this experience finds its way into *The Land of Spices*. Five-year-old Anna Murphy, terrified and bewildered on her first day as a boarder in a convent school, is observed with compassion by the Reverend Mother: 'It was pathetic to be forced, when so small, to become one of a large, alien body, merely because parents had neither the sense nor the sensitiveness to keep a child at home.'

The nuns of Laurel Hill gave Kate O'Brien the only secure version of adult female authority in her childhood. It was not surprising to find that she carried a veneration of the world of the convent into her adult life and into her fiction. Most of the important adult women in her childhood were nuns, her mother's sisters in the Limerick Presentation Convent and her teachers at Laurel Hill. Despite being the youngest pupil there by several years, she accommodated herself to the rules and regulations of the school and it is clear from her fiction that she came to relish convent life. *The Land of Spices* gives us loving detail about the rituals and ceremonies of the school, the use of French during meals, the prayers and ceremonies, the Child of Mary League, the roll-calls of Sunday marks for the week's schoolwork, all ceremonies taken from her time at Laurel Hill. The novel itself takes its major structural events from the yearly events in the convent school year – Foundress Day, Chaplain's Concert – and something of the child's sense of awe lingers.

Kate loved her academic work at Laurel Hill, calling it a 'happy school time'[28] and describing herself as a 'conscientious and rather industrious child. I loved my lessons.'[29] She read voraciously, particularly in French and Irish and poetry, and was a precocious student. Her classmates remembered her as serious, even competitive, and she won several school prizes, including volumes of poetry by Joseph Mary Plunkett and Elizabeth Barrett Browning, which she treasured through all the later upheavals of her life and which were still in her library at her death.

When remembering Laurel Hill in old age, Kate wrote: 'I see myself rather clearly at this time'[30] and, thus, as a writer, her school was central to the formulation of her sensibility. As a novelist, her central concern was with the search for independence by her young Irish women protagonists. Usefully, the nuns at Laurel Hill provided her with an early prototype of an autonomous female vocation, a sustainable life outside family and outside marriage. As a result, she idealised these stern authoritarian woman for their unruffled, poised perfection. Consider this description from *Presentation Parlour*:

> One marvels at the accent of their unmade up faces, tightly bound in linen; at hands which seem massaged and manicured yet most certainly are not; above all the wonder is for the expanse of virgin cloth, never limp, never stained – even as they dash and splash through our common life.

Despite her adult loss of religious faith, Kate O'Brien remained profoundly affected by the nuns of her schooling and also by the Catholic rituals of her childhood in the convent. Her novels are pervaded with a Catholic consciousness and turn on moments of crisis and moral conflict. In Declan Kiberd's view: 'O'Brien, for all her agnosticism, wrote with tender respect for those audacious enough to place their belief in the central mystery of Catholicism.'[31]

Kate clearly loved her schooldays, but she does begin to register some dissatisfaction at her own character, a life-long habit of self-criticism. Her alter ego, Anna Murphy, the protagonist of *The Land of Spices*, shares this quality: 'But the trouble really lay in her continued detachment from the personalities of school. She was genuinely more interested in books, and her own thoughts than in people.' Writing in later life, Kate invariably described herself as solemn or as 'a cross little child' and, in the childhood photographs, her expression is always grave, watchful and even mistrustful. This measured, measuring gaze continued into adult life and her photographs often exhibit this quality of keen appraisal in the deep-set, shrewd eyes. As an adult, she had an appealing, lively sociability but, as a child and adolescent, she seemed quiet and watchful. Distance was taught to her early in childhood and mainly by the nuns of Laurel Hill. In *The Land of Spices*, Anna Murphy is given this precise quality: 'Her tastes were literary and linguistic rather than scientific; she appeared to admire distinction in personalities and achievements – yet for a growing child she gave the impression of detachment which was not very endearing.' This quality of detachment, allied to her sense of personal unease, shaped her as a writer, impelling her towards fictive worlds where the self could be evaded and then refashioned.

The nuns at Laurel Hill were educating the young women of Limerick at a time of nationalist and religious conflict, and some of these conflicts find resonance in her fiction. Limerick was known at this time as a place of deep Catholic fervour, even for a southern Irish city at the beginning of the twentieth century, and Laurel Hill was a bastion of orthodox belief and practice. Sometimes, religious fervour could turn into persecution. As Frank O'Connor described Limerick at this time: 'The religious orders run confraternities which march to church behind their bands, and exclusion from one of these confraternities is almost equivalent to social extinction.... Jews, evangelists and strolling players have all at various times suffered from these outbursts of demented religion.'[32]

When Kate was six, one of the worst episodes of 'demented religion' occurred with the so-called Limerick Pogrom of 1904. A redemptorist priest, Father Creagh, called for a boycott on all Jewish businesses in Limerick, and this led to individual acts of random violence, a falling-off in business and then the forced emigration of eight Jewish families.[33] This ugly episode was symptomatic of a city where, as Frank O'Connor wrote, 'In most Irish cities, nationalism has always come first, religion second; but in Limerick where the two fanaticisms are almost equally balanced, they produce conflict on a very considerable scale.'[34] The nuns at Laurel Hill, the 'French' convent, had to tread a very careful line in relation to this religious extremism and also in relation to the emergent cultural nationalism of Ireland in the early twentieth century. Ireland was still part of the British empire and the nuns were educating the daughters of the Limerick bourgeoisie to be European and Catholic ladies rather than young Irish women. The guiding cultural influence for Laurel Hill at this time was the Reverend Mother, an English woman called Anne Blackett. Blackett, who was from Yorkshire, set the tone with a sense of allegiance towards the British empire, and Laurel Hill looked to London politically. During World War I, the girls at the school knitted mufflers for the Munster Fusiliers and this patriotism led a Dublin newspaper, *The Leader*, to complain that the school was educating Irish ladies to be the wives of bank managers and British colonial governors. In *The Land of Spices*, Reverend Mother Helen Archer, a version of Anne Blackett, muses:

> ...it could not so glibly be said now that Sainte Famille trained its girls to be the wives of British majors and colonial governors; for at least there was a choice of cultures offered to them....She still held out as strongly as ever for the European and polite tradition initiated one hundred and fifty years ago at Rouen – indifferent alike to the future needs of Gaelic Leaguer or British officer.

Anne Blackett was an important figure from Kate's time at Laurel Hill, perhaps the most important, described by her as 'a controlled and just eccentric governor, a tiny and disconcerting pillar of control and reserve'.[35] Fifty years after she had left Laurel Hill, Kate wrote an account of her schooldays called 'Memories of a Catholic Education'. Her adulation for Anne Blackett remained undiminished.

> Reverend Mother was not just English; she was late Victorian upper class English almost one might have said (wrongly) to the point of caricature. Unfortunately in appearance she suggested Queen Victoria ...this little nun had a very hard role in the Ireland of my childhood. She was cold, inexpressive and non-intellectual...she was, from an Irish point of view, unprepossessing.[36]

Talking of the other nuns teaching in the school, Kate makes the extraordinary claim that: 'no one of them, mature and witty women, understood her [Blackett] and admired her as I did, a mere child'.[37] Kate's birthday was also Anne Blackett's feast day and this coincidence delighted Kate.[38] In *The Land of Spices*, Helen Archer is Anne Blackett transformed, with one telling difference: Helen is as beautiful as Anne was undistinguished.

In spite of Anne Blackett's strong imperialist interests, Irish language and Irish literature were taught at Laurel Hill in the early years of the twentieth century, reflecting a changing cultural and political climate in the country. The second half of the nineteenth century saw that artistic renaissance called the Celtic Revival, and a renewed interest in Irish writing was paralleled by a renewed interest in the Irish language. The Gaelic League was set up to provide a linguistic revival to complement the anticipated political independence and, by the time Kate came to Laurel Hill, the Irish middle class were educating their children in the Irish language. This jarred somewhat with the European system of education at the French convent, and her fiction records this clash of ideologies. The Reverend Mother in *The Land of Spices* tells the young nationalist chaplain Father Conroy: 'Our nuns are not a nation and our business is not national matters.'

This business of being a European Catholic, in the manner taught at Laurel Hill, proved a defence against the colonial stigma of 'mere Irishness' during Kate's working life in Britain and was a key element in her elevation of the newly emergent Irish bourgeois. In her own life, she had direct personal experience of crucial episodes in the struggle for Irish independence: the aftermath of the 1916 Rising, the War of Independence and the Civil War and she knew some of the political leaders of the new Irish state. None of this experience would find its way into her fictions. Her few episodes dealing directly with debates about cultural nationalism are handled with disapproval and distance. Yet, as a convent schoolgirl, she was an enthusiastic scholar of the Irish language:

> When I was at school, Irish was an obligatory subject only for university matriculation. The standard of Irish required was ludicrously low... there was a nun in my school, Mother Lelia, a niece of Sir Samuel Ferguson. Somewhere around 1910 or so, I think, she became completely bitten by the Irish Revival and in no time at all she had a few of us kids as Gaelic enthusiasts.[39]

Her interest in Irish aroused her competitive instinct:

> Now at that time, there was a weekly paper published in Dublin called the *Claidheamh Soluis* and there were competitions every week, all to be submitted in Irish. Now for the boasting. I was always winning these competitions. In second place, again and again, was this boy with a London address who mystified us. How was he learning his Irish? However I kept beating him – and schooldays passed and I grew up and went away and lost my Irish. In 1948, returning from years of life in England, I met, for the first time, and in the Green Room of the Abbey Theatre – Michael MacLiammoir. 'I've sought you all my life, Caithlin Ni Bhriain, you maddening blue stocking of the old *Claidheamh Soluis*![40]

Anne Blackett was dubious about her favoured pupil's interest in

Irish: 'Reverend Mother reflected in wonder and distaste about the Revivalist passion. She used to ask me about it, "Do you like this language?" "Very much, I find. It is very difficult but so is Latin." "Ah yes, but Latin is important."'[41] Later in her writing career, Kate came to share Anne Blackett's negative view of the politics of Irish cultural nationalism.

Laurel Hill was important to Kate's imagination and is remade again and again in glowing terms, but her old school was not always appreciative of the attention from the former pupil. An unaccredited story survives of a reproving letter sent to Kate from a later Reverend Mother, asking why she wrote such scandalous books. Kate's reported response was a telegram with three words: 'pounds, shillings and pence'. Mother Patrick O'Brien, a schoolfriend of Kate's who later became a nun in the same order, gave an interview at the end of her life about her former classmate. She took great exception to the portrayal of various clergy in her novels and believed that Kate took 'outrageous liberties'[42] with the characters derived from her time at Laurel Hill. Successive generations of students at Laurel Hill were told of this banned former student in disapproving terms or never heard of her at all. However, since the centenary of her birth in 1997, Kate O'Brien has been reclaimed with pride by Laurel Hill, with the school library renamed in her honour, housing a permanent exhibition about her life and her literary achievements.

The French convent was one source of female parenting for Kate; her aunts at the nearby Presentation Convent were another. Two of her mother's sisters, Mary and Fan Thornhill, were nuns in the Presentation order and lived near to Boru House in their convent. (It is a telling indication of the class position of the Thornhills that these women were Presentation nuns and not members of the wealthier Faithful Companions of Jesus at Laurel Hill.) The O'Brien children were regularly brought to the parlour in the Presentation Convent to be inspected by these aunts, another ritual of advice, concern and unease. 'There I learnt such intricacies and convolutions of human feeling. That parlour was a place where my aunts were to be seen, to be observed in action and always in relation to us and the anxieties and pleasures, which we caused in them. I know that I would face it as in the past, exciting and wondering and with all my nerves exposed.'

This anxious awareness of her aunts continued into her adult life, because her Aunt Fan lived on into her nineties. Therefore Kate's adult visits to Limerick included visits to 'Presentation Parlour' and, when she published her first novel, Fan was eager to read it. Kate's sister Nance would allow her elderly aunt to read it if only she promised to read just the sections that Nance had marked out. Censorship of Kate's novels began early.

Laurel Hill gave Kate O'Brien a great deal of confidence, but, to some extent, it also limited her. For one, she never came to question the authority of the nuns or acknowledge the underlying power structures and exactions of religious life. She recounted her final meeting with Reverend Mother Anne Blackett in the summer of 1916 when the issue of her loss of religious belief was raised. It is not clear precisely what Kate lied about to Anne Blackett but what is clear is that the Reverend Mother intruded on the young girl's private conscience and forced some sort of saving lie about her loss of Catholic faith:

> I told her a lie on that day when she forced me to speak about my non-belief and my private sins and she accepted my lie and said she expected it and went on talking as if I had never uttered it. She never smiled; she said none of those bright things one came to read later from English Catholics. She spoke, I think, in grief – and I was not able to help her. And she knew that. I was never to see her again after that painful conversation under the elms of the Visitors Walk. After twelve years I was going out of her house an unbeliever – my silly lie had been to no avail.[43]

Kate wrote this when she was in her sixties and long established as a novelist, but, still, she was childlike in her unquestioning respect for the codes of the convent school. She justifies Anne Blackett's interference in the private matter of belief and denigrates her own youthful attempt at self-protection by calling it a 'silly lie'. In this way, she never outgrew Laurel Hill.

As a novelist, she returns again and again to the convent school, in novels like *The Flower of May*, *As Music and Splendour* and *The Land of Spices*. Holy women abound in her work, either as nuns or as secular figures of austere spirituality and authority. Nuns gave Kate a version of secure authority that was lacking in Boru House, and so family is often the millstone or the stumbling-block for her young female protagonists. The nuns represented emotional distance. Kate valued this and saw it as the one precious necessity for the creative life. Writing about Joyce, she defined the artistic life thus:

That is the business of being an artist…you move into life out of childhood into the attentiveness of adolescence and self-consciousness and then you find a great pressure upon you from outside life. You realise that you are engaged with the world in some way removed from the commonplace. You begin to see that your fate is not to accept everyday life and get a living out of it but rather to express and enlarge it, in terms of your free imagination.[44]

Kate O'Brien, the daughter of a self-made Limerick merchant, learnt to dispense with any bourgeois notion of earning a living. Instead, she sought to express and enlarge her life through her fiction.

Her life in Limerick came to an abrupt end in June 1916, when her schooling at Laurel Hill finished and, in the same month, her father died. Tom O'Brien's death precipitated a financial crisis in the family firm and Boru House had to be sold in 1918. By the time her Limerick home had gone, Kate was already away at university in Dublin and she never lived in the city again. Yet Limerick was to possess her imagination as 'Mellick' for all her writing life.

2

Earning a living: 1916–26

The freedom of university life in Dublin came as a shock to Kate after the intensity of boarding-school, but it was a shock that stimulated and excited her. John Henry Newman had founded University College, Dublin, in 1854 as the Catholic University for Ireland. As a Jesuit-run college, it had already produced many important figures in the making of modern Ireland: writers like James Joyce, statesmen like Eamon de Valera and Pádraig Pearse the 1916 Rising leader, to name a few. The Jesuits left in 1908 when the college became part of the newly constituted National University of Ireland and was renamed University College, Dublin (UCD). Women were first admitted as full students in 1908 and, by 1916, when Kate arrived, there were over a thousand students at this rapidly expanding institution. During her time there, some of these students were housed at 86 St Stephen's Green, in the heart of Georgian Dublin, and she lived at one of the nearby women's hostels.

Kate was now orphaned and without any financial support from home. Her friend John Jordan wrote that she had won a Limerick County Council scholarship to attend university, but her name is not included in the relevant lists of scholarship holders in the UCD calendar, though she did win a college scholarship in her second year.[1] A schoolfriend of Kate's believed that the Bishop of Limerick, Dr O'Dwyer, paid for her university education.[2] This was possible, as her father and Dr O'Dwyer had been friendly, and the bishop had taken a keen interest in her education at Laurel Hill. She came up to Dublin in the autumn of 1916, when that city was, as she described it, 'a bleeding smoking theatre of tragedy' in the aftermath of the 1916 Easter Rising. The Rising, a desperate attempt at armed revolution, had taken place six months previously and the subsequent execution of the leaders had left Ireland in a state of unrest. War was still raging in Europe, and Kate's three years at UCD coincided with times of political turmoil in Ireland, as the struggle for independence gained momentum in the final years of British rule. The university was central in this struggle for independence, and the political atmosphere there in the autumn of 1916 was strongly sympathetic to the executed leaders of the Rising. University staff and students had been involved directly in the Rising. Indeed, during Kate's time at UCD, fellow students successfully ran for parliament, for Sinn Féin, in the 1918 election. It is curious that little of the atmosphere of these politically fraught days finds its way into her fiction.

However much she enjoyed the experience of university life, the national struggle held little interest for her as a writer. Her attention was focused on the recreation of her lost world, the Limerick bourgeoisie, and on her imaginative connection with Europe. However, it is only in her last novel, *As Music and Splendour*, that she began to reflect this sense of youthful fun and enjoyment of student life in her writing. Laurel Hill had been a concentrated, even claustrophobic, school, with a surplus of teachers and a small number of students, but at university she was one of many and, imaginatively, she seemed to herself to have disappeared. Remembering this time at university and recalling her friends and classmates, she wrote, 'I see them much more clearly than I see myself in that landscape.'[3]

Her recorded memories of her university years are happy and carefree, markedly different to those of the discipline and rules at Laurel Hill. This sense of lazy, warm student bonhomie surfaces in her travel book, *My Ireland*: 'We in University College were full of ourselves and as happy as Larry.' Elsewhere she remembered 'the rough and tumble place was not a convent or a seminary. It was a seemingly ill directed or if you like non-directed place of learning – but it was open.'[4] Kate recalled the cramped lecture halls and the dingy tutorial rooms of her university years with some pleasure. At university, she relaxed in her attitude towards her studies: 'I do remember this about myself, from having being a really industrious and hard-working schoolgirl, I became almost overnight a lazy and sceptical student.'[5]

Kate made a virtue of her new-found slackness as a student. For example, she took Latin in her first year at university and, like all her classmates, used a standard translation or a 'key' instead of translating the work herself:

> We seemed mostly to read Livy...that we knew no Latin, reading

> Livy was a great responsibility. There was among us a copy of Kelly's Key [an English translation of Livy]. People were bad at showing each other the place in the key and they were imbecile in that they read Kelly's version clearly and fluently. . . . I always hesitated and thought it all out and delivered the passage in likelier words, may I say, than Mr Kelly's. . . . 'Thank you, Miss O'Brien,' the lecturer growled, 'You're the most intelligent reader of a key I've ever listened to.'[6]

Contemptuous of the poor standard of Irish being taught, Kate stopped going to lectures and then found herself being reprimanded by the President of UCD, Dr Coffey, for her non-attendance. However, despite her presentation of herself as a poor student, she does record her debt to teachers like Professor Roger Chauvire: 'Listening to Chauvire on French writing in the seventeenth and eighteenth century, I grew up.'[7]

The poet Austin Clarke, her lecturer in English Literature, delighted her one day by announcing that her English essay showed an outward manifestation of inward grace. She writes again and again of the pleasures of intellectual companionship: 'It was on the bridge in Stephen's Green that Violet Connolly, on a freezing cold morning, met me and said: "Look, look here" – and we sat down and read, a little navy blue-book, that first printing of Gerard Manly Hopkins.'[8] In this new atmosphere, Kate blossomed socially. At this age, slim, dark, with deep-set blue eyes and straight dark hair, her good looks, intelligence and sense of fun made her popular with fellow students.

Dublin was important to her for other reasons. In *My Ireland,* she remembers her first time at the Abbey Theatre as a moment of aesthetic revelation, when she saw Shaw's *Man and Superman*:

> I went into the theatre that Saturday afternoon a nervous, green convent-school creature, just up from Limerick, and I suppose I came out looking much the same. But in fact I came out afraid to breathe; I felt as if I had been filled with some very brittle burning kind of light . . . It was no especial word or idea heard that lighted me up. . . . Simply it was the rush of air, the windows opened on extravagance and storm of idea. . . . I have never forgotten the shock of it or the tingling refreshment. . . .

In the autumn of 1919, Kate graduated with an honours degree in English and French: 'all I took of it was a Second Class Honours BA.

And I remember when Professor Robert Donovan – how kindly! – sent for me and told me that to his regret he could not give me marks sufficient to gain me a First, I thought life was over. Truly I did. I thought that to get a Second was a kind of death.'[9] In her graduation photograph, her classmates look guarded, amused or even glum, but Kate looks directly at the camera with an expression of tentative hope on her face. Now twenty-two and having spent eighteen years in the protected world of convent school and university, she had her independence and a living to make: 'Some of my friends had fixed vocations, I know, but I don't remember any particular ambition in myself. I was careless about what the future would be...My impression is that I was rather slack about all that, even after I got my degree I took my time about the business of making a living, it seemed an unattractive business, or so my lazy and prophetic soul told me.'[10]

Kate spent the first half of 1920 in Fermoy with her Aunt Annie, now widowed and struggling to maintain a failing business and a young family. In *Presentation Parlour* she wrote: 'I stayed in her house for some months at the beginning of 1920 – I was just down from the university, and slack about setting out for England to choose a job.' As a university graduate, she had the option of a teaching or a public service career in Ireland, but she decided on a life in Britain instead. She had been to Grenoble in France briefly in the summer of 1919 as part of her university studies in French but had never lived outside Ireland. Of her siblings, only Nance and Gerry still lived in Limerick. In 1910, Nance had married Stephen O'Mara, the son of a prosperous Limerick merchant family and an active Irish nationalist. Michael had moved to New York, May and Clare had already gone to England to find work, and, after the failure of the family business, the eldest brother, Jack, followed them.

After some hesitation, in the summer of 1920 Kate joined her sisters in London and embarked on a journalistic career, reviewing freelance for *The Sphere*. This part-time work ended when, in the autumn of 1920, she answered an advertisement in the *New Statesman* for a job as assistant translator on the foreign news page of the *Manchester Guardian Weekly*. When Kate joined the *Manchester Guardian* in late 1920, it was fast approaching its centenary (May 1921). This liberal and free-thinking journal was still under the editorship of the distinguished C.P. Scott, who had been in command of the paper since 1872. For an Irishwoman starting her professional life in England, it proved an enlightened place to work, for the newspaper had a history of committed support for the struggle for Home Rule in Ireland. As one historian of the newspaper put it: 'The Irish Question was to the *Manchester Guardian*, and in no figure of speech, a liberal education.'[11] In retrospect, Kate considered this first job a lucky start: 'everybody was very kind to me. I found that my French was enough, my German wasn't and anyhow I couldn't translate things like "Russian Rolling stock".'[12] Financially, the job was also a lucky start: 'I very much enjoyed my large salary, I had five pounds a week and five pounds a week in Manchester in 1920 was riches! I remember I used to come down to London for weekends with my sisters and spend money. Great fun.'[13]

This was her first experience of working in England. Domestically, she lived in a succession of lodgings, small flats and rented cottages for all her working life there. In her fiction, she made much of the assured and gracious domestic world of the Irish bourgeoisie but, in fact, she wrote her novels in a series of flats and small homes in London and the Home Counties, with no servants and an uncertain income. Manchester also taught her much about being Irish in Britain at a time of great political tension. During her time in Manchester, the lord mayor of Cork, Terence MacSwiney, imprisoned in Brixton jail in London, was on hunger strike. His protracted fasting and eventual death in late October 1920 caused public discord in Britain and in Ireland. Kate's Irishness made her vulnerable to racial baiting:

> There's one hideous memory associated with the *Manchester Guardian* that autumn, Terence MacSwiney was hunger striking in Brixton Jail and along my corridor in the *Manchester Guardian* every morning there came a little man, a horrid little man with a hideous face and hideous grin. He used to open the door of my room and yell in at me, 'Sixty-one days fasting and you still think he's fasting, Miss O'Brien.' 'Sixty-eight days and you believe in that man.' Oh, we used to get into a terrible state, my two colleagues were dreadfully upset and I used to burst into tears of sheer rage. But we never could stop that awful little morning joke. I never could forget him.[14]

Manchester provided her with the material for her first play, *Distinguished Villa*, her only work set in an English lower middle-class milieu. Although the play was written several years later and set in Brixton, she drew on her experience of boarding-house life at this time. One newspaper reported: 'In lodgings in Manchester... she became deeply interested in the life of small people and like Frances, the delightful woman in *Distinguished Villa*, she had always liked to look on at the story.'[15] Kate's description of the English lower middle class as 'small' revealed her contempt for any class other than the civilised Irish middle class, or the European equivalent, and their faithful working-class servants. Late in 1920 the *Manchester Guardian Weekly* shut down its foreign news page and, in January 1921, Kate moved back to London to live in Streatham.

For the next six months she taught at the Institute of the Blessed Virgin Mary, a Catholic school run by the Ursuline nuns in England's Lane, Hampstead. Teaching was more secure than journalism and one of the few stable professions open to the liberal arts graduate. However, Kate lasted only two terms as a teacher. She had loved being a pupil in a Catholic convent school but disliked being a teacher. Her memory of the school itself was not a particularly happy one: 'run by some snob nuns. One compensation was the nuns' sideline, a branch for refugee Russian, Polish and Hungarian children, by far the most intelligent.'[16]

Kate was popular with some of the children: 'I taught English and History and all the mixum gatherum one used to teach in convent schools in those days.'[17] One of her pupils at this school was a thirteen-year-old called Mary O'Neill, who kept a diary of these six months called 'A Catholic schoolgirl's diary'.[18] In this diary, Mary O'Neill recorded her growing admiration and eventual 'schwarmerei' for the 'beautiful young woman teacher'. Despite her name, Mary O'Neill was English, her father being the deputy editor of the *The Observer* and her mother, Elizabeth O'Neill a historian, a graduate of Manchester University and author of *A Nursery History of England* (1912).

In her diary, Mary O'Neill recorded the arrival of Miss O'Brien, the new English, French and History mistress, and charted the gradual cult of the 'beloved' that grew up around Kate. The girls found out her age (twenty-three) and her first name (Kitty) and were pleasantly scandalised when she said 'Good God' in class and told them that she might be shot, because she was going to Ireland for Easter. The 'Beloved' Miss O'Brien was encouraging and friendly to her students, but her application as a teacher was not striking. The diary records a visit by the school inspector during a French class that left the class 'disgraced' and the 'Beloved' teacher and her pupils in tears. When Kate accidentally dropped a gooseberry in class, Mary and her friends preserved it in spirits, calling it the 'Sacred Gooseberry' and fighting for weekend possession of the relic. This obsession came to the notice of some of the parents and Mary O'Neill's mother came to talk with the Reverend Mother. Reverend Mother's comment was, 'The truth is that the beloved is very beautiful.' The diary ended with the tragic realisation that the 'Beloved' would not be returning to teaching the following term. Mary's despairing cry, 'I wish I were dead, this is the end of everything', finishes the diary and her account of an infatuation.

However, Kate kept in touch with Mary O'Neill after her teaching at the Institute of the Blessed Virgin Mary ended in July 1921. Kate wrote to Mary in August, on her return from a summer holiday on the Rhine, and again in December from Washington DC, where Kate was working as an assistant for her brother-in-law, Stephen O'Mara, Nance's husband. Stephen, a close friend of Eamon de Valera, had been elected lord mayor of Limerick in March 1921 after the murder of the two previous incumbents.[19] In August of the same year, the Minister for Finance, Michael Collins, announced in the new Irish Dáil that Stephen O'Mara would take over the coordination of the Bond Drive, a fundraising campaign in America for the new Irish state.[20] As part of this arrangement, Kate was employed to go to Washington with Stephen and Nance 'as a kind of secretary'.[21] Nance and Stephen O'Mara were important to Kate, because their house in Limerick was now the only home base she had in Ireland. She respected Stephen, a well-educated but conservative Catholic businessman, for his political acumen and his intellectual abilities, even though they often clashed on matters of censorship and issues of artistic freedom.

Kate recalled her time in Washington in an interview with John Jordan:

> It was there that she met Harry Boland, an intimate of both Michael Collins and de Valera and a prominent member of the IRB. I think only when she was speaking of Harry Boland did I detect a slight glistening of the eyes – 'Whenever he took me to New York with him, we'd go to see Sophie Tucker – you know, the Red Hot Momma – he loved her.'[22]

A story from her time in Washington was that, reputedly, Kate wore the Russian crown jewels at a fundraising event for the Irish Bond Drive. Irish Historian Dermot Keogh records that Russian jewels were in the possession of the Irish delegation in Washington: 'a story broke in the press, involving the Russian crown jewels. When de Valera was in the United States in 1920, he loaned some money to a Soviet agent and was given jewels as security in return. The jewels were brought back to Ireland and handed over by Harry Boland.'[23] As one of the few young women in the Irish Bond delegation, Kate may easily have been involved in this stunt. When Harry Boland was preparing to return to Ireland in December 1921, Kate wrote to him from Washington, flirting with him by thanking him for 'my perfectly beautiful golf sticks...you kind, kind, kindest man!...You never knew how much I loved you – did you, Harry? – until you started going away. What a wet, red-eyed object I was today.'[24]

Kate returned to Ireland in January 1922 and, after a brief visit to her Aunt Annie in Fermoy, found that she had no desire to live and work in Ireland. In March 1922, writing to Harry Boland, now an important figure in the turbulent new Irish state, she thanked him for his recommendation for a job in the Irish foreign ministry but demurred 'I am not keen enough on the new government to wish my hand to become its servant.'[25] Kate's friendship with Harry Boland had a tragic ending:

> On a July evening in 1922 in London, Kate saw the name of Sophie Tucker in lights in the West End and in a spontaneous gesture of nostalgic affection, wired to Harry Boland. She learned later that at about 2 a.m. that night or rather morning, Boland was mortally wounded in a swoop by Free State troops in the Grand Hotel in Skerries.[26]

Now an independent and assured young woman, she applied for a job as a governess, or a 'Miss', in the Basque country that summer and was accepted: 'I was in a condition of hesitation and I wanted to be out of England and left to myself for a while.'[27] Her post was as English teacher to the thirteen-year-old son and sixteen-year-old daughter of a wealthy Basque surgeon in the village of Portugalete, near the seaport of Bilbao. The position of 'Miss' was one of the few careers open to middle-class Irish women, but, with a university degree, Kate felt herself overqualified for it: 'I was what was called a "Miss" but because the family required rather special tuition in English Literature for their very intelligent son and because I had a degree in that subject I got double the standard "Miss" salary.'[28] This time away was crucial for Kate in her formation as a novelist. The vitalising experience of living in another culture drew her out as a writer and provided her with an imaginative impetus. It gave her a distance from the Ireland she sought to remake in her fictions.

She spent her time there living in the house of a man of some note in the Basque region. Dr Enrique Areilza, born in 1860, was an eminent surgeon and a liberal reformer, influential in the setting up of a free hospital for the miners working in this heavily industrialised region. Apart from his interest in social reform, Areilza was also connected with the literary journal *Hermes* and friendly with the writer and philosopher Miguel de Unamuno. Unamuno was a key figure in the so-called 'Generacion del 98', 'the Generation of 98' a literary and artistic movement celebrating the austerity and rigid purity of the Spanish landscape. In *Farewell Spain,* Kate O'Brien mentions her reading of Unamuno and other poets of the 'Generacion del 98' at this time – in her fiction, she also appropriates this notion of an austere Spanish landscape for her own literary purposes. In addition, she was interested in the cause of Basque cultural nationalism and her writings on Bilbao draw a parallel with the politics of the new Irish state and those of the Biscayean region, a region alive with political debate. One day, she asked her young pupil to bring her on a visit to the bar of the Basque nationalist club and was surprised and pleased to see a picture of Terence MacSwiney, garlanded with Sinn Féin and Basque flags. In *Mary Lavelle*, her novel inspired by her time living in Portugalete, her heroine muses, 'She heard the Basque speech in the market place; amusedly once through the oration of a Basque nationalist, she heard the names "Arthur Griffith" and "Pádraig Pearse".'

It is unclear precisely how much time Kate spent in Portugalete with the Areilza family. Her pupil, José María Areilza, later remembered it as fourteen months. However, she had travelled out in September 1922 and was back in London by May 1923, which makes it, at most, an eight-month stay. Her student in Bilbao, like Mary O'Neill, left an account of his time under Kate's tutelage. Speaking in Limerick nearly seventy years later, José María Areilza recalled Kate as:

> ...a tall young woman, with very black shiny hair, cut à la garçon, with very white skin, light grey, almost blue eyes, a small expressive mouth, and a forceful, yet warm, voice. Her gait was athletic and decisive. Her clothes were nearly always a pleated wool skirt and a long casual jacket. She usually wore low-heeled shoes and grey stockings. She was a lively woman and very friendly to both of us.[29]

José Maria Areilza was also privy to Kate's first attempts to become a novelist: 'but you could also tell by something visible in her character that she had a considerable inner life.... She confessed to me that literature was the very thing she aspired to do in life and that to this end she wrote several pages a day as a discipline.'[30] In the mornings, she taught him and his sister *Emma* and *Julius Caesar* and, in the afternoons, she explored Bilbao and the surrounding countryside with her young charges. These afternoon wanderings were important for Kate. In *Farewell Spain*, she remembered herself at this time:

> I, on the other hand, mooned along in a state of immaturity.... I was a considerable ass; very vague withal, and unaware of my asininity. And I was often lonely and bored. But I see now... that I was pleased, in my roots, with the unexpected Spain I had found – and glad to an extent I would not realise for years to have opened up acquaintance with a country I was to love very much.

Sometime in the spring of 1923, after seven months or so in Portugalete, Kate left and returned to London: 'I loved the life; my pupil was of blazing intelligence; and I think that had not personal and family matters brought me home within the year, I'd have been very happy to have stayed a long while in Spain as a "Miss".'[31] As with Mary O'Neill, Kate remained in correspondence with José María Areilza and his sister after she left Portugalete, although they eventually lost contact with one another in the upheavals of the Spanish Civil War. José María Areilza was to have a varied political career; the most controversial moment of this career came in July 1937 when he was appointed mayor of Bilbao after its capture by Franco's troops. Areilza welcomed the troops with the ringing statement that 'Bilbao is a town redeemed by blood', going on to denounce what he called 'the imbecility of Basque nationalism'.[32] In 1941, hoping to be made Spanish ambassador to Fascist Italy, Areilza co-wrote the ferociously imperialist text, *Reivindicaciones de*

Espana. However, after World War II, in 1947, he began his diplomatic career with a posting to Argentina. When he was Spanish ambassador in Washington in 1950, he received a letter from Kate:

> I have seen your name mentioned in the British press as being the current Spanish Ambassador to the USA. I felt that I had to write to you, in the hope that you are the same boy I tried to teach good English back in the 1920s. My short stay in your family home is printed indelibly in my memory. That period was so important for me that I used it to write an almost autobiographical novel called *Mary Lavelle*.[33]

Contact between teacher and former pupil was re-established and Kate sent him a copy of this, her third novel. His recognition was immediate: 'There, on those pages, nearly all my family, my father, my mother and my sister, were portrayed under different names and with variations of characters and circumstances, of course.... The home of my adolescent years is evoked in masterly fashion down to the last detail.'[34] However, Kate and Areilza never met again, despite her many visits to Spain through the 1960s and early 1970s, perhaps because of their very different political positions and because of her opposition to Franco.

Kate decided to leave Bilbao suddenly, putting an abrupt end to a happy and creative time in her life. Areilza mentions that, during her time in Bilbao, she had been in correspondence with a young journalist: 'we would discuss her literary projects and personal problems for hours. She also told me about a sentimental relationship she had had with an English journalist who worked, if I remember rightly, on the London *Observer* and she regularly got copies of that newspaper in the mail.'[35] Kate's reason for leaving was that she had decided, suddenly, it seems, to get married.

On 17 May 1923, in the registry office in Hampstead in London, Kate married Gustaaf Johannes Renier. She was twenty-five, he was thirty and both gave their occupation as journalist. Gustaaf Renier was Dutch, living and working in England as a freelance writer, and it must have been in the summer of 1922 that Kate met him, before her departure for Spain. When she moved to Bilbao, Gustaaf wrote proposing marriage.[36] Kate's decision to leave Spain after only eight months was clearly a result of this pressure. The marriage was short-lived and little is known about their domestic life together, apart from the fact that they were both short of money and, early on in the marriage, Gustaaf gave Kate a present of a potato-peeler![37]

Born in 1892, the son of a sea captain, Gustaaf Renier was educated in a Catholic school and destined for the priesthood. However, by his own account, he was sent home from school because of a sexual involvement with another male student.[38] Like Kate, Gustaaf Renier was a lapsed Catholic and he began his journalistic career in London representing a Dutch newspaper. His marriage to Kate ended, according to her friend Lorna Reynolds, after eleven months, in April 1924. It is clear that this marriage was a mistake for Kate and she left him within the year, living apart from him for the rest of her life. She never remarried. However, they did not divorce for another fourteen years. In all her autobiographical writings, she never refers to this period of her life and thus the reasons for the early ending of her marriage can only be inferred. In Gustaaf Renier's autobiography, published ten years after he had married Kate, there is, surprisingly, no mention of her. This silence is notable despite the fact that they were still in contact and that she was by then a well-known dramatist.

Kate never wrote of Gustaaf but some second-hand accounts of the end of the marriage do exist. After they had parted, Gustaaf wrote to Kate's sister Nance: 'Kitty says she has never been happy with me, that she is not made for matrimony and cannot live with me under false pretences.'[39] Lorna Reynolds, wrote: 'it was a very short and stormy relationship, lasting just eleven months. She used to joke, if one asked her why she left her husband, and say it was because he counted the strawberries: "one for you, one for me, two for you, two for me".'[40] A fellow student at Laurel Hill heard of the marriage and remembered two versions of the break-up. One was that a woman with some children had arrived at the home one day out of the blue and announced herself to be Renier's wife. Another story was that Kate had left him for a woman, leaving him a note on the mantelpiece. The Irish novelist Paul Smith wrote: 'her taste in men was indeed bad, even for a writer lady. She was married once to a man in London who would only eat steak and lettuce three times a day, insisted on going round three-quarters naked with a shaven chest and played too much tennis. He had girls everywhere, one in London and another in Manchester and had great difficulty in keeping them apart. The marriage broke up.'[41]

Gustaaf's second wife, Olive Renier, also a writer, gave her opinion that:

He [Gustaaf] had an agonizing personal experience of the strange legal habits of the British state when his marriage to Kate O'Brien was terminated by her departure and he was involved in complicated divorce proceedings. It was indeed many years before it was even possible to get a divorce for desertion, and only post Second World War changes in the divorce laws rendered unnecessary the bitter public washing of dirty linen which such legal actions involved in the twenties.[42]

Olive Renier also wrote that Gustaaf returned briefly to the Catholic Church in the months after Kate's departure, a short-lived return. However, there is evidence that Gustaaf and Kate remained in friendly contact for some years after the separation. After 1924, Gustaaf lived in Great Ormond Street in London, close to Kate's Bloomsbury flat. By 1930, he had completed his doctoral studies and was lecturing in Dutch history at the University of London. A letter survives from Gustaaf to Kate with helpful research advice on the historical background for her first novel, *Without My Cloak*. Gustaaf was also in contact with other friends of Kate's; her lover Stephie had a number of formal photographs of Gustaaf in her possession, and in 1933 Gustaaf presented Kate's former pupil Mary O'Neill with a copy of his biography, *Oscar Wilde*.[43] Gustaaf waited until 1938 to divorce Kate, with no cause given, and then in 1939 he married Olive Corthorn, twenty years his junior and the god-daughter of Olive Schreiner, the author of *An African Farm*. Like Kate, the second Mrs Renier also wrote an autobiography, entitled *Before the Bonfire*.

Gustaaf Renier also found success as a writer. His book, *The English, Are They Human?*,[44] was published in the same year as *Without My Cloak* and he went on to publish another twenty-four books, mainly historical and biographical studies. Two of these subsequent works, *Oscar Wilde* and his autobiographical *He Came to England: A Self-Portrait*,[45] offer an insight into his character and there is clear evidence in this work that Gustaaf Renier was either homosexual or bisexual. He may also have been the inspiration for Kate's portrayal of Henry Archer, the homosexual father in *The Land of Spices*. The resemblance between this fictional character and Gustaaf's own self-presentation are striking. In addition, these resemblances correspond with the portrait of Gustaaf in the memoirs of his second wife, Olive.

Gustaaf Renier's *The English, Are They Human?* was a popular work and so, in 1933, he published *He Came to England: A Self-Portrait*, a fictionalised version of his own life (*The Times* called it 'Mr Renier's autobiography').[46] He was a competent, fluent biographer and essayist, but his autobiography is truly unpleasant and arch. In this version of his life, Renier indulged in self-dramatisation and veiled autobiography: 'These, then, are the brittle waters of a life seen with the eyes of fancy.'[47] Described as a self-portrait, *He Came to England* has a Dutch protagonist called Gerard, who has moved to London to work as a journalist. Gerard writes of his education as a Catholic and his brief period training for the priesthood in a seminary, but, as the story advances, he outgrows his Catholic faith: 'Though he had broken the mould long ago, his mind had kept the shape.'[48] Marginalised in his native Holland, Gerard moves to London, works as a journalist, pursues studies at the London School of Economics and writes a best-selling study of the English. No mention is made of a marriage, but Gerard does have a woman companion called Joy and a soulmate called David. (The book was dedicated to David Hallett, who co-translated a number of books with Renier. Hallett shared a home with Renier and his second wife for much of the 1940s.)

Telling his life story in the third person, Gerard reiterates his unconventionality, his unorthodox bohemianism. At one point, he makes the startling announcement that 'Later another friend had said of him "Gerard is a homosexual who happens to desire only women". This also was true.'[49] In the book, Renier circles around the subject of his protagonist's homosexuality, but refuses finally to commit himself to a clear sexual identity. Renier's complex relationship to his own sexuality can be inferred from the fact that he was married twice. However, there is a clear homosexual subtext in his memoir. Renier repeatedly stresses his bohemian disregard for the distinctions of social class and there are a number of episodes where Gerard befriends young working-class men: inviting an electrician to lunch with him, patronising a young Italian. This free-spiritedness and fellowship is in fact a form of sexual cruising, as when he meets the young Italian 'Gerard held out a coin to him but the forefinger of his right hand said "no" while the big eyes smiled and were understanding.... Gerard was utterly incapable of placing him; the presence of Joy his wife precluded the hypothesis to which his refusal of alms might have given rise.'[50] (This tortuous prose is typical of much of Renier's memoir.) Renier's second wife, Olive, makes clear in her autobiography that her husband had a life-long bond with

David Hallett, a bond that endured over his two marriages: 'There were, however, crises, such as that of Gustaaf's marriage and its almost immediate collapse, when Gustaaf turned to David for support.'[51] Indeed, Gustaaf's second marriage was something of a *ménage à trois*, since he and Olive and David Hallett all worked together at the BBC Monitoring Service in Eversham during World War II and shared a house in Twickenham from 1949 onwards.

Linked to this is Renier's 1933 *Oscar Wilde*, displaying a remarkably enlightened view of Wilde's homosexuality and which must have influenced Kate O'Brien's later radical representations of sexual identities. Renier argued for toleration instead of legal prosecution and saw Wilde's homosexuality as innate and natural. His belief was that 'Wilde's sexual psychology did not result from a sudden deviation due to insanity and that it was not a chance development in middle age, but that it was part and parcel of his personality.'[52] Renier attempted to overturn conventional prejudice against homosexual men and women:

> The popular mind harbours many misapprehensions on the subject of homosexuality. It is, for one thing, often confused with sodomy which as a matter of fact is probably as prevalent (or as rare) in heterosexual as in homosexual relations. And then there is the confusion between effeminacy and homosexuality in men, and ill-poised masculinity and homosexuality in women.... There are, among women, homosexuals who are perfect needlewomen, who love children, who are completely feminine. Among men there are homosexuals who are all-round sportsmen, soldiers, explorers, capable of all the energy and initiative we have come to associate with the term 'manliness'.[53]

Not surprisingly, Renier's views on Wilde's homosexuality caused a great deal of controversy. Although Compton McKenzie[54] called it a 'brilliant piece of biography', not everyone agreed with him and Wilde's friend Robert Sherard went to the trouble of publishing a pamphlet called *André Gide's Wicked Lies about the Late Oscar Wilde*,[55] where he took Renier to task for his frank portrayal of Wilde's sexual life. So angry was Sherard about the biography that he resorted to a personal and xenophobic attack on Renier: 'The Dutch Doctor Renier sailed into English waters with a mudsquirt dangling from his masthead and a tub of French sewage conveniently placed for the befoulment of a broken marble column that only calls for tears.'[56]

There is a remarkable similarity between Renier's own auto-biographical self-portrait, the memoir of him left by his second wife, Olive, and the character of Henry Archer in *The Land of Spices*. Many of the opinions and traits that Gerard claims himself are echoed in Archer's characterisation. Indeed, Archer could conceivably have written *He Came to England*. Both Henry and Gerard advertise their disregard for bourgeois convention and express individualism through atheism and scholarship. In *The Land of Spices*, the central moment is Helen Archer's discovery of Henry Archer's homosexuality and this marks the end of her devotion to him. Henry Archer owes much to Gustaaf Renier in terms of characterisation, and Kate's marriage may have ended because of her realisation that her husband was bisexual or homosexual. Her convent education would have kept her ill-informed in sexual matters and, indeed, in her writing Kate often expressed her approval of virginity and of sexual innocence. Thus, such a revelation would have been a significant one for Kate. Perhaps that is why no direct record survives of the marriage or even of her life in the months after the marriage had ended. However, preserved among her papers is a snapshot of her and Gustaaf, facing each other in front of a sun-filled window, both smiling. This photograph survived the many upheavals of her life and was with her to the end.

One legacy of her marriage was the persistent rumour that Kate had given birth to a child around this time. John Jordan, speaking at the 1988 Kate O'Brien weekend in Limerick, suggested that she may have had a child. Further to this, the adoption of a son, Peter, by her childless, wealthy sister, Nance O'Mara in the spring of 1927 led to speculation that young Peter O'Mara was Kate's own child. There is no record of Peter O'Mara's birth, since he was a foundling with the given name of Peter Johnson, taken into care by the National Children's Adoption Association in London. When Nance O'Mara adopted him, Peter was believed to be around eighteen months old. This means that he was born some time in late 1924 or early 1925, in the year after the break-up of Kate and Gustaaf's marriage. Without a birth certificate for Peter O'Mara, it is impossible to prove or disprove the claim that he was Kate's own child, but the lack of any personal record of Kate's whereabouts at the time when he was born may be significant. In the papers of Nance and Stephen O'Mara, now in the possession of their granddaughter, there are no letters between Kate and her sister during the period after her marriage – 1924/25. Also, the question arises as to their reason for adopting a child in London. The wealthy and politically influential O'Maras would have had no difficulty in obtaining a child to adopt in Ireland. On the other hand, adoption was not available in Ireland at this time and Nance O'Mara worked through a reputable London association to obtain her son. It is clear from letters between Nance and Stephen O'Mara that the child was being gradually introduced to his relatives, including his Aunt Kate in London. It is unlikely that Nance would have gone to the trouble of adopting any child of Kate's by means of an official organisation. Without any definite proof as to the parentage of Peter O'Mara, speculation that he was Kate's son can remain only speculation.[57]

When her marriage ended in April 1924, Kate found work as publications secretary to a new philanthropic organisation, the Sunlight League, founded in May of the same year. The Sunlight League was the idea of a Dr Saleeby, a medical reformer (who was married to the daughter of the writer Alice Meynell), and its purpose was to introduce working-class children to the benefits of clean air, smokeless coal and the sun's rays: 'the systematic use of sunbaths as a preventative and therapeutic measure'.[58] Kate was working with the League by July 1924, when she accompanied the excursion to 'London's first Sun-bathing centre for Children'. Living in Great James Street in London, and based in the Bloomsbury office of the Sunlight League, she also doubled as publications secretary for the league's annual journal, *Sunlight*, which was produced when the society had enough money to print it. Kate's articles featured in the first three issues, between 1924 and late 1926, after which a May O'Brien took over Kate's position. Presumably Kate was keeping the post in the family by giving the work to her older sister.

While working for the Sunlight League, Kate put her interest in writing to the test. Among her friends in London was the actress Veronica Turleigh, who had graduated from UCD the year after Kate. Turleigh put a challenge to her. Kate wrote:

> At this time I was mixing with young actors and writers. I used to talk about the theatre a lot and Veronica Turleigh, who was just out of the Academy of Dramatic Art, very young, bet me a pound that I wouldn't write a play in a month to give to her and I did! She took it to an agent, and paid me the pound which was very decent of her, and he read it and sent me twenty-five pounds on its chances, he thought

so well of it. I never before or since heard of an agent doing that . . . it was a young, over-written play, very tragic, very kitchen sink, over-romantic but I do think it had some merit.[59]

Kate's move into professional writing was facilitated by her connections in the world of theatre and also by the fact that she was based in London. *Distinguished Villa* was first performed by a non-professional company, the Repertory Players, as part of a one-off Sunday night series at the Aldwych Theatre, on 2 May 1926. The first performance went unreviewed by the press because of the citywide General Strike, a massive trade union action that brought London to a halt for several days, but it attracted the attention of a new theatrical producing partnership, José Levy and Henry Millar. They were looking for new English plays to present in the West End and, two months later, on 12 July, the play was set to open in the Little Theatre, with a professional cast and director. *Distinguished Villa* very nearly failed to get a first performance because the Lord Chamberlain, Lord Cromer, who controlled censorship of theatre performances, delayed permission for the play to open. In a newspaper interview two days before the opening, Kate explained: 'Before the production of the play by the Repertory Players, certain cuts were made, but unfortunately an uncut copy of the play was sent to the Censor when we asked permission to produce the play. With great courtesy the Lord Chamberlain read the play through without delay and this afternoon telephoned to Mr Levy saying he had no objection to its being produced.'[60]

Distinguished Villa played successfully in London for two months and then toured in February 1927 all over the provincial theatres in England. It was set for an American tour, but this failed to materialise. Nevertheless, her playwriting continued and her second play, *The Bridge*, opened on 31 May 1927. *Distinguished Villa* eventually played in Dublin in the Abbey Theatre in January 1929. The play has an English suburban setting in which a number of unsatisfactory, disparate lives coincide with tragic consequences. Kate contrasts conventional, house-proud Mabel Hemworth with the artistic and perceptive Frances Llewellyn. Kate constructs Mabel as lower middle-class to her soul, concerned with appearance, order, neatness and good housekeeping and unwilling to respond to the affection and love of her husband Natty. Frances Lewellyn, on the other hand, is artistic, educated, bookish, devoted to music and poetry, free-spirited and sympathetic to Natty's nature. Kate's description of Frances is very close to a self-portrait: 'She looks about twenty-eight, and is slim and tall. Her dark brown hair is closely shingled. Her face is leanly cut in noble boyish lines. Her eyes are gentle and merry, her skin pale.... She carries one or two books and writing materials and seems a little diffident.' This diffidence earns Frances the love of two un-free men, Natty, Mabel's husband, and John Morris, who is engaged to Gwen. In one of the weakest scenes in the play, Frances pities Natty for the limitations of his conventional life: 'You're not all right; you're sad and wretched.'

Kate characterises Frances as repelled by the unbearable dreariness of everyday suburban life, and this she tries to offset with art, music and literature. As with *The Ante-Room*, Kate ends the piece with suicide. Natty kills himself, explicitly the victim of Mabel's unrelenting and heartless respectability: 'Natty has killed himself. It could not happen! He knows the delicate state of my health.' Implicitly, Natty is also brought to despair by his admiration for Frances.

The play became a commercial success and, at the end of the first performance, when Kate was called on stage to speak, her unusual beauty and grave manner attracted attention. The next day, found typing away in the office of the Sunlight League, she gave the first of several press interviews. She began a lifelong habit of self-refashioning, giving her age as twenty-seven rather than the actual twenty-eight, and, in one interview, resituating herself as 'the baby of my family' – although she had three younger brothers! Kate was described as speaking with 'a soft Irish brogue'.[61] Another interview provides a striking pen-picture of the suddenly successful playwright: 'Many a frequenter of London theatre queues would recognise her as a handsome girl of 27 [*sic*] with half-cropped hair, dressed in a loose smock-like frock and wearing a huge cowboy brimmed Montmartre-crowned hat at a rakish angle and with the longest of cigarette holders in her mouth.'[62]

(Interestingly, Radclyffe Hall, notorious for her lesbian novel *The Well of Loneliness*, also wore a Montmartre hat for newspaper photographs during the obscenity trial of her novel in 1928. It seems as if Kate was already dressing in a code that was recognisably lesbian.)

In reviews, some reservations were expressed, particularly about Kate's representation of Brixton working-class life. Several reviewers of the play raised the question of her handling of what she herself

called 'a new world – lower middle-class English life, with all its little
tragedies'.[63] James Agate, writing in the *Sunday Times*, liked the play
in performance but shrewdly identified her view of English working-
class life as patronising: 'Is Natty's class bored with Brixton? One
suggests not. Miss O'Brien has forgotten, or perhaps never realised,
those games of nap and solo whist played on newspapers spread in
the train, the Saturday afternoons at Highbury [Arsenal's football
ground] or the Oval [cricket]. Discontent without other capacity is
not to be encouraged, even by sentimental playwrights. I feel that the
people in this play are true less to themselves.'[64]

In the *Sunday Pictorial*, the writer Herbert Farjeon put it even
more bluntly: 'What really grown up person could sympathise with
an idealist who stops a record of Mozart's "Voi Che Sapete" in the
middle because he considers the surroundings of a Brixton parlour
heinously unsuitable?'[65] Most of the other reviewers noted her lack
of social insight and St John Ervine, writing in *The Observer*, said:
'If she can discipline her likes and dislikes and learn to distinguish
between poetry and priggery, she will probably write an accom-
plished play.'[66] Stung by this review, Kate wrote from her flat in
Great James Street to *The Observer* to thank St John Ervine for his
'flatteringly merciless report of my play'.[67] He felt obliged to defend
his view further. With so many reviewers attacking her for her portrayal of English petty bourgeois life, she did not repeat the mistake.

In her novels, she learned to avoid such radical condescension.
Turning to Ireland for imaginative material, Kate used the Irish
bourgeoisie to create characters whose lives are emphatically not
'small' or 'little'. In her first interviews as a newly acclaimed writer,
she was conscious of English literary stereotypes about the Irish and,
when asked about her next literary project, answered sharply: 'I am
now writing a play about Ireland, but it is not an Irish play of the
usual type. All Irish people are not peasants, you know.'[68] (This
protest against Irish peasantry may have had something to do with
the fact that Seán O'Casey was the other great commercial hit of
London theatre that summer. O'Casey had sent her a congratulatory
telegraph. 'Dublin ventures to salute Limerick.') The phrase 'All
Irish people are not peasants' expressed a central impulse within her
subsequent novels: the impulse to teach her English readers that
Ireland had a civilised and educated bourgeoisie, as civilised as any
in Europe. This was to be one of the strongest motiviations in her
novel-making.

3

Writing Mellick: 1926–34

In the years following the success of *Distinguished Villa*, Kate O'Brien found herself as a writer. She began to write novels based in her invented Mellick, exploring the moral conflicts of her Irish middle-class female protagonists. Emotionally, she found support, companionship and a sexual identity as a lesbian within the professional female world of her London working life. These two new factors in her life – the success of her creativity and the realisation of her sexuality – were the most important aspects of her adult life in England.

Although drama was the medium by which she became a writer, it did not sustain her. A subsequent play of Kate's, *The Bridge*, opened in May 1927 at the Arts Theatre Club in London but proved unsuccessful, and her next play, *The Silver Roan*, was never staged. However, the success of *Distinguished Villa* meant that she was now regarded as a professional writer and, in January 1927, PEN, the writers' association, invited her to join. Kate attempted to repeat the commercial success of *Distinguished Villa* when she co-wrote a play on a biblical theme, *Susannah and the Elders*,[1] which was completed in 1931 but never staged. Her literary collaborator, Theodora Bosanquet (born in 1880), was a friend both of Kate and of Mary O'Neill. In many ways, her career is typical of many of Kate's friends. A university graduate, Theodora had worked as a literary editor and secretary for Henry James and, by the time she met Kate, she had already written a life of Harriet Martineau (1927). Theodora went on to publish books on Henry James (1931) and Paul Valery (1933) for the Hogarth Press. At the time of writing *Susannah and the Elders* (1931), Theodora Bosanquet was working as the secretary to the International Federation of University Women in London. The play connects with Kate's later fiction, in that Susannah, a Jewish woman in Babylon, is viewed with suspicion. In this priest-ridden society, Susannah is a learned woman with philosophical interests, but her independence of mind is considered to be compromising to her virtue (Susannah prefigures Ana de Mendoza, the persecuted heroine of *That Lady*).

Around this time, Kate wrote another full-length play called 'Gloria Gish';[2] likewise, this play was never performed and remains unpublished. Although the surviving manuscript, now in the National Library of Ireland, is undated, it is clear from the text that the action is set in the late 1920s and, thematically, the play has much in common with her later fictional concerns. The play is set in middle-class Surrey in the late 1920s and the central character, Gladys, an 'absolute beauty', is the indulged wife of the wealthy industrialist, Bill. The central dramatic interest of the play comes from Gladys's ambition to become a film star and outshine a mythical 1920s screen beauty Gloria Gish. Bill's money is employed to further her ambition, with comic results. Despite the thinness of the plot, 'Gloria Gish' is well written, sharp in tone and shows a lively ear for dialogue.

Drama did not sustain Kate imaginatively. In several newspaper interviews during the run of *Distinguished Villa*, Kate mentioned that she was toying with the idea of writing a novel. She had finished writing for the Sunlight League early in 1927 and, with the money she had earned from her play, she moved from her flat in Great James Street, Bloomsbury, to Ashurst Bank. She was established there by the summer of 1928 and it was at Ashurst Bank that she began writing a novel. She tells us: 'I had a cottage in Kent when I was writing my first book, *Without My Cloak*, I wrote most of it in a cottage on the Kent–Sussex border.'[3] Kate's nomadic work life was beginning, with constant moves and upheavals and intermittent financial crises, but she seemed to thrive on such wanderings and such insecurity and it never interfered with her impressive productivity as a novelist and critic.

Kate first made money as a professional writer by writing for the stage, but it was in fiction that she found herself. Creating a complete imaginative world satisfied her, giving her a place and a stable identity that were lacking in her outer life. Novel-writing occupied her for the next thirty years and her methods of composition were fixed and would always remain the same. She said in a television interview[4] that she wrote very slowly but rarely needed to revise and that, when she began a novel, she never knew how it would end. Her manuscripts attest to this care and often her first drafts were complete and ready for publication. In an essay, 'The art of writing',[5] she noted: 'I work so slowly, on such long and long reflections that were I – as so many do – to make second and third drafts, no book of mine would ever reach a publisher. No, I labour from the very beginning to get said at once, as closely as I can, what I intend to say.' Her pattern of writing was set from this time: 'When I'm working on a novel, I put in a good long spell each night – I write always at night. But I have long intervals when I can't write at all, apart from doing short articles or a short story....If I begin about five o'clock, I can work until about eight and then eat something and begin again about nine. When I have been really writing well, and under the stress of it, I've often worked on until nearly five in the morning.'[6]

Each of her nine novels is realist in form, and her primary focus as narrator is in representing psychological conflict and exploring the interior life of her characters. There is an archetypal plot in each successive novel, usually with a young Mellick girl at the centre who is unquestionably beautiful, intellectual and of fine conscience and bred in bourgeois civility and comfort. In the course of the novel, framed always within a conventional realist progression, the young woman attempts to confront her conventional destiny. She tries to find an independence away from the constrictions of family and of faith. A crisis of passion usually intervenes and the protagonist is inevitably propelled by sexual and emotional conflict into loss and isolation. This leads her towards a cool, detached rationalising of her sexuality and her emotions. Art, in some form or other, aids the young woman in achieving this rationalisation, be it a poem, a song, a line from a play or even a bullfight.

At the end of each novel, love, conflict and passion are over and the protagonist remains alone, shaken but wiser, and enriched with a fuller sense of self. The point of each of Kate O'Brien's novels is this achievement of a fuller selfhood. Sometimes she varies her archetypal plot, making the central character male, as in *Pray for the Wanderer*, or Spanish, as in *That Lady*, but each novel moves towards the same moment – a modernist realisation of essential isolation for the individual, with only the possible consolation of art. She was not a romantic novelist but one interested in representing the consequences of romance and desire within the consciousness of her protagonists. Her novels are reflections on loss, on love and on the failure of desire and the resultant melancholia attendant on such loss. A passage from *Without My Cloak* describes this imaginative texture perfectly: 'His old fastidious love of dropping the exquisite bitter into every sweet was taking a revenge. For nowadays there were moods when he could hardly see beauty for its blinding sadness and when he slipped into his old trick of seeing melancholy, it sprang to take him by the heart.' As her imaginative confidence became more established, Kate's emotional life was also becoming more defined. After her brief and somewhat stormy marriage, Kate's lesbian identity was now becoming established.

Veronica Turleigh was the actress friend from university who had challenged Kate to write her first play. She was also responsible for introducing her to Margaret 'Stephie' Stephens – the woman to whom Kate dedicated her first novel. Stephie lived with Kate at Ashurst Bank during the writing of the novel and was clearly her first female partner. The daughter of missionaries, Margaret Gadney was born in India in 1886 and had graduated from Royal Holloway College, London in 1910 with a degree in languages. With the birth of her daughter, Ruth, in 1916, Margaret Gadney changed her name to Mrs Margaret Stephens, to protect herself and her daughter from the social stigma of single parenthood. At one point in her career, Stephie worked as secretary to John Maynard Keynes, the celebrated economist, but otherwise she made her living as a freelance translator. She may have come to know Gustaaf Renier and Kate through her Dutch translation work. Stephie was close to Veronica Turleigh, Kate's friend from UCD, and came into Kate's life in the mid-1920s. By May 1928, Kate, Stephie and Ruth had made a home together at Ashurst Bank and the three, as a household, were gradually integrated into Kate's family circle. May O'Brien regularly visited Ashurst Bank and Nance and Stephen O'Mara hosted Kate, Stephie and Ruth on a visit to Limerick in the summer of 1930. When I spoke to her as a very old woman, Ruth Whitehead remembered Kate as an integral part of her childhood, a trusted figure throughout her life.

In 1934, Kate and Ruth spent the summer travelling to Spain, where Kate saw her first bullfight in Santander. The memory is recorded in *Farewell Spain*: 'I had never been to one until then.... Ruth, English and seventeen, begged me to let her come, too. I wondered what her mother, a very dear friend, would think. Nowadays, however, that is a quaint sort of wonder. I agreed that she should come.' Stephie also travelled with Kate to Spain and, in

Farewell Spain, Kate recalled going to a bullfight with Stephie too. 'Stephen said, as everyone says, that she thought she ought to see one. I was very doubtful about that.... At the end she was unhappy and profoundly exhausted but she admitted, reluctantly indeed, that she saw seductive beauty in the ring and an inexplicable nobility. "But I don't want to see another", she said and looking at her exhausted face one felt that that was the best.' It is interesting that Kate called her by the masculine 'Stephen' rather than 'Stephie', her usual name. Perhaps the character 'Stephen Gordon', the female protagonist of *The Well of Loneliness*, was in Kate's mind.

Kate left Kent in 1930 and moved back in Bloomsbury, in Gordon Square, but Stephie remained an important figure in her life. She was known amongst Kate's circle as the only person Kate feared, and this relationship continued for the rest of Kate's life; Stephie outlived Kate, dying in 1982. Her daughter, niece and grandchildren all maintained close ties with Kate.[7]

This relationship with Stephie raises the important question as to Kate's own sexuality. It is clear from her novels that she regarded erotic love between women as both possible and natural. As Emma Donoghue notes: 'Kate O'Brien, on the two occasions that she writes about passion between adult women, calls it exactly that; no coyness veils her analyses of lesbian relationships.'[8] Stephie's family remember clearly that all Stephie's sexual relationships were with women. Given the evidence of her life patterns, I maintain that Kate O'Brien was also lesbian and that her sexuality was, as with any sexuality, conditioned by her upbringing, her religious experiences and her culture. She may not have been openly lesbian, but she was lesbian by the lights of her own London life and her own experience.

Only once did she ever write about homosexuality and that in terms that suggested her own detachment from the subject and also her clear sense of the biographical irrelevance of sexuality in the life of an artist. Of the painter El Greco, in *Farewell Spain*, she wrote:

> He is said to have been homosexual, but that suggestion can be of little use to us in considering his work. More mighty than he have been touched with that peculiarity but the residue of all emotional experience tends in spirits large enough to be at last of natural and universal value, whatever the personal accidents of its accretion.

Sexuality was, of course, of great usefulness when Kate wrote of her own characters, but her habit of careful distance about any public revelation of her own sexuality was characteristic of her time and her culture.

The critic Lillian Faderman defines lesbianism as 'a relationship in which two women's strongest emotions and affections are directed towards each other. Sexual contact may be a part of the relationship to a greater or lesser degree or it may be entirely absent.'[9] While Kate never wrote of herself as lesbian in these terms, critics and writers have classed her as a lesbian writer without any hesitation. Violet Powell, in her life of the popular novelist Elizabeth (E.M.) Delafield, is unequivocal: 'Elizabeth's women friends included Virginia Woolf, who published two of her books of literary criticism, and Kate O'Brien, who was to be a rock of support in the last hard years of her life. Both of these writers are known to have had lesbian relationships but Elizabeth herself was always interested in men.'[10] After Kate's death, this perception of her as Ireland's most important lesbian writer was clearly recognised by her surviving friends, however obliquely. A newspaper report on John Jordan's lecture at the Kate O'Brien weekend in Limerick in 1988 said that 'the novelist had certain problems of her own in that she was mannish in her ways and had difficulty in personal relationships. After her divorce from her Dutch husband, she made more friends among women.'[11] John Jordan's indirect and somewhat perjorative references to Kate's sexuality are evidence of the social constraints around homosexuality in Ireland even in the late 1980s rather than of any hostility toward his close friend and mentor.

Why did Kate never define herself openly as lesbian? For one, at this particular time, broader cultural perceptions of love between women were becoming increasingly uneasy and even hostile. In the nineteenth century, romantic friendships between women had been accepted because they were seen as chaste but profoundly emotional. As Faderman suggests, 'these romantic friendships were love relationships in every sense except perhaps the genital'.[12] However, with the increasing interest in psychology and sexology towards the end of the nineteenth century, these relationships became suspect from the outside and women who loved women had to protect themselves from public scrutiny and disapproval. Classified by sexologists as 'lesbian' in the year of Kate's birth, 1897, and often viewed as a morbid medical condition, women who loved other women found that they had lost the protection of this ideal of 'romantic friendship'. As Faderman notes: 'Openly expressed love between women for the most part ceased to be possible after World War I. Women's changing status and the new "medical knowledge" cast such affection in a new light.'[13] Radclyffe Hall's novel *The Well of Loneliness* and its subsequent trial for obscenity intensified this demonising of the lesbian. Significantly, it was published in 1928, the year that Kate and Stephie were setting up home in Ashurst.

Despite this demonising of the lesbian, Kate's sense of her own sexuality was, by the late 1920s, clearly women-centred and this influenced her mode of dress and self-presentation. Hall's protagonist, Stephen Gordon, courageously expressed her sense of sexual difference through the adoption of rational dress, having her hair cropped short and ordering tailored 'mannish' suits to wear. From this time onwards, Kate's habitual dress was distinctly non-feminine. She always wore business-like jackets, blouses and skirts and kept her hair short, adopting a slightly severe but practical style that differed from the more feminised style of her sisters Nance and May. Kate dressed to been seen as an independent professional woman, rather as a woman doctor of the period would have dressed. Sometimes she went even further in dressing differently from the codes of correct feminine attire. E.M. Delafield's daughter, Rosamund, remembered her as 'rather dashing in capes and cloak-like garments'.[14] Kate is also remembered as walking the streets of her native Limerick in mannish trouser suits.[15] Kate never compromised on this distinctive style of self-presentation. The biographer Violet Powell remembers meeting her at a cocktail party at the Savoy Hotel in London and remarked on her disarming disregard for any form of dress except her working clothes, her tweed suit.[16]

Given cultural difficulty with lesbian sexuality, it is not surprising that Kate never defined herself publicly as lesbian. Therefore, the web of interconnected relationships in her life is the only reliable biographical material available for an evaluation of her sexuality. Kate's emotional life, starting in London in the late 1920s and lasting until her death, was sited within an extended circle of professional, university-educated and independent women – academics, painters, writers, translators. This circle provided her with her main source of companionship and support. As Edith Somerville has written of her life partner, Violet Martin: 'The outstanding fact, as it seems to me, among women who live by their brains, is friendship.'[17]

The reappearance, around 1930, of another figure in Kate's life, her former pupil Mary O'Neill, throws further light on the nature of Kate's relationships with women. Mary O'Neill was Kate's pupil in 1921 in Hampstead and later studied at the Slade School of Art under Sir Henry Tonks. Her studies there were interrupted when her parents separated, but she continued to work as a painter and an art teacher and it was her sister Betty who met the now celebrated playwright and reintroduced her into the O'Neill family.[18] Kate became a close friend of Mary's mother, Elizabeth O'Neill, who supported her family by working as an archivist, and as a result Kate was, as Betty O'Neill remembers, 'almost like a father to us'.[19] Kate helped Mary's brother Bill in his attempts to publish a novel and was later to stand as godmother for Betty's son, Austin. Kate formed a life-long relationship with Mary. They travelled together in Spain in the mid-1930s and Mary provided the illustrations for *Farewell Spain* and for Kate's biography of Teresa of Avila, as well as painting in 1936 the study of Kate, now in the National Portrait Gallery in London.

Nonetheless, the relationship between Kate and Mary was much more profound than that of writer and illustrator. They were in constant contact with each other until Kate's death, with daily postcards or letters or phone calls and frequent visits and travels together. In Kate's letters to Mary, there is a constant thread of affection and admiration. Kate refers to her by various pet names, all allusions to Mary's beauty and fairness, calling her 'Bawnie' or 'La Rubia'. A common passion for cats and for feline postcards marked their constant interchange. Sometimes Kate wrote directly to Mary's cat, addressing her as 'Dona Matilda O'Neill'. In Kate's later travels, Mary's flat in Hampstead was her London address and refuge. Their friend, the gay actor, Micheál MacLiammoir, in a letter to Mary, describes her as 'the clearest and dearest image in Kate's life'.[20] The lifelong trust and love between Kate and Mary O'Neill was undoubtedly understood by many of their closest friends. This trust was exemplified when Kate appointed Mary as her literary executor and co-heir.

As Kate became part of Mary's life and a friend of her mother and sister, so Mary was integrated into Kate's own life. Mary painted a portrait of Stephie's daughter Ruth in 1932 and received a copy of Gustaaf Renier's book *Oscar Wilde* directly from Renier. Theodora Bosanquet, Kate's friend and literary collaborator, paid for Mary to travel to Spain with Kate in 1934. Whenever Mary visited Dublin, Nance O'Mara would meet her. Mary O'Neill's friendship with Stephie's family led to a close relationship with Stephie's grandniece, Orlaith Kelly.

It is clear that Kate encouraged her close women friends and her family to form independent relationships. This woman-centred, inclusive web of relationships was necessary in a society where adult women were defined by marriage. This meant that Kate could live as a lesbian, something of a balancing act, rather like the balancing of the Irish and English parts of her life. It says much for her skills with lovers and family that it worked, integrating them all into the everyday pattern of her life. Her London life was key in this process of self-assertion and it says even more for a woman from her conservative Irish Catholic background that she could claim a life as a gay woman as she did. Much of this self-assertion is reflected in the radical achievement of her fictions.

So, as Emma Donoghue has written: 'Reading Kate O'Brien as a lesbian novelist is as fruitful, and as necessary, I suggest, as reading Elizabeth Bowen as Irish, Jane Austen as middle class or Alice Walker as black.'[21] Kate's representations of love between women were radical and sympathetic, compared to the tortured and unhappy women depicted in Djuna Barnes's *Nightwood*, published in the same year as *Mary Lavelle*.

Many of Kate's friends had religion in common: those close to Kate, like Mary O'Neill, Gustaaf Renier, E.M. Delafield and others, were Catholic. English Catholicism was part of this world of woman-centred relationships and Kate's representation of Catholicism in Ireland comes from these English circles. In England at this time, many women-loving women were turning to Catholicism for spiritual support and affirmation. For example, Radclyffe Hall converted to Catholicism in 1912. This seems paradoxical, given the Catholic Church's condemnation of homosexuality. (Radclyffe Hall's biographer, Sally Cline, wrote: 'Today in Anglo-American society, the Catholic Church is seen as a prime enemy of homosexuality among both women and men.' Yet, as Radclyffe Hall's conversion shows, for women at least this has not always been the case. Her conversion was but one among many undertaken by lesbian writers.)[22] Many 'queer' women and men in England in the late nineteenth and early twentieth centuries turned to the Catholic Church for spiritual solace.[23] The aesthetic appeal for gay people came from the fact that the Catholic

Church in Britain was marginal, elitist, ritualised and pre-modern in its liturgy and its music. Evelyn Waugh's 1945 novel, *Brideshead Revisited*, is characteristic of this idealised view of the English Catholic Church. In such novels, the forbidden erotics of same-sex desire were transformed into an aesthetic by Catholic ritual. This aesthetic version of English Catholicism influenced Kate's own fiction. Her imagined Irish Catholic characters, particularly in novels like *The Ante-Room* and *The Land of Spices*, owe much more to Kate's adult experience of Catholicism in England than to her childhood in Laurel Hill. Thus she was able to write about believing Irish Catholics who managed to be both sexually dissident and spiritually independent.

As to her own religious beliefs, Kate was no longer a believing or practising Catholic, but she retained a profound reverence for Catholicism as a form of cultural identity. Irish critic Brian Fallon, writing about her relationship with Catholicism, comments:

> Kate O'Brien...seems in some scarcely orthodox sense to have kept her religious faith, which had been mellowed by the experience of continental Catholicism....She spoke to and for people, who, while they might be critical of many of the Catholic Church's sayings and doings, still counted themselves believing Catholics in spiritual communion with millions around the world. Criticism of Rome did not necessarily imply rejection of it; there was an intellectual reverence for the greatness of its traditions and its enduring relevance.[24]

I disagree with Fallon when he says she retained her faith, but she did write for those who still revered the Catholic Church. Where she parted company radically with other Irish Catholic intellectuals was, unsurprisingly, on the issue of sexuality and sexual freedom.

Living in England, unmarried and financially independent, meant that Kate O'Brien was free to invent her own version of Irish Catholicism. Distance meant that she could invent a version of Irish Catholicism in her novels where individual conscience and personal choice on moral issues was possible. Irish Catholics were outraged.

With an established emotional and professional life, Kate persevered with writing fiction and, on her birthday in 1931, her first novel was published. (In one review[25] she says that the publication date, 3 December 1931, was her thirty-first birthday, but it was, in fact, her thirty-fourth.) *Without My Cloak* was dedicated to

Stephie and was published by Heinemann, who accepted it on the strength of the first eleven chapters – or so Kate claimed. It was a best seller.[26] Heinemann royalties to authors in the 1930s varied between 19 per cent and 24 per cent and so she would have made enough money to live independently as a writer. The book was also critically successful, winning her the Hawthornden and James Tait Black memorial prizes in 1932. *Without My Cloak* helped her to establish a fruitful and successful relationship with Heinemann for the rest of her career. As John St John, the historian of Heinemann, writes: 'Kate was very fond of Charles Evans [commissioning editor for Heinemann], who gave her much personal help.... At one point the firm was to give her an interest free loan of one thousand pounds.'[27]

Without My Cloak follows the fortunes of the Considines, a prosperous Catholic family living in a southern Irish town called Mellick in the latter half of the nineteenth century. To a large degree, Kate identifies the Considines with her own family and Mellick with Limerick; as a result, she is ambiguous in her representation of family life. On the one hand, the narrative, which is realistic in form, traces four generations of Considines. It follows a line of patriarchal descent from father to son, from Anthony, the horse thief, through Honest John, founder of the family fortune, Anthony, the late Victorian consolidator of wealth and position, and finally to Denis, rebel and dissenter. This tale of the Considine struggle from poverty towards bourgeois wealth celebrates the resolve and vigour of the family. In it, Kate uses her own version of the O'Brien's rise from post-Famine peasant destitution to Limerick merchant respectability. Like Kate herself, these Mellick Considines are also proud of the lowly status of their forefathers: 'Anthony was a snob himself, if it is snobbish to take a too-emphatic pride in lowly origins. He exulted, as did all the Considines, in the hard story of his father's life and attached a value that was at least debatable to its material achievement.'

Her need to represent the Irish bourgeoisie as civilised and self-confident is clear, but her view of bourgeois life differed from the conventional literary definition of the bourgeoisie as middle-class, stolid and prosaic. Kate's Irish merchant souls are bourgeois only in name, because she viewed them as natural rulers, serenely resistant to colonial prejudice and secure in their physical beauty and refinement. On the other hand, her representation of the bourgeois Considines was not completely idealised. The title of the novel comes from Shakespeare's Sonnet 34, a poem lamenting emotional vulnerability, 'Why didst thou promise such a beauteous day, /And make me travel forth without my cloak'. Kate presents a saga of middle-class family life where solitude is most deeply felt by those members of the family 'without cloaks', those with imaginations and souls. As the novel progresses, imaginative sympathy moves towards the dissenters and rebels within the family – Eddy, Caroline, Denis – and away from the upholders of a communal family ethos – Anthony, Father Tom, Teresa. As Kate presents it, the price for conforming to a middle-class family ethos is dangerously high to those with imagination. Her protagonists are caught within an oppressive world of family affection and duty and find that they are unable to escape. In the notes she made in preparing the novel, the following words occur: 'The burden of tradition, the cruel bonds of filial love.'[28]

In the novel, Eddy, the homosexual brother living away in London, is the character nearest to Kate herself: 'Eddy Considine was the sort of man who was liked in England for his unmistakable Irishry and admired in Ireland for his total lack of it.' As the narrative gradually reveals, Eddy's life in London moves him further and further away from Mellick and its values. He finds himself tormented by the gap between his London self and his Mellick self:

> He wanted sometimes, or almost wanted, with a great bewilderment, to get back miles and miles from the particular point that he had reached, further back from it than Anthony was or Caroline, back to where the root normality and plainness of his stock was still abounding.

Eddy's life in London is secret and threatening to his Mellick family. His sister Teresa, a stolid Mellick matron, takes a guess at this difference: 'and still there remained something about this brother that dimly frightened the shrewd Teresa. Something vague and unfamiliar about his ways. He positively ought to marry.' Kate's own sense of a divided life between Limerick and Bloomsbury is clearly the inspiration for her representation of Eddy. A crisis comes when Caroline, the beautiful, unhappily married Considine sister, leaves her lawyer husband and runs away to her brother Eddy in London. Her subsequent love affair with Eddy's lover Richard 'outs' her brother, and Kate stresses the unsustainability of such relationships outside the pale of Mellick. Eddy tells Richard: 'I've never loved a woman except Caroline; and you love her, and I love her more perhaps than I love you, more even than I love myself. And these loves of ours are out of order and come to no good.'

Caroline's attempted escape from Mellick fails when her brother Anthony follows her to London and forces her to return to her husband. It is for the next generation to attempt another rebellion against the oppressive conformity of the Considines. The fourth in the line of Considine males, Denis, is destined to inherit the firm. Denis's slow recognition of the oppressive nature of that inheritance is hampered by the overwhelming love his father, Anthony, has for him: 'Suddenly it seemed to him that he hated his father, who had compelled from him so womanish and unnatural a love.' As Kate noted in her research book while preparing the novel, 'to succeed in one love is an immense success and may demand failure in all other loves'.[29]

It is left to Eddy to explain to his nephew the very difficult and contradictory nature of Considine familial love:

> You haven't escaped any more than the rest of us our terrible family affection, our cowardly inability to do without each other. Why, our whole strength is simply in our instinct to be large and populous and united. We cover all our secret misgivings by mass formation.... The compromise that will be required of you in all your years in Mellick will be a long one.

In resolving this deadlock between communal values and individual emotional life, Kate has a failure of nerve. Instead of continuing, the deadlock is broken artificially when Denis falls in love with Anna Hennessy, the daughter of a suitable Mellick family. His love for Anna satisfies his desire for a soulmate and fulfils his romantic ideal. She also persuades him to stay in Mellick. As a novelist, Kate is not yet ready to break with the conformities of her Irish middle-class world.

Unlike many first novels, *Without My Cloak* remained a popular choice. It sold 50,000 in the first few months and the Book Society selected it as 'Book of the Month' and marketed it as, 'in the plainest sense of the word, a thoroughly good novel'.[30] Years later, Kate commented on the commercial success of her first novel: 'I wrote this book so long ago that I have difficulty in imagining it. It seems to have given much pleasure over the years to all kinds of readers.'[31] It was to earn her consistent royalties and was translated into Spanish, Italian, German and even Czech, with a paperback Penguin edition published in 1949. It stayed in print up to her death and was adapted for BBC Radio in April 1969.

After leaving Ashurst, Kate was now living between a rented flat in Chelsea and a cottage in East Anglia. She began writing a second Mellick novel and used her free time as a professional writer to make visits to Spain. She also began to publish her first pieces of literary journalism, short works like 'Return in Winter', an impressionistic piece about life in the countryside, published in a collection called *Contemporary Essays*,[32] which included other young writers like Edmund Blunden and Graham Greene. Like many first essays, 'Return in Winter' lacks the clarity of her later work but does include the revealing statement that 'to fib without lying – that is the creative writer's job'.[33]

In 1934, Kate moved back to Bloomsbury in London. In an otherwise nomadic existence, she made her home there for the next few years, staying on until early 1940, and making a circle of friends which included other young writers like John and Barbara Gosworth and the poet Anna Wickham. This was an unusually settled time for her, where she wrote and travelled and lived as part of a literary circle, a sub-Bloomsbury group:

> In the 1930s, I was tenant of a top floor flat at no 33, Great James St, Bloomsbury, and the Gosworths, John and Barbara, occupied the flat below me...there were some celebrities, major and minor, dwelling among us then. Dorothy Sayers next door to the 'Rugby'...who rode a devil of a motor bike....I for one remember them in vivid light – for they were vivid and my impression is that there was much summer weather in our street. Music from non-stop gramophones, John and his friends Hugh McDiarmid [Scottish poet and founder of the Scottish Nationalist Party], Audrey Beecham, chanting their lines and dashing around wreathed in long, inky galley-proofs; Mary O'Neill running up the stairs like 'The Angel of the Lord' as Anna Wickham called her; Anna Wickham herself, her arms full of wild rhodo-dendrons, stolen as she crossed the Heath! Anna, writing sudden wonderful satires on the panelling and John, her Boswell, flying to copy it down; Anna on sentry-go up and down outside no 33, lest any of us refusing to open doors to her at eight a.m. should escape her excessive need of her, Anna crying out, à propos of a novel of mine that she was reading 'I am lonely for the Irish Bourgeoisie'.[34]

The poet Anna Wickham, with her 'excessive need' of Kate, was a vivid presence in those years in Great James Street. Born Edith Harper in London in 1884, Anna Wickham[35] was a poet, a friend and admirer of the lesbian writer Natalie Barney and, for a while, a passionate admirer of Kate. (In later life Kate recounted the story of Anna Wickham's first meeting with Barney in Paris, where Anna had gone on a pilgrimage to meet her idol: on arrival, she had thrown her arms around Barney, accidentally smashing the two bottles of wine she had brought as tribute and drenching them both in wine!)[36] Wickham lived with her sons on Parliament Hill in London during the 1930s and became a friend of Kate's, sending her poems and letters expressing her devotion. Sometimes calling her 'Madonna Berg', Wickham's love letters and poems to Kate were increasingly urgent: 'I begin to want to have phrases between us. I love you and no one may know',[37] but it was a relationship that didn't last beyond Kate's move to Oxford at the start of World War II.

Kate soon ran into trouble with money, a constant feature of her working life. Although she worked hard at literary journalism, she was always spending money, constantly travelling, and soon she ran into debt. This constant lack of money was due partly to the fact that she had no regular income and was paid at freelance rates. Freelance work included short fiction writing for journals and Kate published a short story called 'Golden lady' for a series in the *News Chronicle*. Other writers in this series included popular novelists like Storm Jameson and L.A.G. Strong, an indication of Kate's growing reputation as a commercial and accessible novelist. The stories were later collected in a volume entitled *The First Class Omnibus*,[38] edited by Helen Gosse and published in 1934. Unusually for Kate, 'Golden lady' is an archetypal Irish story in the same genre as Frank O'Connor and Sean O'Faolain, a tale of repressed love in a Irish farming family. In 'Golden lady', two brothers fall in love with the same woman and the elder brother loses interest out of love and loyalty for his sibling. This anticipates the emotional tangle of Kate O'Brien's second novel, published in 1934 under the title *The Ante-Room*

This novel is also set in Mellick and continues the saga of the Considine family, but it focuses on one branch of the family, the Mulqueens. The narrative concentrates on three days when the members of the Mulqueen family are waiting at the deathbed of their mother, Teresa. This intensification of narrative focus allows Kate to develop the clash between family affection and individual desire more completely. As with *Without My Cloak*, Kate allowed no escape from this deadlock between family and individuality. Kate dedicated this novel about doomed love between a woman and her sister's husband to her own sister Nance and her husband: 'To Nance and Stephen O'Mara, under whose kind roof the greater part of this book was written. I dedicate it with my love and gratitude.'

With a deathbed at the centre of the action and an adulterous passion as the emotional interest of the narrative, *The Ante-Room* is a dark, even gloomy, novel. As with the Considines, there is solitude for every member of this prosperous family and each bond of love intensifies rather than relieves the isolation. Like *Without My Cloak*, unreasoned family love is the theme here. The mother of the family, Teresa Mulqueen, loves her stricken son Reggie, but uncertainty as to his future after her death makes his love painful to her and prolongs her deathbed sufferings. Teresa's preference for her invalid son has cost her the normal love and respect of her other children: 'Firmly, ruthlessly, without a word of pity or sentiment, she [Teresa] had built for her wasted son a life that was safe from life. She had built it with a concentration of purpose which had almost cost her the love of her other children and had certainly caused the withdrawal of their confidence.'

Reggie is syphilitic and his mother plots to marry him off to the young and ambitious Nurse Cunningham, a project that prolongs her life in a tortured and self-denying way. However, the central relationship in the novel is that between Agnes Mulqueen and her sister Marie-Rose. Agnes's feelings for her sister are overwhelming and passionate: 'Still, in the hour of waking, she sometimes reflected coldly upon the unrelated phases of her life, through which the only unifying thread was Marie-Rose.' Agnes's passion for her sister is put to the test when Vincent, Marie-Rose's disaffected husband, falls out of love with his wife and in love with Agnes herself. This passion is intensified when Agnes returns his love. Agnes is the first of a series of O'Brien protagonists who fall for married men (Mary Lavelle, Ana de Mendoza). Adulterous passion is always approved of and even ennobled by Kate O'Brien's authorial voice.[39]

The authorial voice contrasts Marie-Rose and Agnes in terms of femininity and in terms of beauty – Marie-Rose is the feminine and pretty sister, Agnes the austere and androgynous beauty – and this polarity between versions of womanhood continues throughout her fiction. Irish critic Patricia Coughlan comments: 'In her novels, the physical descriptions of central female characters extravagantly stress their visual attractiveness' and she remarks on 'the sensuous narcissism of Marie-Rose'.[40] As a novelist, Kate O'Brien insisted on portraying characters who were perfectly beautiful and who gloried in this physical perfection, a symptom of her novel as a place to idealise.

Her insistence on female and male beauty is linked to her insistence on the material confidence of the Irish bourgeoisie. In one incident in *The Ante-Room*, she uses her Mellick beauties to score a point against imperialist Britain. A distinguished English surgeon, Sir Godfrey Bartlett-Crowe, pays a visit to Mellick to stay with the Mulqueens. His British expectations of savagery among the Irish provincials are comically overturned:

> But to plunge right into the murderous and stormy south, to stay in the home of a real Irishman, a Catholic, to attend the wife of a small town merchant and waste twenty-four hours, and perhaps encounter danger in doing so – that at first blush had seemed an absurd suggestion.

As Sir Godfrey gets over his initial fear and settles down to the comforts of the Mulqueen home, his thoughts turn to the erotic possibilities of this strange, uncivilised land: 'Sir Godfrey was a connoisseur of women up and down the social scale, but he had never met a colleen. Amusedly in the train, he had wondered about the species. Shy and wild no doubt – perhaps even barefoot – and in need of masterly coaxing.'

Kate overturns the Englishman's stereotypical view of the Irish 'colleen' with an emphasis on the beauty and cool self-possession of Marie-Rose and Agnes. Sir Godfrey finds himself at a disadvantage: 'These ladies were not shy and wild, and though they had a brogue, Sir Godfrey felt that its movements were too subtle for immediate imitation.'

During his stay in Mellick, Sir Godfrey becomes hopelessly infatuated with Marie-Rose, to her amusement, and this passion disempowers him. He is glad finally to leave Mellick: 'The sooner an ageing, restless, conceited man with an ageing, restless, conceited wife, forgot the soft sweet Irish rose, the better.' The natural superiority of the Mellick woman overturns the colonial relation and tilts emotional power back to the Irish.

As the novel ends, the various agonies within the Mulqueen family intensify: Teresa's death, Agnes's adulterous passion, Reggie's fear, Marie-Rose's marital gloom. Little direct acknowledgement is made of this agony in the family. The only moment of direct emotional appeal comes at one point when Marie-Rose sings Schubert in the parlour after dinner. Music becomes a covert way of communicating between the two sisters and, in this, Kate is drawing directly on the musical evenings of her own childhood in Boru House:

> Marie-Rose, singing, wondered at herself with faint irony, and yet knew that out of some crazy loneliness she was singing to her sister, in denial of her own present life of contempt and irritation, and to praise that which could never be again, the harmony of innocence and irresponsibility in which Agnes and she had flowered, their spirits nurturing each other.

Agnes honours the silent pleading from her sister and chooses familial love over personal desire when she breaks with Vincent. Vincent's despair at this rejection leads to his suicide:

> Dear love, last night–Du bist die Ruh. Die Ruh. He remembered leaning on a gun in the garden at home on a sunny day, leaning like this and talking to his mother. It was summer and she was sewing. She had said, 'Don't lean on it, Vin, It will mark your face.' Darling mother. He smiled. He could see every detail of her smile. Darling mother. He pulled the trigger, his thoughts far off in boyhood.

Suicide is the only escape from this stalemate, or so it seems in this novel. *The Ante-Room* is a novel in which Kate O'Brien idealises the Mellick bourgeoisie and, at the same time, suggests an emotional conflict within this world that can be broken only melodramatically.

Unlike the more popular *Without My Cloak*, Kate was pleased with *The Ante-Room*. The unity of time and place appealed to her, as did the pervasive melancholy of the novel. In a letter to her friend John Jordan,[41] she makes the point that she is a better novelist than her admirers know, or indeed her despisers, and goes on to describe the novel as masterly. At the end of her writing career, she wrote of it as an unappreciated work but her purest, strongest and best-formed, doubting, in hindsight, the wisdom of Vincent's suicide at the end, but still calling it 'a damm good example of a tragic novel'. Later, Jordan wrote that it was always customary to speak of *The*

Ante-Room as her best novel.[42] Vivian Mercier reported: 'Miss O'Brien says, and I agree with her, that *The Ante-Room* is her best novel.... Only in a predominantly Catholic country could she have developed her attitude to the whole problem of sex. She is preoccupied with sin without being puritanical.'[43]

Kate returned to the stage with an adaptation of *The Ante-Room*, which opened in August 1936 at the Queen's Theatre in London. This was the first of her novels to be adapted for the stage and, although she did have two co-adaptors, she claimed in a note on the manuscript of the play version that she did most of the adapting herself. The play was the first production by H.M. Tennent and was directed by Guthrie McClintic. (McClintic was married to the stage actress Katherine Cornell and, ten years later, Kate was to adapt her novel *That Lady* for Broadway, with Katherine Cornell starring and, again, Guthrie McClintic directing.) The distinguished cast included Jessica Tandy as Marie-Rose and Dana Wynyard as Agnes. Despite this, the play failed to please and was, in Kate's own words, 'a sickening flop'.[44]

A young actor called Denys Blakelock played the part of Reggie and he became friendly with Kate, a friendship that lasted intermittently until her death. A Catholic, like many of her English connections, and gay, Blakelock remembered her at this time as 'a romantic personality. She might have materialised from the pages of one of her own stories. Her voice, with that slight yet unmistakable cadence of the cultured Irish, was one of the most charming I have ever heard. It would have served her well had she decided to become an actress, instead of becoming the scholar and incomparable writer she is today.'[45]

She was already developing a professional confidence in her dealings with actors, directors and publishers and this description of her voice accords with her many radio broadcasts that still survive. As an Irishwoman living in England, Kate's ability to modulate her accent – her control of her self-presentation – was already marked. With two novels published and her Mellick world established, Kate O'Brien now began to expand her imaginative horizons and incorporate more of her life experience into her fiction. Her first Mellick novel had ended with a conventional marriage and the second with a despairing suicide. In her next work, she turned away from Ireland and towards a Spanish setting as a way of altering her imaginative world. Just before her marriage, Spain had offered her a brief escape, a breathing space. Now, as a novelist, Spain offered her a way out of the deadlock of Mellick.

4

Banned: 1934–41

By the mid-1930s, Kate O'Brien was well established as a professional writer and the idea of Spain was to transform her imaginative concerns. Placing her Irish protagonists within a Spanish milieu energised her as a novelist and she returned with a new intensity to her familiar preoccupations; the formation of individual conscience, the transforming nature of art, the cruelty of passion and the variety of sexual identity. Spain mattered to her as an Irish writer living in Britain: 'We, a little provincial clutter, as might be thought an outsider, have always had the knack – in our religious history as well as in our literary – of catching on to Europe – of by-passing our British conquerors in our thought and reaching out to Spain and France.'[1] Spain allowed her to transcend the limitations of her imagined Mellick by suggesting a historical link between Catholic Ireland and the humanist civilisation of Catholic Europe. However, this imaginative transformation was to bring her to the attention of the Irish censors.

With this growing confidence as a professional writer came an evolving personal confidence. Mary O'Neill wrote in the *Dictionary of National Biography* that Kate had been reserved as a young woman but subsequently had developed a confident social manner, which served her well in her search for freelance writing and as a traveller. She spoke and dressed and lived as an independent woman of intellect. Therefore, by her own account, she was comfortable going alone to the theatre and the cinema, and even drinking alone in pubs, at a time when lone women were made to feel suspect in such public venues. She had very little interest in the domestic world, apart from a hospitable generosity in providing food and drink for guests, and she had no time for private hobbies or pursuits. Apart from reading and writing, she liked spending time talking and drinking with friends. She could be intellectually intimidating, sharp in her opinions and most decided in her intellectual preferences and dislikes. Her friend, the Irish writer Benedict Kiely, remembered her as 'a handsome, well-built woman with a mannish hairstyle who had a direct way of speaking. She put you on your toes and kept you there.'[2] She could be dismissive in adult company, but there are several accounts of the young children of her friends finding her likeable and sympathetic and she was particularly sensitive to the awkwardness and shyness of adolescence. As part of her social manner, she sometimes presented herself as a humorous, self-deprecating woman of the world, at ease in a bohemian milieu and not easily shocked, and she deliberately constructed this social self, altering and shaping it in relation to her position as a woman writer.

In her letters and in some of her studio photographs, she consciously experiments with self-presentation. In a series of publicity shots that are now in the National Portrait Gallery in London, Kate tried out versions of herself: The Distinguished Woman Writer, The Bohemian Artist. She also adapted her tone in letters to suit her correspondent. When writing to her older sister May, for example, she was loving, meek and even platitudinous. In contrast, her letters to literary connections like John Gosworth and John Jordan were racy, flippant and amusingly dismissive. Her creation of a humorous, assured and lively public persona was her defence for an uncertain self. It is only in her fiction and in some of her critical writings that a distinctive 'voice' emerges, the voice of an isolated, melancholic yet courageous sensibility.

Based at 33 Great James Street, from 1934 onwards, an accepted writer of two well-received novels, Kate was now living and working in a literary circle, though not exactly the Bloomsbury circle of nearby Gordon Square and Tavistock Place. In 1933, the writer Marie Belloc Lowndes, a sister of Hilaire Belloc and once a friend of Oscar Wilde, had written her a letter praising *Without My Cloak* and asking after her new novel. The PEN club was a common interest for them both and this friendship flourished, lasting until Marie Belloc Lowndes' death in 1947. Rupert Hart-Davis, the editor of Wilde's letters, was another literary connection from this time.[3]

Her new freedom as a professional writer allowed her the opportunity to return to Spain. She had not been back since her time as a governess in Bilbao in 1922.

Ten years later I returned as an ordinary traveller... and then I think that for most of the summers of '33, '34, '35 until the Spanish Civil War broke out in July 1936...I used to fool around the cities of Castile. Taking my time and spending little money. I was fascinated and very happy.[4]

When travelling, Kate liked to sit at a pavement café, book and cigarettes at hand, observing the passers-by. Mary O'Neill accompanied her in 1934 and Stephie and Ruth came with her to Santander. In November 1934, Kate was featured in press photos of the Heinemann writers' party as 'the author of *Without My Cloak*, just back from Spain'.[5] Her travels in Spain also produced one of her first short stories, 'Overheard', which was published in 1935 in *Time and Tide*.[6] These visits continued as she worked on her third novel, *Mary Lavelle*, a book that marked a change in her imaginative explorations. Throughout the 1930s and, in particular, after the publication of *The Ante-Room*, Spain became her inspiration.

So what exactly did she mean when she talked about 'her' Spain? She was attracted towards the essential soul of Spain, as she saw in it a lonely, noble spirituality derived from its austere landscape and expressed in the lives and beliefs of its great mystics and writers, St Teresa of Avila, Cervantes, John of the Cross. Kate's Spanish landscape is often Castile, a landscape described by her heroine Mary Lavelle as 'immediately appealing, pastoral, austere and tender'. However, her Spanish intellectual and spiritual heritage is exclusively Catholic. She allows no other landscape or traditions within the Iberian Peninsula to find a place in her Spain. Agatha Conlon says in *Mary Lavelle*: 'Ah, but Castile is good. It's the best of Spain. "Castile and the Bullfight".' (It is clear from Kate's description of her reading of Spanish literature that she draws heavily on the mythologising of the Castilian landscape by poets like Unamuno.)[7]

Her first Spanish novel, *Mary Lavelle*, is set in 1922, the year Kate spent as a governess in Bilbao, and the heroine is twenty-four, Kate's age in that year. The setting for the novel is taken directly from her own experiences as a 'Miss', with Bilbao renamed as Altorno, the seaside village of Portugalete as Cabantes and the Areilza house as Casa Pilar. Mary Lavelle has three teenage girls in her care, the daughters of a wealthy family, the Areveagas (they study *Emma* with Mary Lavelle, as did the young Areilzas with Kate).

In the novel, Mary, the daughter of a Mellick doctor, journeys out to Cabantes to work as a governess for a year. She is to be married, and her fiancé, a suitable, conservative, unimaginative Mellick man called John, is very much in love with her. Mary's decision to go to Spain troubles him, but she insists:

> To go to Spain. To be alone for a little space, a tiny hiatus between her life's two accepted phases. To cease being a daughter without immediately becoming a wife. To be a free lance, to belong to no one place or family or person.... She would be unobserved, uncherished, and, she hoped, unreproved. She had in fact put on a cap of invisibility, from under which, however, she could use her unlearned eyes with circumspection and in peace.

As she relaxes into this new country, Mary finds herself drawn towards Spain and soon starts to outgrow her Mellick identity: 'Although she did not observe the fact, she was growing up fast in this foreign soil, much faster than she or John, when they argued about the value of such growth, could possibly have anticipated.' Mary's hope of a 'cap of invisibility' vanishes when she becomes the focus of a number of obsessive loves, her great beauty attracting her employer, Don Pablo, his married son, Juanito, and her compatriot, Agatha Conlon. On the evening of Mary's arrival in Don Pablo's house, he falls for her:

> Yet this evening, strolling without premonition on to the terrace to see the ferry depart for Torcal, he had encountered that against which he believed no man, however old or wise or tired, can be adequately armed. He had met beauty, mythical, innocent, shameless.... A girl in a pale blue cotton dress and tennis shoes.... Her hair, of goldish brown, was curly and clung to her head like a Greek boy's. Her blue eyes, boyish too, androgynous, were wide and shy, but darkened by dark lashes and by shadows of fatigue. Her mouth was a wide red bow. Her carriage of head, neck and breast most virginal and pagan. He had never seen before in the flesh ... the old eternal poetic myth of girlhood.

Despite these intrusive loves that surround her, Mary Lavelle develops imaginatively and morally in Spain. Crucial to her development is her experience of the bullfight. In Kate O'Brien's description of the bullfight, there is an eroticised masochism, a celebration of ritualised brutality, which reveals much of her own

attraction towards Spain, and this aesthetic awakening for her
central character is perhaps the most radical element in her fiction
up to this point:

> The matador drew his enemy to his breast, and past it, on the gentle
> lure; brought him back along his thigh as if for sheer love; let him go
> and drew him home again.... Again and again in classic passes he
> allowed the horn to skim him, then drawing back from the great
> weary but still alert antagonist, he profiled and went over the horn, as
> gently as an angel might, to kill.

Kate constructs the spectacle of the bullfight as epiphany, a
coming to knowledge for the young Mellick woman, remade by the
spectacle of Spanish art:

> Burlesque, fantastic, savage, all that John had said – but more vivid
> with beauty and all beauty's anguish, more full of news of life's
> possible pain and senselessness and quixotry and barbarism and glory
> than anything ever before encountered by this girl; more real and
> exacting, more suggestive of wild and high exactations, more
> symbolic, more dramatic, a more personal and searching arrow to the
> heart than ever she had dreamed of.... Here – and Mary, to whose
> youth all knowledge was new, received this sudden piece of it as
> crippling pain – here was art, in its least decent form, its least
> explainable or bearable. But art, unconcerned and lawless.

With this aesthetic revelation, Mary is moved 'outside' herself and
confronts the moral problems created by Spain. In the Mellick
novels, these moral conflicts end in deadlock and tragedy, but, in
Spain, a more expansive moral world is possible. One of these
conflicts arises when Mary decides to pursue a sexual affair with a
married man, Juanito, the eldest son of the family. Representations
of sexual love are rare in the novels of Kate O'Brien and they are
always illicit, mostly outdoors, often spied upon and rarely
pleasurable. Her description of Mary's love-making with Juanito is
a characteristic example of this kind of writing and is less than life-
enhancing. There are direct echoes of the cruelty of the bullfight, a
necessary cruelty as Kate O'Brien saw it:

> He took her quickly and bravely. The pain made her cry out and
> writhe in shock, but he held her hard against him and in great love

compelled her to endure it. He felt the sweat of pain break out over all the silk of her body. He looked at her face, flung back against the moss, saw her set teeth and quivering nostrils, beating eyelids, flowing, flowing tears.... She was no longer Aphrodite, but a broken, tortured Christian, a wounded Saint Sebastian.

This moment of passion has tragic implications since, indirectly, it causes the death of Juanito's father. Towards the end of the novel, when Mary decides to leave Spain, Don Pablo unwittingly stumbles across the evidence of her adulterous affair with his son and, in his agitation, succumbs to a heart attack. The rituals of pain and death in the bullfight echo in the love-making scene and then onwards into the death agonies of Don Pablo, linking the aesthetic cruelty of the bullfight with the destructive nature of sexual passion.

Lesbian love is the other moral issue in this novel, the avowal of desire of one woman for another, and this other love story acts as a subtext within the dominant heterosexual romance. The story of this woman, Agatha Conlon, is linked closely to that of Mary Lavelle and, in a sense, the fate of each woman parallels the other. If the twenty-three-year-old Mary was a version of Kate herself in 1922, then Agatha Conlon, in her late thirties, is another version of Kate herself as she writes the novel in 1936. Agatha is not Kate's first homosexual character – Martin Devoy and Eddy Considine in *Without My Cloak* precede her – but this is her first portrayal of a lesbian. Her characterisation is, for its time, remarkably open and enlightened. As Emma Donoghue argues: 'Agatha is no stereotype and, compared to the tortured lesbians of Djuna Barnes (1936), for example, she is full of life.'[8] Agatha declares her love for Mary clearly and without evasion:

I told you a lie that day. You asked me if I'd ever had a crush .... And I said that I'd never had a crush on a living creature. That would have been true up to the first day I saw you. It's not true any more.... Are you shocked? I like you that way a man would, you see. I never can see you without – without wanting to touch you. I could look at your face forever.

Instead of horrifying and alienating the convent-bred Mellick girl, this declaration has the effect of bringing Agatha and Mary closer together. As Emma Donoghue points out, 'Mary has realised how similar their situations are; as she tells Agatha, "You take one kind of impossible fancy, I take another".[9] Agatha Conlon is the first 'holy woman' or secular nun in Kate's fiction, the first of a linked series of independent-minded ascetic women. Later examples of 'holy women' include Helen Archer, Ana de Mendoza and Eleanor Delahunt, characters inspired, partly, by Kate's admiration for Teresa of Avila, a woman who made herself powerful in a male world and supreme within female communities. These 'holy women', severe, noble and proud are counterfoils to more conventionally feminised beauties, and this dichotomy – mythic beauties in opposition to harsh holy women – continues in her later fiction. It is also significant that Agatha articulates Kate's own love for Spain and that it is Agatha who takes Mary to the bullfight.

At the end of the novel, these conflicting passions prove to be too intense and Mary leaves Spain. However, the novel is open-ended because Mary decides not to return to Mellick and a safe bourgeois marriage:

> She was going home with a lame and hopeless story, a wicked story that would be agony to John, and had no explanation, no defence. And afterwards – she would take her godmother's hundred pounds and go away. That was all. That was the fruit of her journey to Spain . . . . She was going home to her faithful lover with a brutal story.

Despite this heavily melodramatic ending, the novel represents a radical imaginative departure for Kate O'Brien as a writer. All her novels after *Mary Lavelle* have this open ending, this movement away from Mellick and Ireland and towards voluntary exile in Europe.

Mary Lavelle was banned by the Irish Censorship Board on the grounds of obscenity on 29 December 1936.[10] It was her first novel to be banned in Ireland and, unlike *The Land of Spices*, it was never the subject of a revocation order and so remained on the list of forbidden works. Despite this, *Mary Lavelle* proved to be one of her most popular novels, the Spanish setting and the doomed romance both attracting a wide audience. It was the first of her novels to be translated into German and Danish, simultaneously with publication in London in 1937, and it was one of the first to be reissued by Arlen House and Virago after her death, on the revival of her works in the 1980s. *Mary Lavelle* continues to sell well and was filmed in 1995, under the new title *Talk of Angels*, with a relatively faithful screenplay by the Irish dramatist Frank McGuinness where the action of the novel is shifted from 1922 onwards to the outbreak of the Spanish Civil War in 1936.

The Irish Censorship Board was not obliged to give its reasons for banning the book and so it is difficult to know what precisely antagonised the censors. There had been no direct censorship in pre-independence Ireland, only the prosecution of suspect books by judge and jury which was common under British rule. However, after the setting up of the Irish Free State, the 1929 Censorship of Publications Act provided for the banning of books in Ireland on the grounds that they were 'in general tendency indecent or obscene'.[11] This resulted in the extensive banning of novels and the consequent alienation of Irish writers from their society. Under the 1929 Act, a Censorship Board of five had to consider any publications brought to its attention by customs officials or by a member of the public and to judge them on grounds of decency and morality. The composition of this Censorship Board was secret and it was answerable only to the Minister for Justice. As Julia Carlson puts it: 'In effect, the Censorship Board has licence to operate in virtual secrecy. Once a publication is banned, its importation, sale, advertisement and distribution are prohibited.'[12] This control of public reading was in line with a number of repressive, paternalistic measures in post-colonial Ireland and, not surprisingly, many writers protested. Despite the fact that the Irish Academy of Letters was set up in 1932 by Yeats, Shaw and others, partly as a protest at the censorship, the wholesale banning of novels continued. Between 1930 and 1939, 1,200 books were banned in Ireland.[13]

For Kate O'Brien, the banning had a number of unpleasant consequences. It entailed a loss of readership and income. As Donal O'Driscoll notes: 'Official censorship was backed up by unofficial censorship; writers and artists harassed and stigmatised, while libraries and booksellers were pressurised into not stocking or removing from their shelves titles which had escaped the official net.'[14] In addition, the ban upset her Limerick relations, but Kate played down the personal consequences of this experience in later interviews, stressing her ideological opposition:

> I object to censorship, it is as simple as that. I think that it's a foolish imposition, people have always had the ordinary censorships of decent society, religion, conscience and the law and it seems we can't

manage with those weapons to protect ourselves from what we object to . . . . I've been censored, I don't know if I've suffered.[15]

The publication and subsequent banning of *Mary Lavelle* prompted her brother-in-law Stephen O'Mara to take her to task in a passionate and closely argued letter, telling her 'your Don Pablo is untrue, your Mary is untrue, your Juanito is untrue, and finally your Miss Conlon is untrue'.[16] O'Mara, a great admirer of his sister-in-law's novels, objected to the scenes of adulterous love-making. He argued with her that the sexual encounter with Juanito is uncharacteristic and violates the integrity of her character as constructed it up to this point, 'If anyone seduced Juanito in the wood, it certainly was not Mary Lavelle; it was quite a different girl – one whose chief characteristic from early youth was solitary brooding and secret self-education in sexual knowledge.'[17]

O'Mara, a devout Catholic educated by the Jesuits in Clongowes, was very much a man of the new Ireland of the twentieth century and a close friend of Eamon de Valera. His objections to *Mary Lavelle* give a significant insight into contemporary Irish unease with the radical elements within Kate O'Brien's work. Not surprisingly, he found Agatha Conlon's declaration of love to Mary Lavelle most shockingly uncharacteristic:

> Miss Conlon deserved better at your hands . . . . Conlon, at the age of 50 was far too nice – too religious and too 'good' to utter the word 'Sodom' to Mary; her [Conlon's] bluntness and outspokenness and straightness in word as well as in thought would have kept her within the bounds of her standard of decency – and her standard as we know was that of Catholicity.[18]

Stephen O'Mara was sincerely troubled by these new elements within his sister-in-law's fiction. In fact, he pinpoints precisely those aspects of imaginative innovation that would transform her fictions. 'Why have you done this?' he laments in a subsequent letter. 'It is not necessary for a work of art; on the contrary, art is obfuscated by the introduction of a sensational factor.'[19] Kate's defence of her novel is masterly and uncompromising, despite the fact that, as she puts it, 'With one's own kind, always, I can only say that I at least will be forever absolutely shy of my writer-self.'[20] Her belief in the validity of her art is unshaken by his criticism: 'If I thought it "nasty", I'd not have published it. It is brutal – in a sense. I used the word before you did, in the book's own text...I have undertaken the examination of violent feeling, violent courage, violent youth, and used a violent music.'[21]

Despite her bruising encounter with Irish censorship, Kate O'Brien continued to move within Irish literary circles. In March 1937, she chaired a lecture at the Minerva Club in London on Irish Women Writers, given by the Irish feminist Hannah Sheehy Skeffington. Sheehy Skeffington dubbed Kate 'The Irish Galsworthy' and deplored the recent banning of her novel in Ireland.[22] Her work as a professional writer developed further when, in September 1937, she began to review fiction for *The Spectator*,[23] at the invitation of the literary editor, Derek Verschoyle. Her reviews appeared twice monthly, alternating with reviews by Belfast novelist Forrest Reid and during a period of ten years she reviewed up to eight novels per month, amounting to nearly a thousand novels during a time when the upheavals of world war were placing writers under particular pressure to react and to explore new forms of the novel. Throughout all these reviews, there is little sense of weariness or routine glibness and her responses were always marked by a distinctive clarity and a characteristic assertion of her own expectations of the novel form. In her evaluation of other writers, Kate is attractively decisive, swift to praise or dismiss, light and witty and always grounding her judgements within her own experience as a writer. Her reviews were conscientious, often moving from the specific details about each writer to some general meditation on writing fiction. Throughout, her critical persona is confident and recognisable and her sustained and wide-ranging review writing made her a successful critic, so much so that she continued to write for *The Spectator* when Graham Greene took over the literary pages in 1940.

Her reviewing continued for the next ten years, until 1947, quite an achievement in the face of the upheavals of war, her own constant movements and changes of address and the publication of her next four novels and a book of essays. Her reviews covers all genres from high modernists as diverse as Mann, Woolf, Colette, Joyce, Rhys, Faulkner and Bowen to popular fiction writers like Norah Hoult, Nevil Shute, James M. Cain and Daphne du Maurier (whose work O'Brien disliked intensely). Ireland and Spain are often the subjects for her critiques, but she was equally at home with American and European fiction and had a keen eye for the quality of new writers like Patrick White and Samuel Beckett. Her exuberant praise for Beckett's *Murphy* in March 1938 stands out, partly because Kate was usually reserved as a critic and partly because she was one of the first critics to recognise Beckett's worth: 'Murphy at least for this humble examiner, sweeps all before him. Rarely, indeed, have I been so entertained by a book.... It truly is magnificent and a treasure, if you like it.... He is a magnificently learned sceptic, a joker overloaded with the scholarship of great jokes.... For the right readers, this is a book in a hundred thousand.' She was less enthusiastic about Flann O'Brien's *At Swim-Two-Birds*, 14 March 1939, declaring: 'For my part, I long ago heard all I am ever likely to respond to, in just or in earnest, of the heroes and heroics of ancient Ireland' and went on to say that she liked 'Mr O'Brien's realistic passages and his lively undergraduate rudeness'.

She was not above reviewing friends, praising Stephie's 'remarkably beautiful' translations of Dutch novels in 1939 and 1940 and devoting a whole article to Enid Starkie's autobiography *A Lady's Child* in November 1941, calling it 'rich and varied' and writing that 'in it, we see, as seldom in autobiography, the innocent mind ruthlessly and humourlessly preparing itself for the talents and responsibilities of maturity'. Hemingway's 1937 novel, *To Have and Have Not* brought from her mixed praise in her review in October of that year, where she attacked his 'sloppiness over his tough guys and "rummies" but admitting that 'the whole book is very readable and deft if you like Mr Hemingway's sentimental tough manner. Personally I do, as entertainment, while deploring the author's lazy surrender to himself.' Graham Greene's 1940 novel *The Power and The Glory*, reviewed in March of that year, was much nearer her own preoccupations – 'it offers the Catholic rather than the Calvinistic message about sin' – and she approves of the novel's exploration of the 'humble and contrite heart. Rarely can it have been exposed to our consideration with a more delicate understanding, with more unmerciful mercy.' Her account of John Steinbeck's celebrated *The Grapes of Wrath* in September 1939 acknowledges that 'he tells a terrible, moving story of universal and immediate significance', but she then goes on to ask, 'Why, then, am I not enthralled by his book? Simply, because, right or wrong, I dislike his manner of writing, which I think epitomises the intolerable sentimentality of American realism. I think he wrecks a beautiful dialect with false cadences; I think he is frequently uncertain about where to end a sentence and I think his repetitiveness is not justified by emotional result.' Perhaps her most illuminating and self-revelatory review was her essay in July 1942 on Elizabeth Bowen's family history *Bowen's Court*, which provoked her into writing of her own childhood knowledge of the same landscape around Bowen's Court and the Ballyhoura Hills and of her own Thornhill ancestors, Cromwellian settlers near Bowen's own home ground in north Cork. She writes admiringly of the memoir: 'I respond with a doubled ease to many of these pages – not solely because of their intrinsic, rich evocation of scene and custom'. She goes on to make a sharp political and class distinction about this shared history: 'I do admittedly read Miss Bowen's précis of periods of Irish history in some measure by the uncertain candle of inherited prejudices and emotions...yet, I am rewarded and perhaps admonished by her apprasial of the Gaelic Revival and her later summary of "the troubles"' and concludes that the book is 'itself one more of those very gifts and embellishments – an amende honorable of singular beauty and distinction'.

However, the turbulent political events in Spain were to engage her attention throughout 1937. The Spanish Civil War broke out in July 1936 and, like many writers,[24] Kate O'Brien felt compelled to respond in print. Her travels in Spain in the 1930s gave her ample material for commenting on the conflict. The result was *Farewell Spain*, published in August 1937, just after the fall of Bilbao to the Nationalists. *Farewell Spain*, which opens with this event, is a text overshadowed by the horrors of contemporary war and full of dread for the future. Despite this, she celebrates her Spain: 'For me, however, it has been Spain. So true is this that I have hardly seen any other countries. . . . My love has been long and slow – lazy and selfish too, but I know that wherever I go henceforth and whatever I see I shall never again love an earthly scene as I have loved the Spanish.' Throughout, she links her personal love for Spain with her hatred of this 'display of militaristic absolutism against democracy'. She goes on to denounce the war: 'A war such as General Franco's, openly aimed at the murder of every democratic principle, and for the setting up of his little self as yet another little Mussolini – such a war strikes not merely at the death of Spain but at every decent dream or effort for humanity everywhere.' It is unfortunate that she even entitles one chapter, a chapter of denunciation against Franco, 'Arriba, España', since this phrase was adopted by Franco's troops as their battle-cry, a fact that was noted by one contemporary reviewer.

Despite the polemic that motivates her writing, *Farewell Spain* is a leisurely and perceptive account of Spain, full of anecdotes and personal observations of buildings, paintings, writers, towns, food, drink and, above all, of the Spanish character as she conceived it. Kate used much of her own life in the travel book, reminiscing about her time in Bilbao as a governess, and writing about Stephie and her daughter Ruth accompanying her to the bullfight. Mary O'Neill, who illustrated the book, appears in a number of episodes as a beloved travel companion.

This was Kate's first sustained piece of travel writing and her critical voice here is shrewd, individualist, detached and well informed. *Farewell Spain* further opens out the landscapes of *Mary Lavelle* – Bilbao, the cities of Castile, the paintings in the Prado in Madrid, the bullfight – all the familiar elements portrayed in *Mary Lavelle*. Her cities of pilgrimage are all in Castile or the Basque country: Burgos, Madrid, Avila, Salamanca, Toledo and Bilbao. No mention is made of Catalonia or Andalusia. (If you follow her path and visit these places, there is, visually, a claustrophobic atmosphere to her Spain, an intense and unrelentingly narrow spirituality in the images and buildings she admired.) She takes on a number of diverse subjects – contemporary politics, historical personages, the tradition of Spanish painting. The originality of her critical perspective is most apparent in her chapter on Philip II. Kate challenges the traditional belief that 'Philip II of Spain was a cold, unattractive and sinister riddle'. Instead, she sees him as admirable and his building of the palace of El Escorial as worthy: 'He had the more difficult thing to say but actually in some ways the more durable and sane.' She acutely identifies the flaw at the centre of Philip's concept of kingship: his fear of his common humanity. 'He saw eternity by no means as release from self but as the phantasmagoric setting for a demonic war about that self. It never occurred to him that the true blessing of death would be the end of self-importance.' Crucially, her reading of Philip's character comes from a clear sighted under-standing of the dangerous egotism at the heart of authoritarian rule. Her admiration and understanding of Philip does not, in the end, blind her to his overweening egotism.

Philip II is one of the many Spanish men she discusses and, indeed, most of her admiration for the spirit of Spain is for men. For Kate, the lone Spanish man is the true embodiment of the Spanish spirit. When she does consider Spanish women, it is usually collectively and with less admiration. In one chapter, she relates an episode at a railway station when Mary O'Neill's beautiful blonde hair excites the admiration of a crowd of young Spanish women:

> There are girls, linked together as usual in fives and sixes, in their usual shiny make-up and with their hair carefully waved and fixed against their heads. Very neat, as usual, and moving easily and gaily – full of pleasure in themselves. But to my mind shrill and disappointing as their lovely, distinguished country never is.

The one exception, it seems, was the mystic and reformer Teresa of Avila, 'a genius of the large and immeasurable kind of which there have been very few, and only one a woman'. Unlike her account of Philip II, Kate's portrayal of Teresa of Avila, the sixteenth century Spanish mystic and religious reformer, is unreserved in its admiration:

> Although impatient of book learning, she was a formidable match for inquisitor or Salamancan doctor. She was a fighter and a schemer, a soldier and a most restless diplomat.... She was a feminist – 'I will not have my daughters women in anything, but valorous men' – Though of women qua woman she thought very little.... Certainly she was the greatest woman in Christian history.

She celebrated Teresa's achievements as a secular figure, the woman who gained power and respect in a man's world, the Spaniard formed by the harsh, austere Castilian landscape that had nurtured her. This veneration of Teresa of Avila, which influenced Kate O'Brien's fictive representations of women, continues in her later writings, with a series of radio talks on the saint for Radio Éireann in 1969[25] and a short biography published in 1951.

A detailed and perceptive review of *Farewell Spain* in *The Spectator*[26] by John Marks, found fault with Kate O'Brien's limited, partial view of Spain in the travelogue and compared the book unfavourably with the achievement of *Mary Lavelle*. This reviewer admired her style – 'She writes with vision and with feeling' – but was critical of her accuracy: 'All her bullfighting facts are wrong – and many things she misses or misrepresents.' He picks up on her prejudice against the Moors in Spain – 'This latter prejudice amounts to a phobia with her' – and goes so far as to question her political convictions and her attack on Franco: 'The reader can't help suspecting that the tragedy of the Civil War distresses her too deeply for full conviction in her cause.' However, his overall impression is that 'now, more than at any other time, the memory of her sentimental journey is worth sharing'.[27]

In the end, the Spanish Civil War was, as Kate had feared, to be the downfall of the Republic. While she was writing, the Nationalist forces had Madrid under siege and the Spanish Civil War was still unresolved. However, in April 1939, Madrid fell to Franco and the war ended with the subsequent surrender of the Republican armies. When Franco's regime came to power in Spain, Kate's official standing with the authorities became an increasingly difficult one, even though she and Franco actually shared a very similar sense of the glories and splendours of Spain's Catholic past. Furthermore, her great interest in Teresa of Avila was, unknown to her, shared by Franco. In February 1937, as she was writing *Farewell Spain*, a somewhat ghoulish episode involving the dictator and the mortal remains of the great saint occurred. Franco's biographer Paul Preston tells the story:

> At this time the nationalist press began to circulate a story which linked Franco's destiny with the intercession of the saints. Allegedly, in the chaos of defeat, the military commander of Malaga...left various items of luggage behind him when he fled. In a suitcase left in his hotel was found the holy relic of the hand of St. Teresa of Avila which had been stolen from the Carmelite convent in Ronda...It was sent to Franco, who kept it with him for the rest of his life. The recovery of the relic was the excuse for the exaltation of St Teresa as the 'Saint of the Race', the champion of Spain and her religion in the Reconquista....Franco himself seems to have believed in his special relationship with St Teresa....The Bishop of Malaga granted permission for the relic to remain in Franco's possession and it never left his side on any trip which obliged him to sleep away from home.[28]

Later, John Jordan wrote:

> As regards the title of the travel book, it is not to be taken as an overt comment on the issues of the Civil War. She would have gone back to Spain had she got a sponsor. To jump forward a decade, when she did try to return to Spain in 1947, she was refused entry on the grounds

that Generalissimo Franco had taken exception to her treatment of Philip II in her novel *That Lady* (1946). Eventually, through the intervention of the Irish Ambassador to Spain, she returned to Spain in 1957.[29]

John Jordan was a close friend of Kate's and much of this information would have come directly from her. Speaking to the Association of Professional and Business Women in Canterbury in March 1972, Kate herself claimed: 'I've never been persona grata with the Franco government – it's the only feather in my cap that all my works have been long ago banned in Spain and so remain.'[30]

There is, in fact, no record of *Farewell Spain* ever having been banned in Spain or in any other country. The Spanish Civil War continued for nearly two years after its publication in 1937 and so there would have been no official Nationalist censorship in place to ban it. Not long after the ending of the Civil War, World War II broke out and Kate spent the war years in England, unable to travel even to Ireland. Thus, her first opportunity to travel to Spain would have come in 1947. Jordan's suggestion that Franco took offence at *That Lady* is debatable, as it was actually approved for publication in Spain on 12 July 1946 by the Ministry of Education. In allowing for the publication of the novel, the Ministry insisted that a note be appended reiterating that this is 'not a historical novel but pure invention'. The internal memo notes that, if the novel is not published in Spain, an Argentinian publisher would publish it without smoothing over those concepts which might bother a suspicious Spaniard![31] (An internal reader's report appended to this licence to publish *That Lady* calls it an entertaining novel but with some scenes that are a little 'raw'.) Permission to import copies of *The Last of Summer*, *The Ante-Room* and *Without My Cloak* was also granted to her by the Spanish authorities and so her work was freely available in Spain and was also translated. The only form of censorship recorded was that permission was refused for the book jacket of *Without My Cloak* on the grounds of immorality![32] Far from being outlawed, her fiction was as available in Spain as in any other country. Even the Hollywood film version of *That Lady* in 1955 was granted permission to be screened throughout Spain, despite what Kate described as 'the initial fuss with Franco.'[33]

In her later writing life, she went on producing travel pieces and talks, all reflecting her great interest in Spain.[34] In March 1959, on the occasion of Franco's opening of his Civil War memorial grave-yard next to El Escorial, his so-called Valle de los Caidos (The Valley of the Fallen), she was provoked into writing a series of articles for the *Manchester Guardian*. Franco's veneration for Philip II, another common interest with Kate, led him to situate the Valle de los Caidos near to El Escorial and she took exception to this.

Kate was deprived of any contact with her Spain for the next twenty years and censorship had the effect of making her impulse towards Europe suspect within her own country. In her next two novels, she refocused her attention on Ireland. In writing novels about the modern Irish bourgeoisie, Kate was creating a literature from scratch. Much of Irish writing in the nineteenth century had been from the perspective of the Anglo-Irish Ascendancy, novelists of the Irish landlord class like Maria Edgeworth, George Moore and Somerville and Ross. In many of these writings, the emergent Irish Catholic bourgeoisie was depicted either as lovably idiotic or else as grasping, unscrupulous and vulgar, and thus a looming threat to the established order of colonial rule in Ireland.[35]

This demonising of the Irish bourgeoisie was also a common feature in nineteenth-century Irish political life. At the same time, the Irish middle class lacked a literary voice from within. There were a few Irish bourgeois writers before Kate, like Limerick-born Gerald Griffin, whose 1829 novel, *The Collegians*, also sought to affirm the civilised nature of the Irish middle class for an English reading public. However, when Kate started writing her Mellick novels in the late 1920s, she was bringing an entire genre into being, the Irish bourgeois novel. (She had few predecessors in this genre, but one worth noting is the early twentieth-century Irish novelist Katherine Cecil Thurston.)[36]

As her fellow Irish novelist, John Broderick wrote:

> For over a century the Catholic middle class have been the dominant influence in Ireland; and for the past sixty-five, the ruling class also. Yet they have been little written about; and compared with the bourgeoisie in France and England, who have produced, with a few exceptions, all the great novelists of the last two centuries, they have been singularly slow in producing creative writers. It is true that they have given birth to the greatest novelist of the century in Joyce; but he is outside the mainstream of fiction and of writers to be compared with novelists like Mrs Gaskell, Trollope, Galsworthy, Graham

Greene and Evelyn Waugh. Of these, Kate O'Brien is the best known and also, I think, the best.[37]

Joyce did provide something of a model for Kate O'Brien in his depictions of Irish middle-class domestic life. Set pieces within his fiction like the Twelfth Night family party in 'The Dead' and the Christmas Dinner scene in *A Portrait of the Artist as a Young Man* have the same celebratory mood as much of her fiction.

With the banning of *Mary Lavelle*, Kate O'Brien's attitude towards the ruling class in Ireland changed. Her relationship with the Ireland of the 1930s was now a hostile one, increasingly antagonistic towards the kind of Ireland that de Valera and his supporters, among others, were creating. Earlier in her own life, Kate had had links with those who fought for Irish nationalism. For example, her female cousins in Fermoy had been on clandestine missions on behalf of the local IRA during the War of Independence, an episode that finds its way into *Mary Lavelle*. So Kate had had some sympathy with the desire for Irish political independence. Her brush with censorship changed this.

Her response, in her next two novels, was to contrast the cultural insularity of the Irish Free State with the enlightened, European Catholicism of her imagined bourgeoisie. She began to differentiate between the 'Eternal' Roman Catholic Church and the narrow-mindedness of the new Irish Catholic state. While de Valera was creating an imaginary sense of nationhood by idealising Gaelic rural self-sufficiency and frugality, Kate was actively countering this with her mythical version of an Irish bourgeoisie, made noble by a kind of gentrified austerity and by the civilising traditions of European Catholicism.

Despite her disillusion with Ireland, her working life in England continued to prosper. In 1938 she was still living in Great James Street, preparing a new novel for publication and continuing to review for *The Spectator*. There is little evidence of her social life at this time, but much of her journalism survives and attests to a busy work schedule.

In April 1938, Kate published *Pray for the Wanderer*, probably the least successful of all her novels. The reason for this artistic failure was undoubtedly her negative experiences of censorship and her consequent haste to produce a novel of protest. Usually, in writing her novels, Kate was slow and painstaking. Her surviving manuscripts attest to this, each one clear and almost without correction, the first draft as clean as a completed version. Yet the writing of *Pray for the Wanderer* was, for her, different in pattern. At the close of the novel, Kate gives the length of time taken writing it as 'July–December 1937'. In an essay on her fiction, the critic Vivian Mercier, who had been in correspondence with her, mentioned that *Pray for the Wanderer* had been written 'in five months, unlike the other novels, which usually took two or three years: this haste is evident throughout'.[38] Her experiences of censorship, as well as the outcome of the Spanish Civil War and the deteriorating situation in Europe, combined to make her fearful and angry in her writing. In this novel, her protagonist Matt muses on 'the warm, personal principle now about to die, perhaps the individualistic thing, the piled-up memory, the piety, the long-held, bitterly wronged sweetness of personal liberty now going out everywhere'.

She wrote *Pray for the Wanderer* in the light of this anxiety and the novel suffered accordingly. Vivian Mercier, who knew Kate and admired her work, considered this to be her poorest novel and writes:

> Personally I am convinced that the cause was the banning of *Mary Lavelle* in the Irish Free State. Miss O'Brien has clearly made her hero an author – and a banned one at that – so that through his mouth she may register her protest against modern Ireland's love of censorship.[39]

Pray for the Wanderer is also unusual for an O'Brien novel in that it is set in the year of its composition, 1937. Another distinctive feature is the use of a male protagonist, but a protagonist invested with much of Kate's own experiences. The novel features Matt Costello, an Irish writer living in London, who returns to visit his brother's home in Mellick. Costello is a self-portrait of Kate. He is a provincial Irishman from a wealthy horse-breeding family, who achieves success as a writer after years of bohemian struggle in Paris and Madrid. Like Kate, Costello has been living in Bloomsbury for six years, the themes of Costello's novels, the 'problems of the Catholic conscience', are her own themes. The novel opens as he travels home to Ireland to recover from a broken love affair.

Costello returns to an Ireland that is antagonistic to his writing and on the brink of a significant act of self-definition: the Irish Constitution of 1937. Costello muses:

Yet here around him this pretty scene of ease and natural hope, this sample of continuity. In a dictator's country, too. But a more subtle dictator than most – though he also, given time, might have the minds of his people in chains. He did not bring materialism out for public adoration, but materialistic justice controlled by a dangerous moral philosophy, the new Calvinism of the Roman Catholic...a clever man, Dev. Indeed a statesman, but twentieth-century.

In this climate of 'new Calvinism', Matt Costello attempts to defend his work. There is a tension between his Mellick self and his London self and the troubled relation between Irish writer and Irish state dominates *Pray for the Wanderer*. In a crucial scene in the novel, Father Malachi, a Franciscan priest, challenges Matt. Kate presents this austere young Franciscan in terms of admiration: 'The ring of dark hair round his tonsured head was curly, his eyes were deeply blue and all his strong features were in the heroic tradition. He might have sat for Augustus Caesar in his prime, Matt reflected.' This intellectually gifted priest defends censorship and it is curious that Kate idealises the Irish Catholic bourgeoisie, even when creative freedom was being denied. The impressive Father Malachi quizzes Costello as to the worth of his novels. Costello's defence of his art is clearly Kate's own:

> Any books, mine or Amanda Ros's or Virgil's exist solely to demonstrate the artist's desire and ability to write them. They are a fruit of the creative function, as irresponsible if you like, as other fruits of creation...I believe that it is useful at present to be an individual, to be non-doctrinaire...I speak only of myself when I say that my job is to re-create life, not as it is, good God, but as the peculiarities of my vision and desire assume it. I give you life translated to my idiom. You take it or leave it.

Amanda McKitterick Ros was an Irish novelist of sentimental, somewhat far-fetched and idiosyncratic popular tales, born in Ulster in 1860 and widely known, if not exactly well respected. Juxtaposing her with Virgil would have been suggesting two ends of a very wide scale of literary accomplishment for Kate O'Brien's contemporary reader of *Pray for the Wanderer*.

At the end of the novel, Matt Costello decides to return to England, unresolved:

> Oh green and trim Free State! Smug, obstinate and pertinacious little island, your sins and ignorances are thick upon your face and

thickening under the authority of your 'sea-green incorruptible'! But your guilts seem positively innocent, your ignorances are perhaps wisdom when measured against the general European plight. How odd if the distressful country, the isle of Saints and Doctors from which Patrick banished snakes, should prove a last oasis, a floating Lotus Land when the floods rise!

In a review in *The Spectator*, called 'The Irish bourgeoisie', Evelyn Waugh praised the novel for helping to 'wake England to the realisation that there is, and for over a century has been, a very considerable Irish bourgeoisie'. Waugh went on to point out that the main fault with *Pray for the Wanderer* is the protagonist. Waugh disliked the novel's romanticised hero and he shrewdly deconstructed him. 'He is immensely lifelike but he is second rate; one seems to have met him before, this moody, prosperous ex-gunman, with his forelock hanging on his face, his pride in his own virility, his Irish accent that has survived the cafés of Montparnasse; one knows him and he is a bore'.[40]

In her own life, despite her busy writing schedule, Kate's finances continued to be unstable and, in June 1938, the Royal Literary Fund granted her £100, at the recommendation of neighbours in Great James Street, the Gosworths. That year saw another change for Kate, with the legal ending of her marriage to Gustaaf Renier after fifteen years. On 20 October, Gustaaf petitioned for divorce, naming Kate as respondent but with no co-respondent named and no grounds given for the ending of the marriage. With this divorce, all contact with Gustaaf ceased, although he continued to live and work in London with his second wife until he died in 1962. Kate spent Christmas 1938 in Norfolk with Mary O'Neill and her mother.

Further recognition for her writing came when Kate was awarded the Femina Vie Heureuse, a French literary prize, in 1939. She was holidaying in Limerick when war was declared in September. She could have stayed in Ireland but made the decision to return to London, writing from her sister's Nance's house in Limerick to her London friend Barbara Gosworth:

> My thought has been with 33, Great James St. all these nights and I feel terribly nostalgic at not being in my right and customary place right now.... I'm still vainly pursuing some desperately needed money and I have no idea what will happen to the quarry I'm after now. I simply must get solvent and earn a living. What jobs will there be, do

you think? I'll be looking for something writerish, if you know what
I mean. I mean I'm not going to be a Police Canteen Woman or a
sergeant of the Waacs.... Let us have a few last nights of the old stuff
– when Milton and Anna Wickham and Ginger Rogers were still a bit
more important than Hitler![41]

Kate travelled back to London in mid-October. She was already in
financial difficulties, trying to pay rent and repay loans to friends,
but the outbreak of war meant that many of her usual sources of
income were thrown into doubt. By December 1939, her financial
situation had become desperate and she moved out of her flat in
Great James Street, remonstrating by letter with her friends for
giving her no send-off. Her letters at this time reflect her problems
with money, her inability to repay loans and a facility to beg, plead
and even cajole creditors which would continue with her for the rest
of her life.

Her new home was in Oxfordshire, in the countryside, at End
Farm in North Leigh near Witney. While living there, she finished
her new novel, *The Land of Spices*, in September 1940. From End
Farm, she moved to a labourer's cottage, perhaps choosing such
rural isolation as a way of avoiding her creditors. A letter to Barbara
Gosworth at this time reveals the full measure of Kate's insolvency:

I do not answer your letters because they fill me with despair, and
what use is my despair to you? You want some money – God knows
I bet you do – and I have none....I had the good fortune, a week
before the blitzkrieg cottage racket started, to find this labourer's
cottage, for 3/6d a week. It is entirely primitive and inconvenient, but
it is a roof over my head which I can manage to pay for. I also had the
good fortune to persuade a sister of mine to pay for the removal of my
furniture and books – most of the furniture being hers, and she being
anxious lest it should be blown skyhigh in Gt James St. So here I am
– and here the writs find me. The Inland Revenue is taking me at last
before the High Court judge this coming month. I have no money to
give them and I don't see what the judge can say.... Things are very
lonely and miserable – for everyone, I gather. Gott Strafe Hitler.[42]

Kate stayed on in Harcourt Cottage until mid-November 1941,
getting little war work despite her hopes, and had to live as best she
could on her writing. Then she moved back to London and, from
there, went on to spend Christmas with Mary O'Neill and her

mother in Norfolk. Kate was now in her mid-forties, with no income and no permanent home. As she later put it herself, 'I've been a mover all my life, not exactly by choice – indeed there have been uprootings from places which I thought would break my heart. I have found that my now ageing heart, which was always vulnerable and, in my understanding of it, faithful, is also tough.'[43]

When Kate moved to Oxford in early 1940, she met the scholar and writer Enid Starkie. Starkie, an exact contemporary of Kate's, was born in Dublin in 1897, the daughter of the Resident Commissioner for Education, Dr William Starkie. Enid followed an academic career, moving to England to study French at Oxford, eventually becoming a fellow of Somerville College and achieving success with books on Baudelaire and Rimbaud. According to her biographer, Joanna Richardson, Enid Starkie began an affair with an unnamed woman around this time:

> For Enid, quite apart from the War, 1940 was a year of much significance. In January, she became involved in a love-affair with another woman. It was not, for Enid, the first affair of its kind but it was clearly the most intense and disturbing liaison of her life.... Enid was well aware of the principles which were involved in this liaison; she had been born a Catholic, and she could not escape a feeling of guilt, sometimes a sense of degradation.[44]

There is no direct evidence that Kate was this woman, but the dates fit since she and Enid Starkie met for the first time around then. The friendship lasted for the rest of Enid's life, but the love affair ended sooner, as Enid's biographer records:

> In September 1941, Enid herself was driven back to painful solitude. Her violent love affair abruptly ended. Quite suddenly, she was abandoned for another woman. She had believed that her relationship was permanent.... The bitterness remained with her long after the love affair had ended. Enid wrote: 'When you are gone all I will think of is the past with you. The way life was experienced with you and then all the pain. All the bitter hurt in memory. You have no gift of friendship. Only to the present lover do you give anything. Yet the others continue to love. For they had with you an illusion that nothing else comes up with.'[45]

One of the strongest characteristics of Kate's emotional life was her ability to retain former lovers as close friends and her relationship with Enid Starkie followed this pattern. Kate was writing *The Land of Spices* at this time and mentioned in a letter home to her sister Nance that Enid, a French scholar, was checking the French in her novel.[46] As already mentioned, Kate reviewed Enid's autobiography, *A Lady's Child*, for *The Spectator* in November 1941 and it makes a very interesting comparison with *The Land of Spices*, published in the same year. In her memoir, Starkie is clear in her portrayal of the cruelty and unhappiness she had experienced in her upbringing and this clarity contrasts with Kate's world of distinction and Catholic civility. Enid Starkie's honesty in evaluating her childhood came from the security of her class, because the Starkies had a clear social position in Dublin as the family of a professional man. Enid writes of an act of cruelty by her nurse: 'This experience engendered in me the conviction that all grown ups were cruel, and indeed until I grew up myself I thought the process of growing up was one of gradation in cruelty.'[47] Throughout her memoir, Starkie makes clear that she rebelled against the snobberies of her class. Kate, on the other hand, used her fictions to consolidate an insecure and vanished provincial world.

In later life, Enid and Kate stayed in contact. In this later relationship between the two women, there was a slight element of amused contempt in Kate's attitude towards Enid. This slight contempt is evident in Lorna Reynolds' description of Enid's visit to Kate in Roundstone in the 1950s:

> Kate O'Brien never lost her admiration for Enid Starkie's relentless application to work nor for the intelligence that set the pursuit of truth above all other aims. But it was an admiration that operated best in absence. I remember that towards the end of the Roundstone days, it was at last possible for Enid Starkie to come on a long proposed visit.... Our hostess came into the room, clutching her head and saying 'My God, I don't know how I'm going to endure it. She is sitting up in bed, talking already'.... She was worried also about the effect Enid Starkie would have on the village; for she was dressed for her country visit in the costume of a French sailor, complete even to the matelot's cap.[48]

There may also have been an anxiety that Enid Starkie's unconventional dress would in some way compromise Kate and her other woman friends, with Lorna Reynolds taking her cue from Kate's own view of Enid. When Enid Starkie died in 1970, Kate attended her memorial service in Oxford and also wrote about her in her *Irish Times* column, 'Long distance':

> About two years ago, she came to lecture on Flaubert at the University of Kent at Canterbury and she stayed with me here.... I wanted to get her to bed early – but could I? She was intellectually ablaze that night – and talked as brilliantly for hours on end, as I have heard her talk. And she was incapable of being trivial.... She was truthful, sometimes to the point which one might think naïve.[49]

The Land of Spices, written in Oxfordshire in 1940, is Kate O'Brien's most beautifully written novel and her most closely auto-biographical. Written at a time of upheaval and financial insecurity, it is, nevertheless, her most successfully realised act of imagining. Published in February 1941, *The Land of Spices* is set in the Mellick convent of Sainte Fontaine, a French school for Irish girls run by an order of nuns called the Compagnie de la Sainte Famille. *The Land of Spices* follows the life of the young protagonist, Anna Murphy, who, like Kate herself, goes to school at the age of six in 1904 and leaves at eighteen in 1916. The English Reverend Mother of this Mellick convent, Helen Archer, is forty-three when the novel opens, Kate's age at this time.

The theme here is education, particularly the empowering quality of female education and mentorship. The link between Anna Murphy and Helen Archer is established in the opening scene of the novel, when Archer, an Englishwoman running an Irish convent, despairs of her life in Ireland: 'She knew, early she had come to know, that at best she was a respected symbol in this house, at worst an Englishwoman.' Helen Archer's isolation is partly racial, but mostly she is disliked for the European system of education she adopts for the young girls of Mellick. The more nationalist-minded nuns and priests of Mellick distrust her European-centred system of education and the chaplain, Father Conroy ('a country boy, fresh from Maynooth'), articulates this distrust. 'It seems a shame,' said Father Conroy, with pointed playfulness, 'it seems a shame that our own Irish girls have to go off to do their religious training in a barbarous place like that!' Reverend Mother counters such attacks with reminders of Ireland's old connections with Europe: 'Certainly Ireland helped in impressing Christianity on Europe. So why should the Irish not go back now, and reclaim for Ireland some of the cultivated thing it planted?'

Kate constructs a self-contained aesthetic world in the Mellick convent. The motto of the school is 'La Pudeur et La Politesse' (Modesty and Civility) and the emotional and cultural atmosphere of the convent comes from this ethos of restraint and discipline. Kate stresses the use of French names and food in the Irish provincial convent and approves of the rigid code of behaviour for the students and the austere and distancing control of the nuns. The narrative begins with Helen Archer's crisis of faith: 'she was at the end of self-control, hated Ireland, hated being hated; that she must feel the dew of grace again, feel it tenderly in her heart – at home, under skies that loved her'.

This crisis is checked when the young Anna Murphy chooses to recite Henry Vaughan's poem 'Peace' at a school gathering:

> Reverend Mother's eyes fell on her.... She thought gently that it was pathetic to be forced, when so small, to become one of a large, alien body, merely because parents had neither the sense nor the sensitivity to keep a child at home. She reflected that the confusions created by parents for children are the most deep and dark of all, and that the relationship of parent and child is grievously important. She thought with sudden bitter sorrow of her father.... Reverend Mother heard, on the little voice, wild floods of memory and cataracts of memory. Much more than memory.... She saw this baby in herself, herself in those tear-wet eyes.

The reciting of the poem calms Helen and she resolves to stay in Ireland. From this initial moment of identification between woman and child comes an unspoken affinity, a distanced mentorship. In the novel, the progress of Anna's life in Sainte Fontaine is towards adulthood and independence and this independence is achieved with Helen Archer's tacit assistance. Anna Murphy is watched over by Helen Archer, guided through the crisis of her brother's death, and assisted in her desire to attend university, despite family disapproval. In a novel where familial loves bring grief and betrayal, the bond of female mentorship is presented as the only reliable enabler of independence.

Anna's choice of Vaughan's poem is not accidental: Kate O'Brien fills the novel with intertextual references. Milton and Schiller are also key points of reference and, indeed, the title of the novel comes from the closing of George Herbert's poem 'Prayer': 'Church bells beyond the stars heard, the soul's blood/The land of spices;

something understood.' Taken together, all these poems create a web of literary references from seventeenth-century devotional English poetry, giving the novel an almost Protestant sensibility. This connects with Kate O'Brien's portrayal of Helen Archer and, indeed, with her representations of Catholics in general. When she writes about issues of Catholic faith and conscience, she allows her Catholic characters possession of their own souls. Her Irish Catholics have independence of belief and confidence in their right to moral self-determination and they exercise this right without hesitation. In this, Kate was remodelling her own upbringing at Laurel Hill, submerging the reality of the Irish Church in the twentieth century. In fact, her version of Irish Catholicism owes much to the Catholicism of her friends in England.

Writing to her sister Nance, Kate explained why some sections of the novel contained untranslated letters in French: 'I was uncertain about leaving so much French in the English edition, but I felt that for this particular book it was helpful, if not necessary, for the establishment of the nun's mind and her nostalgia.'[50]

This invented version of Irish Catholicism is used to strike against the Ireland that censored her. *The Land of Spices* is her counter-attack against the narrowness and bigotry of de Valera's Ireland as she experienced it. The system of education portrayed at Sainte Fontaine is her ideal of intellectual, European Catholicism. Helen Archer's description of the mother house of her order in Bruges reflects this:

> There was an austerity over Sainte Fontaine that almost spoke aloud of distrust of life, discomfort in it. It was old and graceful, but with the grace of hardened asceticism, not of mellowness. Its noble architecture, rigorous garden and almost empty rooms had taught the young novice more categorically even than did the Early Fathers those lessons of elimination, detachment and foregoing for which, as it happened, her hurt spirit craved somewhat hysterically at that time.

In Sainte Fontaine, this ideal system of education manifests itself in the teaching of manners, language, literature and social behaviour, but it is also a system of emotional education. This is an education where shock is contained and made safe. In this context, the central episode in *The Land of Spices* presents a moment of trauma and this moment propels Helen Archer into the religious life. The relationship between Helen Archer and her father is one of the most striking in Kate's fiction. Since female education is her theme in *The Land of Spices*, Helen's own upbringing is crucial as an account of the destructive nature of patriarchal and familial systems of education. Helen's relationship with her father is emotionally intense: 'In childhood, she thought her father very beautiful. It always delighted her to come on the sight of him suddenly and realise, always with new pleasure, that he was different from other men, stronger and bigger, with curly silky hair and eyes that shone like stars.'

There is a curious lack of insight in Kate's presentation of this relationship between Henry Archer and his daughter. Kate seems unaware, in her analysis of this relationship, of the manipulative and exclusive hold that Archer establishes over his daughter's affections. Henry Archer, a former Cambridge don who has brought his wife and child to live in Brussels, is a figure from late Victorian decadent literature. Archer sees himself as pagan, is described as reading the Greeks, and is represented as a Wildean figure of exquisite Hellenic beauty, of aesthetic and bohemian tastes and with a suspect past. In exile in Europe for some unspecified reason, Archer directs his daughter's liberal, bohemian education and force-feeds her into an understanding of Europe: 'Without mercy he fed and loaded her mind. She was free to read anything but she had to read the works he prescribed and discussed with her. He took her all over Belgium and into Holland and the Rhineland in pursuit of art and architecture and history.' When Henry Archer expounds his views on existence, there is a startling resemblance to Gustaaf Renier's authorial voice in the autobiographical *He Came to England*.

Helen's idyllic life ends when she discovers the true nature of her father's sexuality and the reason for his exile from England:

> She looked into the room. Two people were there. But neither saw her; neither felt her shadow as it froze across the sun. She turned and descended the stairs. She left the garden and went on down the curve of Rue Saint Isidore. She had no objective and no knowledge of what she was doing. She did not see external things. She saw her father and Etienne in the embrace of love.

This moment of revelation is one of the few moments of sexual directness in Kate's fiction. As always, her fiction represents the erotic as traumatic and destructive in its effect on the unwitting spectator: 'So that was the sort of thing that the most graceful life could hide! That was what lay around, under love, under beauty.' Henry Archer's sexuality is destructive to those around him, yet he dies happily unaware of the damage he has caused. Kate O'Brien's representation of Henry Archer's homosexuality merits comment, since she constructs his sexuality as a selfish and destructive element within the narrative. Therefore, one could argue that, in this novel, male homosexuality is presented in a negative light. In fact, the emotional crisis is the inevitable result of Henry Archer's control of his daughter. In a sense, the fact that he is homosexual is only incidental.

From this overwrought coming to knowledge, Helen Archer turns to the religious life to punish her father. This places her within a position of power and influence for the education of the young but, because of the intense bond with her father, Helen's mentorship of Anna Murphy is distanced, 'For she was confident that a soul, left to itself, has good chances of recovering in some measure from any sickness – whereas rash manipulation may establish a deformity.' Helen, through careful watching, helps Anna through the sudden shock of her brother's death and fights for Anna's right to a university education. At the end of the novel, Anna leaves the convent to pursue a life of study, thanks to Helen Archer: 'Anna's schooldays were closed and there was no plea against the advance of life and the flight of innocence. She had been taught to be good and to understand the law of God. Also she had been free to be herself. Her wings were grown and she was for the world.' This is the first novel where Kate O'Brien begins to construct the idea of female mentorship and, in addition, her first novel to suggest the vocation of female creativity. In the final chapter, there is a hint that Anna may become a writer. Therefore, Helen Archer enables her to pursue her artistic vocation.[51]

In a review, the Irish poet Austin Clarke (her former lecturer at UCD) praised the novel for the integrity of her representation of the spiritual life: 'In religious subjects, we have been dominated for years by the English convert mentality and have developed a self-conscious feeling of inferiority. But as writers, we have one considerable advantage over the converts. We have not to despise or disparage our earliest impressions in childhood.'[52] Clarke's one criticism of the novel centred on the reference to Henry Archer's homosexuality:

> There seems to me one artistic flaw in this book, the nature of the
> shock which drove Helen Archer, the beautiful, intelligent young

English girl into a Continental Order in a mood of agonised revulsion. It is an outwards shock, purely pathological and mentioned in a single, euphemistic sentence. A more personal experience would have given more scope for analysis and brought us nearer the girlhood of Helen Archer.[53]

The *Irish Independent* carried a review entitled 'A Masterpiece Spoiled', where the reviewer admired the book but felt that:

One could with charitable tolerance overlook some irritating passages. To use the word 'loutish' in reference to a priest, and put into the Bishop's mouth words about education and the Irish language which are little better than gibberish, might be forgiven. But there is one single sentence in the book so repulsive that the book should not be left where it would fall into the hands of very young people.[54]

The offending sentence, unquoted by the reviewer was, 'She saw her father and Etienne in the embrace of love', and it led to the banning of *The Land of Spices*.

By 1943, many novels had been banned in Ireland. *The Land of Spices*, which was published in February 1941, was banned by the Censorship Board on 6 May the same year. (It was published without difficulty in the United States that June.) Kate herself was out of Ireland when the novel was banned and she remained living in Oxfordshire for the duration of the war. The banning led to a public outcry in Ireland. It was felt that the Censorship Board had gone too far in labelling this novel as obscene, and a sustained campaign of protest was begun by, among others, the novelist Sean Ó'Faoláin. Writing in *The Bell*, Ó'Faoláin expressed his outrage: 'The official notice declares this book to be banned in Eire because it is "in general tendency indecent". Clearly this is a lie.'[55]

There followed a series of attacks on censorship in the pages of *The Bell*, with Shaw, O'Casey and others defending freedom of creative expression; one lone voice, Monk Gibbon, defended censorship on the grounds of necessary state control.[56] Finally, in November 1942, Senator Sir John Keane tabled a motion in the Irish Senate criticising the Board of Censorship. He used the particular incident of the banning of *The Land of Spices* as the focus for his opposition.

In the Senate debate, Sir John Keane spoke of *The Land of Spices* with great respect:

I have read it carefully and I may not be a very good judge but I
consider that its general motif is almost religious.... As anyone who
has read the book will agree, the Reverend Mother depicted in it is a
most noble character. She goes into the convent and takes the veil
because she discovers, to her great surprise, that her father is given to
unnatural vice. How she makes this discovery is important. If
references to unnatural vice ran frequently through the whole book,
and was dwelt on persistently I could understand, possibly, the
grounds for objection. But it is a single reference and it is commend-
ably short... for that phrase and that phrase alone that book is
censored. Where that book can be held to be in its general tendency
indecent or in the words of the definition 'to incite to sexual
immorality or unnatural vice or is likely in any similar manner to
corrupt or deprave' I cannot see.[57]

However, Sir John Keane's motion was defeated. Professor
William Maginnis, another senator and a member of the Censorship
Board, took up the cudgels and, in the words of Terence Brown,
'Professor Maginnis, who spoke for four and a half hours in defence
of the Board and all its works, had carried the day'.[58] There was a
slight amelioration in censorship as a result of these debates and, in
1945, the Irish government brought in a Bill allowing for the
establishment of an appeals board. In 1946, Kate was persuaded to
lodge an appeal against the ban on *The Land of Spices*.

My novel, which they censored very severely during the war, that
eventually was unbanned. Sean Ó'Faoláin and other admirers fought
a great battle, it went on for two or three years.... Nothing happened
until I came back to Ireland in 1946 and Sir John Keane heard I was
in Dublin and made me come and see him. He said that I must fight it
myself, I must appeal it myself. There was no appeal board then but
he told me that if I wrote appealing against the judgement and sent a
five-pound note as a sort of a bona fide, he would present this appeal
to the Senate. If they got the book released, I would get my fiver back.
So the book was released and I got my fiver back! Sir John said I had
to do it, for the honour of the thing. It was a victory against the
censorship and it was fought for me, not by me, but by my friends.[59]

This episode was crucial for Kate O'Brien's public profile in Ireland
as a controversial writer. The novelist Benedict Kiely remembered
the effect of this episode of censorship for other Irish writers: 'The
banning of Kate O'Brien's *The Land of Spices*, that was the first

censorship ban that I think I was conscious of and conscious of as a complete and total outrage.'[60] Censorship marked Kate's break with her contemporary Ireland. After this, her protagonists looked only to Europe for independence.

5

Resistance writing: 1941–50

The war years were a time of upheaval and instability for Kate O'Brien but also of great creativity in her writing. Her correspondence shows her constantly on the move from 1941 onwards, staying in borrowed apartments or lodging with friends, like the novelist E.M. Delafield in Devon and Mrs O'Neill, Mary's mother, in Norfolk. Despite continuous displacement and impoverishment, she produced novels at the rate of one every two years – *The Land of Spices* (1941), *The Last of Summer* (1943) and, most importantly, *That Lady* (1946). Her wartime writing was a kind of resistance writing, a response to censorship, to war and to her unstable working life. Her protagonists in these wartime novels – Helen Archer in *The Land of Spices*, Angele Kernahan in *The Last of Summer* and, crucially, Ana de Mendoza in *That Lady* – are all idealised figures of independence and autonomy, stable figures at a time of great personal disruption.

Just how unstable her wartime life was is clear from letters to her friends like the poet John Gosworth, a neighbour from happier days in Great James Street:

> I hate being out of touch with my real friends and feel the separations of the war – as well as all it must mean in discomfort and disorientation for someone like you. I only hope that you keep some notebooks by you and that, however bitter the sum of your reactions to this ordeal may be, you are writing things down, in verse or prose.... Your terribly gentle and modest request for some of the money I owe you has touched me very much, my dear.... The very least I can do is to send you the miserable ten shillings a week you say would be of use.... Our whole world is surrealised! I alone, since no one seems to want my services remain at my profession – and I feel ashamed of my luck, think of you all. I am, however, an Air Raid Warden and a firewatcher! Great James St is empty – I have walked

through it sometimes like a ghost. Bloomsbury is a heap of very, very ancient ruins. I often return and walk about there for a day or two sucking sorrow. But we all will return.[1]

After the success of *The Land of Spices*, Kate signed a contract with Doubleday, her American publishers, for a new novel, to be called 'Summer's Flower'. (This contract undertook to pay her $1,250 plus 15 per cent royalties.)[2] This novel, completed in September 1942, was published in April 1943 under the title *The Last of Summer*. Kate took the plot of this novel from a romantic legend from her own family history. In *Presentation Parlour*, she tells how a Miss Anne Liddy had been the love object of Kate's uncle, Johnny O'Brien:

> On one of his visits home, he met the severe and ambitious Miss Anne Liddy, and gave her to understand that he was in love with her. Be that as it may, she married not him, but his foolish elder brother. He, Johnny, married a French ballerina or music hall artist and died young abroad, of tuberculosis.

In the novel, Hannah O'Reilly, a beautiful, ambitious young Mellick woman, attracts the attentions of all three of the wealthy Kernahan brothers of Waterpark House. She is engaged to marry the handsome, rakish Tom, but he breaks off the engagement and the mortified Hannah recovers her dignity by marrying his elder brother Ned, the owner of the house. Tom leaves Ireland, marries a French woman, an actress with the Comédie Française, and dies young. As the novel opens, in September 1939, Tom's daughter, Angele Kernahan, a theatre and film actress, comes to Ireland and pays an unexpected visit to her father's home, Waterpark House. There she encounters her Aunt Hannah, now widowed and the matriarch of the house. Drama ensues when Angele falls in love with her cousin Tom.

The Last of Summer is almost contemporaneous with its composition, set in 1939 and written in 1941/42. The action is filtered through Angele's perspective and the result is a curiously distanced view of Ireland, where the familiar Irish middle-class setting is seen through the admiring but alien eyes of the young French woman. At the beginning of the novel, Angele, a stranger to her father's country, walks towards Waterpark House, his childhood home, and appraises the beautiful countryside from the point of view of an outsider. Some

Irish country children taunt her and this immediately alienates her and sets her apart:

> She felt tears of fury in her eyes .... In this shaft sped by a rude little girl – no novelty – she felt without reason a greater force than could have been intended; she felt an accidental expression of something that had vaguely oppressed and surprised her, these ten days, in the Irish air – an arrogance of austerity, contempt for personal feeling, coldness, and perhaps fear from idiosyncrasy. In this most voluptuously beautiful and unusual land.

In this 'beautiful and unusual land', Angele finds much to admire. Life at Waterpark is gracious and there is an authorial emphasis on the careless elegance of this life, the equal to any good European bourgeois home. The socialising of the young people of Waterpark – the car trips, swimming, dancing, picnicking – is stressed and this emphasis on social pleasures and the merry-making of a group of young people is the first instance of Kate O'Brien's emerging interest in a kind of European bohemianism. As the Irish critic Anne Fogarty describes it, 'her heroines ... are roving and restless. They are flâneuses who wander the streets of the numerous cities, including Paris, Rome, Naples, Venice and Milan, which form a backdrop to their lives. By adopting the streetwalking existence, they extend themselves, but also plumb the depths of those feelings of homelessness and destitution.'[3]

As the narrative progresses, Angele falls in love with her cousin Tom and, consequently, Hannah battles for possession of her son. The love affair between Tom and Angele is the weakest element within the novel and the real focus is on the battle of wills between Hannah and Angele. Hannah Kernahan is Kate O'Brien's most intriguing characterisation in this novel, a woman of great charm and beauty, perceptive and civilised, yet dishonest and cruel. At certain points in the novel, Angele recalls hearing her own actress mother recite lines from Racine's *Phèdre* and Kate deliberately includes these intertextual references, making Hannah parallel with the incestuous and obsessive Greek heroine (it is a measure of Kate O'Brien's development as a novelist that an earlier parent who loved his child unreasonably, Anthony Considine, is never interrogated in this way, whereas Hannah Kernahan's possessiveness is clearly identified for the monstrous egotism that it is).

Like many mothers in Irish literature, Hannah is associated with Ireland and, in particular, with Ireland's stance of neutrality during

World War II. Hannah's selfishness is seen in her attitude towards the coming war in Europe. When her son Martin insists that war in Europe is happening, she is stubborn: 'We're not having it, Martin. It's nothing whatever to do with us. A plague on both their houses.' For Kate's reading audience, particularly in England in 1943, such indifference to the Allied position would have been ill received, to say the least.

In the end, Hannah triumphs, putting an end to the engagement between Angele and Tom and breaking her son in the process. Angele leaves Ireland for Paris just as war is declared and resolves never to return: 'it's hopeless...a fighter would stay and fight....It's hopeless anyway, against her. Better let it all go. It's too much. I haven't the courage, I haven't the brains.' In Anne Fogarty's words: 'The parting irony of the novel is that the place of refuge from the oppression of the Irish family romance is a Europe poised on the verge of war.'[4] Those young people with imagination and independence of mind make their way to the Continent. Those left behind are weakened and somehow lessened. As one character remaining in Ireland comments sadly: 'It seems we will be lonely here in our neutrality.'

This is the novel where Kate finally confronts the more negative aspects of her Mellick world, where the values of the Irish bourgeoisie are questioned, found to be insular and rejected. Kate O'Brien's physical distance from Ireland during the writing of the novel, her experience of living in poverty in wartime England and the alienating experience of censorship all combined to bring her to this imaginative point.

The Last of Summer was well received and the success of this novel brought her some financial security because on 15 April 1943 she signed with Doubleday, her American publishers, for her next three novels. She managed to sell the Spanish rights in July 1943 and the book was later translated into Swedish, Dutch, German and even Czech, allowing Kate to repay debts to her friends that autumn. As a result of this success, she adapted the novel for the stage, with the aid of fellow Irish man, the theatre producer John Perry. The stage version of *The Last of Summer*, directed by John Gielgud, opened at the Phoenix Theatre in London on 7 June 1944. In letters, Kate worried that the feared German invasion might distract audiences from a mere play.

The Last of Summer was reviewed in the *New Statesman and Nation* by William Whitebait, who highlighted the uneasy transition of the material from novel to stage: 'With the help of Mr John Perry, Miss Kate O'Brien has provided a precis of her novel, but the result is too leisurely to be a play. Two acts empty of suspense are devoted to preparing some excellent scenes in the third. Moreover we fail to accept the author's point of view.'[5] He went on to praise Gielgud's direction and Fay Compton's performance as Hannah and, with some wit, the reviewer commended the portrayal of Jo Kernahan: 'Miss Hazel Terry plays a girl about to become a nun with a quiet realism that will shock those who take their views on convents from Protestant films.'[6] Another reviewer, Herbert Farjeon, again commended the acting, particularly of Angele and Hannah, but found the production values of the play and the elegance of Kate's Kernahans of Waterpark questionable:

> We find ourselves asking whether Mr John Gielgud, the producer, and Mr Michael Relph, the designer of the set, have ever set foot in Ireland, ever seen a garment with a tear in it, a tablecloth with a stain on it, or a garden with a weed in it. Everything is spick and span, everything is 'swell', and there is lots of taste, all good. But might it be said of the true Ireland that it has less taste and more beauty than any other country in the world?[7]

What this reviewer seemed to find most implausible was Kate's portrayal of the Irish bourgeoisie as elegant and tasteful.

From her letters at the time, Kate expressed a wish to get a full-time job, in order to survive financially, but her war work was only ever freelance. (Mary O'Neill, on the other hand, found work as an illustrator on Laurence Olivier's film production of *Henry V*.) The only tangible result of Kate's work for the Ministry of Information was her essay 'English Diaries and Journals',[8] published in 1943. It was published in booklet form as part of a series called *Britain in Pictures*, edited by W.J. Turner. These booklets celebrated various aspects of English life, history and culture; contributors included John Betjeman, Elizabeth Bowen and Graham Greene. Kate's contribution was far more substantial than an exercise in literary patriotism. 'English diaries and journals' was her longest piece of critical writing and one of her most enjoyable, opening with the bold assertion: 'Let me begin with the hard saying that the best English diaries have been written by bores . . . . A good diary is not necessarily literature; for of its nature it must be free of most of the disciplines and tests of a work of art.' Her thesis was that diarists are mainly secondary artists, never attaining the higher vocation of fiction writing. This hierarchical view of creativity sustains her in her survey of diary writing from the English civil war to her contemporaries. Of Fanny Burney's diaries, for example, she wrote: 'they are the best of her and her chief claim to immortality. They are so much better than most diaries because they are imaginative, free and subjective; they are, in fact, the work of a writer, which most diaries are not.' As with her best critical writing, Kate revealed much of herself, commenting on John Evelyn's happy, fulfilled life that 'the average human being may be forgiven if he turns from the bright prospect with something like a shudder'. (Not true. Many people find the spectacle of happy life bearable, novelists included.) Connected to this is her comment on Samuel Pepys:

> Who is there who has not shuddered to imagine some sudden impossible revelation to the world of his actual self.... The self we know, but which, while we alternately inflate and enjoy it or miserably writhe against its monstrous embrace, we are at least determined no one else shall come within miles of knowing?

In this passage she was revealing much of her own struggle with a dreaded 'actual' self. This discomfort with her own sense of self accounts for the change in tone in her letters, her disparaging references to her appearance, her need to idealise within her fiction. Another theme to emerge from this survey was the suppression of female creativity by male relatives, and she cited as examples Fanny Burney's domination by her father and Dorothy Wordsworth's by her brother. Kate argued that this blocked creativity – all the unwritten novels and poems – communicated itself through their journal writings:

> There is too much suppression everywhere in Dorothy Wordsworth of what clearly must have been a most distinguished and original mind.... But she did not write verse and she undertook to be William's angel – so egoism and intellectual restlessness were subjugated by responsibility and by love.

The following year, this essay was republished in a volume she edited called *The Romance of English Literature*, where essays by Elizabeth Bowen, Graham Greene and Lord David Cecil were also republished.

Little personal evidence survives of Kate's life during World War
II, but it is clear that her sustained efforts to survive financially were
finally paying off. Her journalistic work took a new direction in late
1942 when she was invited to contribute to a BBC discussion
programme on drama. Following this, Kate became a regular voice
on the BBC, reviewing fiction for the Home Service from 1943
onwards and talking on programmes such as *What I'm Reading
Now* and *Old Favourites*. She had a regular spot on a programme
called *Book Talk*, for which she was paid twelve guineas per
appearance. (Sometimes she talked about books she had just
reviewed for *The Spectator*.) Her broadcasting work for the BBC
was infrequent but steady and she was often called in for literary
discussions on *Woman's Hour*, right up to the late 1950s. She was
an excellent radio subject, lively and independent in her thinking,
with a beautiful, deep, resonant voice, and she worked extensively
with the BBC and Radio Éireann for the last thirty years of her life.
Her distinctive accent was part of her attractiveness, mostly English
in pronunciation with a hint of her Limerick origins in the soft
endings of her words. It could be best described as having English
vowels but Irish consonants. Apart from her review work, she
regularly submitted her own fiction to the BBC for radio
dramatisation, but only *That Lady* and *Without My Cloak* were
accepted, the former broadcast in 1953 and 1968, and the latter
broadcast in 1947 and again in 1969.

Later in her life, she was to claim that she worked for the Ministry
of Information. In 1965, she told an audience at the Sir William
Gibb School for Girls, Faversham, Kent that 'I began my talking in
public efforts during the 1939/45 war. I was attached to the Ministry
of Information and for some reason they used me a lot for
broadcasting. Pep talks of different kinds and descriptions of life in
England in those days and of how people were adjusting themselves
to the air raids and so on. They said that it didn't matter that my
accent was foreign – in fact they preferred it so long as I was clear!'[9]
However, her surviving letters from this time make no mention of
any such work.

With an upturn in her finances, Kate was able to afford a room in
Buckingham Street in London, which was convenient for her work
with *The Spectator* and the BBC. She also began a new relationship
around this time. From May 1942 onwards, Kate spent long periods
at the Devon home of the novelist E.M. Delafield.

1. Kate O'Brien, her mother Katty, centre, and her brother Michael in 1902 (University of Limerick, Special Collections Library)

2. Boru House, Limerick, Kate's birthplace (author)

3. Kate O'Brien, third from left, with her brothers Michael, second from left, Eric, fourth from left and Gerard, seated, in 1903/04 (University of Limerick, Special Collections Library)

4. Kate with her brother Tom, in Kilkee, Co. Clare in 1910. (University of Limerick, Special Collections Library)

5. Laurel Hill, Limerick in the early twentieth century (courtesy of Laurel Hill)

6. The chapel in Laurel Hill (courtesy of Laurel Hill)

7. The dormitories in Laurel Hill (courtesy of Laurel Hill)

8. Kate (centre) with her sisters Nance (left) and May (right), early 1920s (University of Limerick, Special Collections Library)

9. Kate and her husband Gustaaf Renier, 1923/24 (University of Limerick, Special Collections Library)

10. Stephie, Margaret Stephie Stephens (courtesy of Caroline Whitehead)

11. Mary O'Neill, 1930s (courtesy of Orlaith Kelly)

12. Gustaaf Renier, 1920s (courtesy of Caroline Whitehead)

13. May O'Brien at Ashurst Bank, 1929 (courtesy of Caroline Whitehead)

14. Kate (centre) with Stephie and Veronica Turleigh (kneeling), 1928 (courtesy of Caroline Whitehead)

15. Kate and Stephie, 1929 (courtesy of Caroline Whitehead)

16. Kate in the late 1920s at Ashurst (courtesy of Caroline Whitehead)

17. Portrait by Lafayette, 1926 (courtesy of The National Portrait Gallery, London)

18. Kate with Ruth Stephens (centre) and Veronica Turleigh (right) (courtesy of Caroline Whitehead)

19. Mary O'Neill in Connemara, 1950s (courtesy of Orlaith Kelly)

20. Kate with her godson, Austin Hall, early 1940s (courtesy of Elizabeth Hall)

21. Kate at work in England, 1940s (courtesy of Orlaith Kelly)

22. Three portraits of Kate by Howard Coster, 1950s (courtesy of The National Portrait Gallery, London)

23. Kate and Joyce Grenfell, Connemara, 1953 (University of Limerick, Special Collections Library)

24. Kate in the early
    1970s (courtesy
    of Mary Steward)

25. Kate's last home, 'Boughton'
    in Kent, mid-1960s
    (courtesy of Orlaith Kelly)

Elizabeth Delafield had been an acquaintance of Kate's from the 1930s but, early in 1941, their relationship developed and they soon became close. E.M. Delafield was the pen-name of Mrs Elizabeth Dashwood, a successful writer and author of the charming and immensely popular *The Diary of a Provincial Lady*, which was first published in the literary magazine *Time and Tide* in the 1930s. Delafield was a director of *Time and Tide* and Kate was a contributor and they also shared an American publisher.[10]

Delafield was fifty when Kate got to know her, seven years older than Kate, and the daughter of a novelist, Mrs Henry de la Pasture. Like many of Kate's women friends, Delafield was a Catholic (at one point in her life, she had been a novice in a Belgian convent). Like Kate's other friends, she had married, but, unlike the others, Delafield still lived with her husband, Paul Dashwood, in a house called Croyle in the village of Kentisbeare in Devon. It was there that Kate recorded finishing *The Last of Summer* in September 1942. Delafield was still suffering from the loss of her only son, who had died accidentally in military training camp in 1940, and in November 1941 she travelled to Oxfordshire to stay with Kate in her cottage. Kate then began to spend long periods of time at Croyle and, when Delafield fell ill in 1942, Kate went with her to Cornwall for her recuperation. Kate moved permanently into Croyle during Delafield's long illness and was accorded the use of the old schoolroom as a workroom, a privilege, as Delafield's biographer notes sharply, 'never attained by the mistress of the house'.[11]

It is not clear whether Kate was a guest or a paying lodger in Delafield's house. In letters, Kate suggested that she was living on total charity, but to another, Barbara Gosworth, she wrote, in June 1943:

> I am pg.ing [paying guest] with E.M. Delafield for some time – though I still have my hovel in Oxon, and go there for an odd week. One reason why I can't write too much now is she, E.M.D., is very ill – very nearly slipped the moorings last week, with a sudden, very bad stoppage of the bowels – and she is out of danger now but extremely ill; and the house is full of nurses and silence and anxiety – and I am very busy, with my own work, with directing this place and the nurses and with her letters and business affairs as well as my own. So I am pretty tired and rushed. But so enormously relieved that she is going to be all right that I don't give a damn.[12]

Despite Kate's hopes, Elizabeth Delafield died on 12 December 1943 and, in a letter to John Gosworth, Kate wrote of her grief, 'our association was quite perfect'.[13] After her death, Kate broadcast a tribute to Delafield for BBC Radio, on the Home Service:

> I remember watching her nipping about in the top branches of the big fig tree in her own garden, not ten weeks before she died. She was chucking the ripe figs down to me, and tying muslin bags on the unripe ones. Eating more than her fair share of figs at the same time – she adored them. That was late September 1943. I knew then, quite well, the doctors' verdict on her; and so indeed did she. But on that sunny September evening, it seemed like the verdict of lunatics. But it wasn't, of course. For she died in December.[14]

Violet Powell, Delafield's biographer, described Kate as someone who was 'known to have had lesbian relations' but added that 'Elizabeth herself was always interested in men'.[15] However, I contend that Elizabeth and Kate were lovers.

Delafield's last novel, *Late and Soon*, was dedicated to Kate and was published in April 1943. The novel features an Irish colonel called Rory Lonergan, the love interest for the protagonist, Lady Valentine Arbell. In *Late and Soon*, the colonel is billeted at the home of Valentine, a widow with a decaying country house in Home Counties England and two grown daughters. By coincidence, this Rory Lonergan had also been her first love over twenty years before in Rome, where he had been a penniless artist and she a diplomat's daughter (this was not Delafield's finest hour in her prose writing). Delafield's principal characters in *Late and Soon* are all identifiably taken from her own life. Delafield herself is Valentine, Kate is Rory, Delafield's daughter Rosamund is clearly the inspiration for Jess and Delafield's husband is reflected in the figure of the general, Valentine's brother. The character of Rory Lonergan in *Late and Soon* is worth considering as a fictional portrait of Kate herself. As Violet Powell points out:

> It is possible that Kate O'Brien, more or less in permanent residence in Croyle, may have supplied material on which Elizabeth built up a portrait of an Irishman from a middle-class Catholic background. Unfortunately neither novelist realised that an essentially Kate O'Brien character would not be convincing when transported into an E.M. Delafield novel.[16]

Delafield's daughter, Rosamund, also believed that the character of

Rory Lonergan was a romanticised version of Kate.[17] Rory Lonergan is in his late forties (Kate's age at the time of the composition of the novel), a southern Irishman who has long since left Ireland to pursue his art in Europe and Britain. Delafield describes him in racial terms:

> Rory Lonergan carried his forty-eight years lightly. He was unmistakably an Irishman – not much above medium height, large-boned and heavily built but without superfluous flesh. His dark, intelligent face had the characteristics of his race: clearly defined black eyebrows and blue eyes, long, straight, clean-shaven upper lip and protruding under jaw. His voice was an Irish voice, deep and with odd, melancholy cadences, a naturally beautiful voice that betrayed the speaker's nationality at once by its unEnglish inflections.[18]

Rory has what Delafield calls a 'brogue' (an Irish accent), which broadens when he wants someone to like him. He is privileged within the household by getting his own office, as Kate did in Croyle, and, curiously, has a child, born in France and brought up by his sister in southern Ireland. Kate's own touchiness about the civilised assurance of the Irish bourgeoisie is reflected in Delafield's characterisation of Rory. In the novel, Valentine's family distrusts the Irishman on racial grounds and Delafield is careful to describe Lonergan as southern Irish, Catholic and middle-class.

At one point, Valentine's brother interrogates Rory about Ireland, and authorial sympathy is expressed in favour of the Irishman: 'He had heard too many Englishmen launch themselves, with an ignorance almost sublime in its unconsciousness, upon the subject of Irish politics, to feel any dismay.'[19] Despite all the fuss her family makes, Valentine ends up married to Rory, with the overt approval of the author. This approval was not shared by critics of the novel and one reviewer of *Late and Soon* went so far as to call Rory Lonergan 'a complacent and humbugging bounder of a man'.[20]

Rory reads like a version of Kate, remade and interpreted by Delafield. It is clear that the writer was an acceptable part of the Dashwood household in Devon. Rosamund Dashwood remembered the many literary women that her mother brought home to Devon from London, which was much disliked and resented by her husband and children.[21] Kate, one of these literary women, was an exception. She was compassionate during her mother's illness, without any bossiness, and helpful with Rosamund's desire to get into university. As Rosamund Dashwood remembered her, Kate was given to wearing elegant, cloak-like garments, used little or no make-up, kept her dark hair short and swept off her brow, outside the feminine in the conventional sense but nevertheless attractive and sympathetic to the teenage girl.[22]

In June 1946, Kate wrote the introduction to an edition of *The Provincial Lady*,[23] published in 1947, where she included the surprising critical opinion that she preferred Delafield's novels to her 'Provincial Lady' diaries. This influence worked both ways, since Delafield was to influence Kate herself in her own work. Delafield's son and daughter believed that her mother was the inspiration for Ana de Mendoza, the heroine of Kate's next novel, *That Lady*.

This was to be a crucial novel for Kate, her triumphant realisation of an empowered female protagonist, and one of her most successful narratives. Unusually, the idea for *That Lady* came to her complete and formed:

> One very bad wet night in January 1940, I was working hard in my flat in Bloomsbury – and I went out in the rain in the blackout to the letterbox at the corner. I imagine that I was in a dull and non-receptive mood – and certainly nothing was further from my upper brain than thoughts of Spain and Spanish history. But suddenly, just as I was putting the letters through the slot, I was invaded by what seemed to be an entire novel, which I was one day to write, and which was to be called *That Lady*. I remember being as if dazzled. I leant against the letterbox in the rain, still clutching the letters in the slot, taking in the whole conception. The woman, the Princess of Eboli, had been visiting and revisiting me for years as interesting, but not my cup of tea. All of a sudden, she and her history took clear possession of me – by that letterbox in the rain. Within a few seconds, I suppose, as it were, I wrote the whole book. And I felt superbly happy. I was too exalted to go home, but there was no fun walking in the rain and the blackout – so I went into the nearby Queen's Head and had a drink all by myself – a deep and happy drink. And I remember the dear landlady, Mrs O'Flanagan, asking me what on earth I kept smiling at on such a miserable night.[24]

The actual writing of the novel took place four years later. As soon as the war ended, Kate travelled back to Ireland, spending the summer of 1945 working on *That Lady* and using the 1877 *Vida de la Princesa de Eboli* as her source of reference.[25] Later she remembered the process of writing: 'On Lake Inchiquin, in the summer of 1945, I wrote most of *That Lady*....I had it all ready more or less. I did the actual writing very fast in the end....It was a lovely summer; the relief of the war being over, you know.'[26]

In essence, the novel was in place from a very early stage, but, her only 'historical' novel, it presented her with technical difficulties: 'I remember that when I finished writing the novel in the autumn of 1945, I said to myself, consolingly, that it was certain that during the rest of my life I would never again undertake any piece of work that could possibly confront me with so many terrible technical hurdles.'[27] Some of this difficulty came from having to deal with real lives and events, seeking to balance historical fact against her own imaginative needs. The 'real' story of Ana de Mendoza and Philip II was largely irrelevant to her purposes, for, as she wrote in her introductory note to the novel, 'what follows is not a historical novel. It is an invention arising from reflection on the curious external story of Ana de Mendoza and Philip II of Spain.'[28]

That Lady is a novel produced by her experiences of wartime censorship, and Kate O'Brien created the emblematic figure of an aristocratic, resistant woman. The historical material that Kate used was, on the face of it, unpromising, since the real Ana de Mendoza seems to have been a difficult and much-disliked intriguer[29] (she was used as the villainess in Donizetti's opera *Don Carlos* and was the subject of other historical works, notably Mignet's 1854 *Antonio Perez et Phillipe II*).[30] The difficult, unlikeable Ana de Mendoza interested Kate because she could sympathise with the idea of public disapproval – she could idealise what she saw as Ana's private integrity.

The novel deals with the period of Spanish history from 1576 to 1592 and centres on the power struggles within the court of Philip II. Ana, the widow of Philip's prime minister and a woman of vast independent wealth, is at the centre of this power struggle. Aged thirty-six and considered odd in appearance, she is idealised by Kate O'Brien for this very unconventionality. Identified as Castilian, Ana shares many attributes with the Castilian landscape aestheticised by Kate in *Farewell Spain*, an austere, sparse, rigorous land:

> She was physically the expression of what that implied. Her beauty, for those who found her beautiful, was, paradoxically, of exaggeration and restraint. She was taller and thinner than is averagely considered seductive in a woman; her bones were narrow, and every feature, nose, chin, hand and foot, was a little longer than it should be. Her skin was

thinly white, with blue veins showing on her temples and her hands. Her left eye was full of light but over the socket of the right one she wore, as has been said, a black silk eye-shade, cut in diamond shape. She had worn this since she was fourteen. At that age she fought a duel with a page in her father's house, and lost her right eye.

Her lover, Antonio Perez, the king's secretary of state, on his first meeting with her, is disappointed because she is 'one-eyed and thin...simple almost to the point of dullness....Doesn't play the great beauty.' However, Perez begins to find her strange androgynous appearance attractive and he finally concedes her 'dangerous simplicity, her gaunt, almost ungainly beauty', and falls in love with her. Ana's lost eye becomes a talisman for her and she touches it in times of crisis. She admits: 'I think it decided everything in my life for me.' Marked physically, Ana also stands outside conventional female behaviour. She is a mother but aristocratic and individualistic, in stark contrast to Hannah Kernahan, the shopkeeper's daughter: 'Ana laughed. She was not at all maternal. Towards her children she behaved as towards other acquaintances or dependants, occupying herself with those whom she liked, more or less ignoring the others.' Her relationship with her ruler, the devout, complicated Philip II, is curious. She is both his obedient subject and his closest friend, a woman he has admired and desired but never loved.

Although Ana possesses wealth and position, as a woman in a patriarchal society she is without autonomy. When she does finally choose to assert her individualism, she does so by initiating a love affair with Antonio Perez: 'I'm nearly thirty-seven and I'm said to have more power in my hands sometimes than any other woman in Spain. Yet this is only the second time in my life that I've decided anything for myself.' (The first time was when she tried unsuccessfully to become a nun at the convent of Teresa of Avila, in the aftermath of her husband's death.) Ana's love affair with Antonio is the dramatic turning-point of the novel, the shaping force in the events that follow. As lovers, Ana de Mendoza and Antonio Perez are signalled as cross-gendered. At first, Ana is dismissive of him: 'He seems to be just a little popinjay, almost a mignon...he runs quite counter to our usual male conventions.' Her maid comments: 'He smells like a woman.' When it finally happens, this love affair is seen as inadequate, not sufficient in itself: 'private life, however deprecatingly one chose to view it, must surely be about something more than the commonplace of any street or bed. There still must be a reason, Ana thought, for being oneself, and this is not it. Suffering perhaps, or conflict or faith or an argument or a test of some kind.' Ana seems to get little pleasure from her relationship with Antonio. She may assert her political right to self-determination, but spiritually she is unable to rid herself of a sense of sin. As she tells her lover, rather sadly: 'My soul has no place in your arms.'

Sexual love, as Kate O'Brien viewed it, was neither sufficient nor permissible in itself. She needed to frame it within some higher justification or purpose. So, when Ana comes into conflict with her king, this justification is found. As an authoritarian monarch, Philip sees no dividing line between public and private life. He spies on Ana, stealing her love letters and then confronting her with the evidence of her love affair. The scene where Ana faces down Philip is the strongest in the novel, dramatising the clash between public duty and private morality. Kate accords the moral victory to Ana. When Philip confronts her with the evidence of her sexual misconduct, as he sees it, Ana denies him any authority over her private life: 'There have been, Philip, as long as I can remember, thoughts, and even acts in that private life, which, presented to the world, would seem to injure this or that.... If I do wrong in it, that wrong is between me and heaven. But here below, so long as I don't try to change it into public life, I insist that I own it.'

Not only does Ana assert ownership of her private life, she extends this into a plea for democracy in Spain, subtly linking sexual and political authoritarianism. She asks Philip to 'Come back to govern us so that we can see what you are doing . . . let us feel the movement of government in Spain again.' For Ana, this is a moment of triumph, the opportunity for political change in Spain, but, for Philip, it is dangerous treason and he punishes her. Ana's resistance to Philip's authoritarian rule is successful, even though it leads to her immediate incarceration and the loss of family, wealth and freedom. She is shut away in prison and left to die. Even her name is expunged from public life and she is known only as 'That Lady'. In spite of this, her stand against the king is seen as a moral victory for individual conscience in the face of state control.

In her prison, loyally accompanied by her daughter and her duenna, Ana creates a female commune, a cell of resistance. In some sense, she is sanctified by this suffering. When Ana, looking worn and ill from her incarceration, is visited by the Cardinal of Toledo, he observes to himself: 'She looks distinguished and ascetic, like a very good nun who has been worked too hard.' Ana has realised her wish and become a nun, a secular one, a holy woman beatified by political martyrdom. The novel ends with the king, successful in his prosecution of the rebellious Ana but alone and stranded in his tyranny:

> He rose painfully from the table and moved without purpose across the room....A bell was ringing from Santa Maria Almudena. He remembered how much more clearly one heard that bell in the Long Room of the Eboli Palace....He looked out at the sunlight towards her empty house, and the glare hurt his eyes and the bell seemed to toll for his loneliness and the sins that drove him on, for ever further into loneliness.

In America, *That Lady* was criticised in journals like the *Catholic Mirror* and the *Catholic Book Club Newsletter* for the independent, self-determining morality of the protagonist. A Father Clement De Muth offered the undoubtedly accurate opinion that 'Miss O'Brien's version of what the Catholic requires by way of repentance is seriously at variance with the truth. Those who read her book must be forewarned that it misrepresents Catholicism on a matter of great importance.'[31] Defending the novel in the *Catholic Book Club Newsletter*, Harold C. Gardiner wrote: 'Her [Ana's] problem is how to reconcile the fact that she knows that she had offended God with the other fact that she cannot disavow the pleasure that was undoubtedly hers. This is a nice psychological point. Miss O'Brien, I feel, handles it with no small discernment.'[32] This conflict between Kate's need for Catholicism as an aesthetic code and the limitations of Catholic morality is never more evident than in *That Lady*.

One could argue that Ana de Mendoza was more of a Protestant heroine than anything else and this leads on to the question of Catholic belief in Kate O'Brien's writing. As always in her fiction, Catholicism operates in *That Lady* as a cultural symbol and her representation of Ana's Catholic conscience drew criticism. Her own relationship with Catholicism as an adult writer was complex. When invited to talk about Catholicism on BBC Radio in 1956, Kate declined, describing herself as a lapsed Catholic who was unwilling

to discuss it, and giving as her reason the fact that her family would be listening in to the programme most eagerly.[33] In relation to *That Lady*, she once wrote that she was even less of a Catholic than she had been when she wrote *The Ante-Room*.[34] She went on to comment that 'all the best are [Catholic] or come from it or go into it'.[35] For her, Catholicism was crucial to her sense of self as a writer, but the moral code of the Catholic Church was a different matter. In a letter to the critic Vivian Mercier, she comments: 'I am a moralist, in that I see no story unless there is a moral conflict, and the old-fashioned sense of the soul and its troubling effect in human affairs.'[36] All these contradictions surface in the tortured reflections of Ana de Mendoza.

That Lady was a commercial success and sold more than any other of her novels, except *Without My Cloak*. It was translated into eight languages and was published in America by Doubleday as *For One Sweet Grape*, a title that Kate took from Shakespeare's 'The Rape of Lucrece': 'For one sweet grape/who would the vine destroy?' This commercial success was reflected in the fact that it was a Book Society choice for May 1946 and was adapted for the Broadway stage. As always, Kate was on the move, with no settled home, but it was now success that was the reason for her nomadic existence. She spent much of 1949 in New York working on the stage adaptation of *That Lady* and it opened there that November with the celebrated stage actress Katherine Cornell in the title role. Kate was uneasy about having adapted the book herself, as her friend the novelist Paul Smith remembered:

> She knew she was in trouble the day she heard the cast first read the play. She knew it, and said it and yet she was frightened, inwardly raging, outwardly pretty passive before the great talents of Guthrie McClintoc who knew about directing, his wife Katherine Cornell, who knew about acting and the producer who knew bugger all about either.[37]

In the published version of the stage play of *That Lady*, dedicated to Katherine Cornell, Kate made her reservations plain about the three-year process of adapting the novel for the stage: 'So, novel into play? It is a difficult thing always – if the one is good and the other aims to be good ... we shall soon know ... whether this novel-into-play is good.'[38] The answer was no. According to Lorna Reynolds, the production lasted for eighty days and did not make Kate O'Brien the money she had hoped for. In a letter to Denys Blakelock in 1954, Kate said:

> The play isn't really very good. The story expands into the minds of Ana and Philip. It should be a good film but it's not good theatre. However a snob historian in Oxford told me that my Philip is good history. But I know that myself and he is not hysterical. He is far more complicated than that.[39]

That Lady was dramatised for radio, televised by the BBC in 1954 and again in 1961 and was filmed in Hollywood in 1955. This Hollywood film version was directed by Terence Young and had Olivia De Havilland, miscast but adequate, in the role of Ana de Mendoza. The rewritten script took great liberties with the original storyline, removing Perez's wife from the narrative thus making his affair with Ana more acceptable. The film, which Kate disliked, was noteworthy only as the film debut of the English actor Paul Scofield, who played Philip II. Paul Smith said that Kate sold the film rights for £3,000 and, when asked in interview if she liked the film version of *That Lady*, replied: 'It was out of my hands, I had nothing to say. They could have done it beautifully, but they did it very ostentatiously, over-rich, not like Spain at all.'[40] *That Lady* was not her only experiment with film. Her literary archive, which was sold to a Chicago bookseller in 1970, included a copy of an undated film script, based on the life of Mary Magdalen, which bears a striking thematic resemblance to her novel on Ana de Mendoza.

One consequence of the success of this novel was that it renewed her popularity in Ireland, both with the Irish reading public and within intellectual circles. In 1945, Kate was able to travel back to Ireland after six years of self-imposed confinement to England. The shock of return was great:

> In May 1945, the month of VE Day, I returned to Ireland after a total absence from my native country of five-and-a-half years.... I was in Ireland, as it happened, in September 1939 when World War II broke out. I returned to London in October of that year, and thereafter, as I say, saw nothing of my native country until I sailed into Dunleary [*sic*] Harbour on an evening of May 1945. It was to sail back far, and shockingly, into the overlaid and the forgotten. I remember how the cleanliness startled me. The season was in leaf, and all the gardens,

public and private, were Victorian tended and radiant with flower. This was indeed a far, far past – and very ghostly. Had Ireland been living within this golden ambience throughout the six worst years of human history? Well no. Rigidly, and under many stresses, de Valera had kept the people out of active war. He was proved right in this, of course.... But it didn't take long to find, among the poets and the middle-aged writers anyway, certain shock and sorrow that kept us up to date even then.[41]

Kate began spending long periods back in Ireland. In September 1945, in a hotel in County Clare, she wrote a poem for a fellow guest, Frank Richardson. A keen angler, Richardson had taken a lock of her hair and had made a trout fly with it, calling it 'O'Brien's Glory' and presenting it to her. In celebration, she wrote 'Jay's Hackles, Mallard's Wing and Pheasant's Tail':

> With a wisp of my poor 'glory' folded in:
> This fly – is it dry or wet? – may not prevail
> Against the cunning trout of Inchiquin.[42]

She was in Ireland in 1947, in County Wicklow, when she heard that she had been made a fellow of the Royal Society of Literature. Kate's renewed interest in Ireland was partly due to a number of new friend-ships she had made in Dublin, with young writers like John Jordan and Paul Smith and, most importantly, with the academic and critic Lorna Reynolds. The man who was responsible for introducing her to these new Irish friends was Micheál Mac Liammóir.

Micheál Mac Liammóir, who had started life in London in 1899 as Alfred Willmore, moved to Ireland in the late 1920s, Gaelicised his name, reinventing himself as an Irish man, and, with his partner Hilton Edwards, had set up the Gate Theatre in Dublin. Micheál Mac Liammóir's theatre presented a programme of European and experimental drama in a Dublin dominated by the Irish drama programme of the Abbey Theatre. Micheál, a hugely talented actor and writer, gathered around him a circle of artists and writers in Dublin. Kate reacquainted herself with Ireland and with an Irish artistic world through him. Later, she was to write an introduction for a recording Micheál Mac Liammóir made of Yeats's poetry and to participate in a television tribute to him on his seventieth birthday.[43]

Significantly, Micheál Mac Liammóir and Hilton Edwards were living openly as a couple, no mean feat in a country where homosexuality was criminalised and censorship was brutal. Kate was to find in their friendship an important source of support and community when she returned to Ireland. Within their circle, she made a number of new contacts, many of them younger gay men. Up to now, she had known Ireland through family and old college friends only, but she was finding congenial, unconventional friends, similar to those in her London circle. To some degree, Micheál had a popularity and acceptance in Ireland that Kate had failed to achieve herself. Censorship had branded her books obscene and even her popularity with a wide reading audience worked against her, leading to the dismissive categorisation of her work as that of a 'lady novelist'. Only a few Irish critics, like Vivian Mercier and John Jordan, wrote seriously of her fiction. Even her accent, altered by her years in England, marked her as different. She exuded an air of European civilisation and education that set her apart from Irish people. MacLiammoir, with his actor's ability to please and his instinct for public self-presentation, found himself a place within Irish public life, but Kate's self-presentation could make her a rather intimidating public presence.

The academic Lorna Reynolds was Kate's most important new friend in Ireland. Lorna Reynolds, born in 1911 and fourteen years younger than Kate, was a lecturer in the English Department at Kate's alma mater, University College Dublin. In her book *Kate O'Brien: A Literary Portrait*, Lorna Reynolds describes their first meeting:

> In November 1946 Kate O'Brien was invited as guest of honour to the Annual Dinner of the Women Writers Club in Dublin.... Micheál Mac Liammóir was asked to propose the toast to our guest and I to second it. With her usual graciousness she came up to me afterwards and congratulated me on my speech....A few days later she invited me to lunch, and so began a memorable and stormy friendship.[44]

In correspondence, Kate dubbed Lorna 'Feisal' and signed herself 'Ibn Saud', after the father and son rulers of Saudi Arabia. Both women travelled to France and Monaco in July 1947, where Lorna introduced Kate to an old schoolfriend of hers, the Irish-born Darina Laracy who was married to the Italian novelist, Ignazio Silone. Lorna Reynolds remembered Kate on this holiday as an unadventurous traveller who preferred to sit quietly reading or observing. Lorna and Kate travelled again in Europe in August and September 1949, visiting Denmark, Switzerland, Rome and Venice.

Micheál Mac Liammóir was also responsible for introducing Kate to a new friend, who differed markedly from others of her circle. Paul Smith was over twenty years her junior and had been born in a Dublin slum. He came to know Kate when he was working at the Dublin Gate Theatre as a costume designer for Micheál Mac Liammóir. It was a friendship that lasted, despite the differences between the two. As Paul Smith was to write:

> In a sense, two extremes met in us; she, representative of a prosperous middle-class, conventionally educated, widely travelled, widely experienced, a woman of deep culture and I, a working-class Dubliner, who had never known where his next cut of bread or next pair of runners was coming from.[45]

Describing her as 'the most interesting woman I've ever met',[46] Paul Smith was sensitive to her class prejudices and her idealisation of the bourgeoisie: 'She was a tangled fishnet of contradictions. She liked the rich because she liked the way they spoke.'[47]

Kate found the friendship of younger gay men like Paul Smith enjoyable, especially if they had literary interests, and she encouraged his ambition to write novels. Interestingly, there is no evidence of Kate making connections with other Irish lesbians at this time, as she always had done in London – Ireland simply had little or no lesbian community. Smith's first novel, *Esther's Altar*, set in a Dublin tenement during the Easter Rising of 1916, was published in 1959 to great critical claim. His most successful novel, *The Countrywoman*, published in 1962, caused some confusion when he dedicated it to his mother, who also happened to be called Kate O'Brien.[48]

Like Kate, Paul Smith's work was banned in Ireland and remained so until 1975. His 1972 novel, *Annie*, was reviewed by Kate, who said 'It went straight home to one's central nerves'.[49] He accompanied her to the Dublin production of *That Lady*, with the Irish actress Shelagh Richards in the role of Ana de Mendoza and remembered:

> At the dress rehearsal the day before, Kate had voiced her objection to the heavy ornamentation the leading lady was giving the part. On the first night, she was to sit white-faced and appalled in her dress circle

seat and watch Dublin's answer to Ana de Mendoza exit through the
dead centre, up-stage fireplace and hear the audience bellow its gutty
laughter.[50]

In 1950, Kate made the surprising decision to return to Ireland
permanently, not to her native Limerick but instead to Connemara.
By Lorna Reynolds' own account, it was she who influenced Kate's
decision:

> At this time, she was staying in the Shelbourne Hotel, enjoying the
> success of her latest novel and spending the money she was making
> from its sales like wildfire. Though no business woman myself, I
> thought this reckless...so I advised her to buy a house, in Ireland of
> course, since she seemed to want to live in Ireland. I also, I remember,
> suggested Connemara, thinking it a suitably romantic place for a
> romantic novelist. It was years before I realised I had given her the
> wrong advice.[51]

6

Lotus Land: 1950–60

Years later, Kate was to refer to her ten years in Connemara as time spent in 'Lotus Land',[1] as if it were a place of fatal enchantment where she had dreamt her time away. In reality, her productivity there continued unabated, with two novels, a biography, two full-length essays and over forty short stories, travel essays, radio talks, lectures and articles, all produced between 1950 and 1960. The real Lotus dream was her idea of herself returning to Ireland as a distinguished and wealthy author and running her home with generosity and prodigality, on the scale of her father's Boru House.

Her house in Roundstone was called The Fort and had been a doctor's dispensary before she bought it. It needed substantial re-decoration and furnishing and cost her a great deal to repair, but it was large and overlooked the Atlantic. The house was valued at £7,000, according to Kate,[2] at a time when the average industrial wage in Ireland was around £5–£6 per month.[3] The cost of living was lower in Ireland than in England and so, counting on the success of *That Lady* and her many journalistic commitments, she planned to live with some style in Roundstone. It was rumoured that The Fort was haunted, which gave Kate great pleasure, and she was to grow very fond of her new home. The painter Michael Wishart spent some time in Connemara in 1951 and he and his wife Anne became friends with Kate. In a patronising account of his stay in the West of Ireland, he wrote:

> At Roundstone lived the novelist Kate O'Brien. She had a beautiful old house built out on a rock promontory overlooking the harbour. Like most beautiful old houses in Ireland, it was said, not without reason, to be haunted by bad luck. Kate drank a lot, but still managed to write occasionally. She fell in love with Anne at sight. She was nevertheless very kind to me, and we were grateful for her charming

and relatively stimulating conversation in that land of priests, tinkers, and bookies, with none of whom had we much in common.[4]

The Fort was run with lavish hospitality, as John Jordan recounted: 'Her house there was a perhaps over-hospitable centre for personal friends, transient writers and (it is I who am saying this) nuisances.'[5] She complained in a letter of 'too many friends of old friends who feel that they cannot pass my gate'.[6] In reality, she enjoyed being the chatelaine of a large house. She was also part of village life in Ireland, for the first time in her life.

When writing about her time in Connemara, Kate makes a clear distinction between the writers and artists who visited her and the villagers of Roundstone: 'But what I missed in Connemara was talking with writers and meeting writers. It was all very well living over in County Galway but, you know, most of the people living over there were fishermen, and holiday people and idlers [laughs]. I never met anyone to talk my own language to.'[7] However, the local village people provided copy for her journalistic sketches of Connemara, while the artists found in her a figure of patronage and encouragement.

In 1951, a young Belfast painter, James MacIntyre, spent the summer living on a small island off Roundstone with two fellow artists. On one occasion, Kate invited them to The Fort for supper:

> Kate O'Brien's house sat among trees on a bend in the road about half a mile beyond the harbour. We entered through a tall gate a well-tended garden with a smooth lawn which faced an imposing cream-painted house. A menagerie of cats in shades of black, brown and white stopped chasing their tails through the shrubbery to stare at the three strangers crunching up the gravelled drive. Our hostess was waiting and rose to greet us from a white garden seat near the front door. She wore a long black dress that rustled in the still evening. It was the first time I had ever been in such a large house, one so well-proportioned and furnished with taste and wealth.... I had imagined that anyone who lived in a house of this size and elegance would be aloof and distant with the like of us, but Kate O'Brien greeted us warmly and with such friendliness that I forgot my good intentions and was soon babbling away.... Through a wide panelled door, we entered a high ceilinged room with alabaster cornices and an ornamental centre rose, which supported an enormous etched-glass light fitting. Heavy leather chairs sat on a multi-coloured carpet and the walls were hung with paintings, mostly oils.[8]

Kate treated the impoverished young painters to drinks and a lavish supper, much to their delight, and, on a later visit, she bought some of their drawings and watercolours. A shared interest in art and in Spain enlivened these evenings and even Kate's marriage got a brief mention, but she told them nothing to illuminate the reasons for its short span. The picture of Kate that emerges from MacIntyre's memoir is of a generous, lively hostess who was keen to encourage the young men in their painting.

That same year, the young Irish novelist Val Mulkerns, on a cycling tour of Connemara, called unannounced at The Fort late one September evening. Kate welcomed her and encouraged her to talk about her writing. The younger woman was full of admiration for the 'heavy but still handsome woman'[9] and remembered Kate saying: 'I never wanted to be a mother. I'd have liked to be a father.'[10] The next day, Val Mulkerns joined Kate for a farewell drink in the local pub and the younger woman noted Kate's 'secure place in that little community. "Miss O'Brien" had a word for everybody in the steep main street and in the low-ceilinged little pub which was also a general store. Everybody also had a smile and a crack for her. She gave sweets to a little gaggle of local children and asked me if there was ever anywhere a more wonderfully beautiful lot?'[11]

Secure in her role among her beloved villagers, Kate was happy to befriend young writers, but, away from Roundstone, the relationship between the two women writers altered, as Val Mulkerns went on to relate:

> Somehow, in London however it was different. Over lunch in La Belle Etoile in Soho, I saw a side of Kate which didn't suffer fools gladly and I made a foolish remark about Venice, one of the places she regarded as sacred. Nothing would do me but to invite her to dinner in my flat. She smiled her thanks kindly and said that she never ate dinner these days.[12]

Paul Smith stayed in Roundstone in the summer of 1952, using it as a setting for his 1963 novel *Stravaganza!*, a novel of bohemian life in Connemara. He spent much of the summer in Kate's company: 'On the very evening of our arrival, there was an invitation to a party in her house where she was entertaining, among others, Joyce Grenfell and her husband.'[13] As part of her role as house-owner, Kate took up driving a second-hand Fiat, but, as Lorna Reynolds remembered, this was not a success:

Once, driving by Ballinafad, she misjudged the second curve in the road and, instead of continuing on the road, jumped the bridge and landed on the ground below. A lorry-driver coming from the opposite direction was petrified by what he saw and thunderstruck when the driver emerged unscathed from the car.... 'I remembered', she said, 'the advice of my father. He always said "if your horse is inclined to bolt with you, throw your weight back in the saddle". So I threw my weight back in the saddle and, as you have heard, landed on all fours.'[14]

Connected to her sense of self in Connemara was her writing about the village and the people in Roundstone. In her representations of Irish middle-class life, Kate always made a clear distinction between the Irish bourgeoisie and their servants, and she presented these servants as loyal upholders of a civilised Irish existence. Something of this difference surfaced in her stories of village life in Roundstone which were written for radio broadcasts or magazines. In these stories she positioned herself as an observer of a feudal way of life and represented herself as a much-loved overlord, not unlike Ana de Mendoza in Pastrana. Although she wrote of herself as integrated into the community in Roundstone, talking about 'our lovely village', 'our children' and 'our beautiful Civic Centre', Connemara itself was seen as a place apart, because of 'the accident of detachment from the crowded world'.[15] She usually wrote about Roundstone for a British readership. An article on Connemara that she wrote for *The Spectator* in 1951 sets the tone:

Its general aspect is of lonely and simple majesty. Connemara has a life very markedly its own, an elastic, quiet, unflurryable sort of life which springs from the character of its inhabitants but which after a while admits the pleasant stranger quite cordially to its habit ... it would be difficult for this austere people to share in the agitations and ambitions that torment the busy places of the world.[16]

She seemed to have viewed the people of Connemara as a race apart – simple, unworldly, austere, dignified – and this was from the perspective of a writer who was born less than a hundred miles away. This other-worldliness was also her theme in a radio talk for Radio Éireann in 1956 on the Clifden Pony Show, where, she claimed, 'the West has a certain aristocratic quality in all things'.[17] Other radio broadcasts, like 'Corpus Christi and the Children in

Connemara',[18] and her short story 'Chrissie's First Confession',[19] relied on the quaint ways of the local children and the colour of Catholic ritual to make commercially viable stories. These writings were commercially successful and, in October 1956, she spoke on BBC's *Women's Hour* about Roundstone. The whimsy of stories like 'Return to Boston' and 'Miss Finucane' allowed Kate to represent herself as a part of village life, the trusted recipient of confidences and biographical incidents from the villagers of Roundstone.

During the 1950s, Kate O'Brien's critical voice was gaining strength. Her essays on Teresa of Avila, George Eliot, Greta Garbo, Marie Curie, the Brontës, Maria Edgeworth and George Sand are particularly important in light of her fiction. The figures she admired in these literary essays were women writers, as seen in her 1956 essay 'Writers of letters'.[20] In this essay, she focuses more on women like Teresa of Avila, Madame de Sévigné and Charlotte Brontë than on celebrated men of letters. Kate's journalism always celebrated empowered women – the woman film star, the scientist or the religious reformer – and these figures were paralleled by the young opera singers and university students of her fiction. (To some degree, they were also paralleled by Kate's own life as chatelaine in Roundstone.)

In October 1951, Kate read a paper called 'George Eliot: a moralizing fabulist' to the Royal Society of Literature in London (later published in 1955). In this paper, she reads Eliot in light of her own imagination and decisively judges the good and condemns the unsuccessful in her fiction (she liked *Daniel Deronda* but deemed *The Mill on the Floss* to be artistically unsuccessful). She praises Eliot's young women protagonists for qualities that echo her own fiction: 'Now, George Eliot's young ladies did emphatically go out to confront their destinies. And it is because she saw them do so, let them do so without fear or favour that she led the English novel ahead of itself in the nineteenth century.'[21] Eliot's representation of conscience also earns her Kate's approval: 'For her there were no lovely innocents, no dashing, careless boys. Every character is actuated, to this extent or that extent, by awareness of moral responsibility.'[22] (This was certainly true of Kate's fictions but not necessarily of George Eliot's.)

Religious figures continued to interest her. During this period she wrote extensively about two saints of the Catholic Church, Teresa of Avila and St Francis Xavier. However, she saw them as symbols of secular power rather than as spiritual or devotional figures. Like Joyce, Kate appropriated much of her aesthetic of the novel from her Irish Catholic education. In her 1951 biography of Teresa of Avila,[23] the saint became an emblematic figure for female power and hierarchy. Teresa is, like Ana and other women in Kate's fictions, cool, hard, autocratic but justified, or so Kate argues, as her vision of religious reform resembles the cold, remorseless drive towards the creation of art. As she declared in her opening chapter of this biography: 'I write of Teresa of Avila by choice which is passionate, arbitrary, personal.... I am free here to speak of a great woman. But I am not writing of the canonized saint. I propose to examine Teresa, not by the rules of canonization, but for what she was – saint or not, a woman of genius.' (Interestingly, she allows for only two other women in this category of genius: Sappho and Emily Brontë.) Teresa's genius, as Kate interprets it, was her ability as a woman to make herself powerful in a male world and to found and rule a large organisation of women successfully.

Kate O'Brien is careful when writing of Teresa's mysticism and religious ecstasies to distance her from these experiences. There is a familiar association between Spanish landscape and Spanish character in this biography: the Castilian landscape is seen as strong and ascetic, and these qualities are reflected in Teresa's extraordinary personality. (It must be said that, in writing this biography, Kate cannot have been aware of just how unpleasant she made the saint seem!) The biography was reviewed by the Abbey playwright Teresa Deevy, who made the ambiguous point that readers 'may hesitate, seeing that it has been written by the author of *Without My Cloak* ... here we have the best – the mingling of two personalities ... if you will not read St Teresa, at least read Kate O'Brien. This book repays.'[24]

A similar sensibility, an unquestioning belief in religious rigour and severity, informs Kate's 1952 biographical essay on St Francis Xavier, published in a volume called *Saints For Now*.[25] In this confident, readable essay, she writes approvingly of the surrender of personality which the young Jesuit Francis Xavier endured, praising the Society of Jesus for its 'absolute fidelity to this cold principle of abnegation'.[26] Kate O'Brien's unquestioning belief in the aims of the Society of Jesus, the need for the individual to surrender selfhood within any Catholic structure, is reflected in her fiction and in her depiction of convent education. She believed in freedom in art and freedom of the individual imagination, yet, conversely, she admired the surrender of self that Catholicism demanded. Somewhere between these two contradictory beliefs, Kate O'Brien created her Catholic characters.

As part of her reintegration into Irish literary life, she began to give lectures and public talks at various literary events in Ireland. She addressed the arts festival An Tostal in Cork on 23 May 1957, gave lectures on Spain to the Irish Countrywomen's Association, spoke at the university colleges of Dublin and Galway and even wrote on emigration for the *Irish Digest*.[27] Radio Éireann commissioned a series of radio talks called *Between Ourselves* and Kate showed a keen interest in her Irish literary antecedents by using this opportunity to talk about Irish women writers: Maria Edgeworth (whom she praised for the masculinity of her writing!), Alice Milligan, Speranza and Lady Gregory. In the same radio series, she also broadcast on non-literary subjects like 'Village life in London', 'Motor cars', 'The Irish in London', and there was even one entitled 'A high-brow cat'![28]

This exhausting workload of newspaper and radio reviewing was necessary because of her lack of a fixed income. There is more than a strain of autobiography in Kate's *As Music and Splendour* when Clare Halvey laments the various comic roles forced upon her as part of her work as an opera singer. Kate must have felt a degree of contempt for the kind of writing her freelance status necessitated.

In addition, she began to write and review for Irish literary journals like the *University Review*, *Kilkenny Magazine* and the newly launched *Irish Writing*. She published a short story in *The Bell*, Séan O'Faoláin's literary journal, where the censoring of *The Land of Spices* had been strongly opposed. This short story, '*A Fit of Laughing*', was published in 1952 and was, unusually for her, a story of the Irish countryside, full of the comedy of Hiberno-English. In style, it was much more akin to the Irish stories of her contemporaries Frank O'Connor and Liam O'Flaherty. Her stance on the importance of region and place within Irish writing was also influenced by her reintegration into Irish literary culture and, in May 1957, when she spoke at the Cork Tostal arts festival, she began her lecture by challenging Sean O'Faolain, who had opened the same festival. O'Faolain had announced that region was unimportant for any writer, no matter if they were Irish or French; it mattered only that they were writers. Kate countered this by pointing to

O'Faolain's own work and claiming that his best writing came directly from his childhood in Cork city and the farmlands of his mother's native County Limerick. Places of childhood, as Kate saw it, were central to the writer's imagination.

This growing involvement in Irish literary life was paralleled by her friendships with Lorna Reynolds, Micheál Mac Liammóir and Hilton Edwards, all visitors to The Fort. Another close friend of Kate's during this period was the young Irish poet and short story writer John Jordan. Born in Dublin in 1930, John Jordan was a writer of some precocity who made a point of introducing himself to famous writers. As a teenager, he began a correspondence with the drama critic James Agee, and he met Kate by making his way backstage in 1945 at the Dublin production of *The Last of Summer*. He was embarking on an academic career, so Kate introduced him to Enid Starkie, who assisted him when he went to Oxford to study English in the mid-1950s.[29] Throughout this time, John Jordan visited with Kate in Connemara, not always happily, as their correspondence records. Kate often found herself playing the older, wiser woman of the world, correcting his social behaviour. This unpleasant letter from The Fort, written in 1952, gives a clear insight into Kate's imperious nature:

> Thank you for your letter – not all of which I believe in but the spirit of which I accept. As to 'Absolvo' of course – which of us is to refuse that simple word of his fellow at any time! But do listen to this and forgive me. You should have written four lines of thank you a day or two after you left. But one is actually angered by silence sustained by a departed guest. I was angered into positive dislike of you. All you had to do was write four or five lines and after all, you are a writing chap like myself? – and no bones broken. You silly man. Now you managed to break many bones. Anyway you have me completely embarrassed. Because – what am I to do about your lovely awkward gift? Gide's Journal – I dare not return it to you and anyway I lust after it.[30]

In another letter to him, she compares herself to a queen who has an empathy with a young hero, without, as she puts it herself, 'any sensual hopes of any kind'.[31] This feudal view of herself came to the fore when she lived in Roundstone. John Jordan admired her fiction and wrote about her work for *The Bell* and other journals and Kate, in turn, influenced his writing, as this poem demonstrates: 'poor

Anna Wickham/Hung herself on Haverstock./Lesbos, burning Sappho,/And the tonic sea.'[32] (It is unlikely that Jordan would have known Anna Wickham, except through Kate's recollections.) In one of John Jordan's short stories, 'First draft', a middle-aged writer appears, a Mrs Rose MacMenamin, who has piercing blue eyes and the forwardness and charm of a dedicated drinker. At one point, she announces that she will write her memoirs: 'Well, Dotey, you know the sort of thing, my childhood in South Tipp, and then school and College in Dublin, and then being a "Miss" in Spain, and my marriage with poor Joe and – she finished quite shyly, the men I've known.'[33]

John Jordan helped with her research on Madame Recamier for a series of articles she was writing on famous women. This series, 'Brilliant Women', was written for a popular women's magazine called *Woman and Beauty* and was published in 1952/53. Although *Woman and Beauty* was a commercial and not a literary journal, the standard of Kate's critical writing for this series is on a level with her other work at this time. In her first piece, published in October 1952, she is lyrical about her beloved Greta Garbo when she celebrates what she called 'acting already individualised by reticence, by gentleness, and by a slow unflurried certainty in letting the portrayed character unfold and reach the onlooker's understanding without the most momentary resort to emphasis, but out of a sort of musing authority'.[34] She mourned Garbo's withdrawal from acting (she believed that Garbo would have been ideally suited to play Ana de Mendoza in the film version of *That Lady*, rather than Olivia De Havilland).[35]

Kate's other 'Brilliant women' included an admiring essay on Marie Curie in November 1952, a short version of her lecture on George Eliot in January 1953, an excellent account in February of George Sand and, in March, an essay on Madame Recamier – whom Kate privately considered to be a 'fearful bore'![36] She concluded the series with a realistic but sympathetic essay on Sarah Bernhardt in April 1953. It is significant that a popular women's magazine would have considered her sufficiently well-known for such a commission.

Kate's essays on brilliant women informed her next novel, published by Heinemann in October 1953 under the title *The Flower of May*. The setting for the novel was Dublin in 1906 and the narrative takes place among the Irish bourgeoisie. Kate drew on her childhood experience of visiting her Aunt Hickey in Mespil Road,

Dublin in 1906 and she locates the events of the novel in Dublin rather than in Mellick. The novel deals with the archetypal O'Brien struggle: a young Irish woman who asserts her independence in the face of the constrictions of her family. Fanny Morrow, the young daughter of a Dublin wine merchant, returns home from her convent school in Brussels to attend her sister's wedding. To her horror, her parents decide to keep her at home, leaving her education incomplete: 'In a sentence, Fanny had been instructed to understand that home was enough; and she had instantly apprehended, even as her father spoke, and without trial, that it was not.' The narrative follows Fanny's gradual move away from family and from Ireland and the realisation of her independence in Europe. Fanny's friendship with Lucille De Mellin, a wealthy young Belgian woman, is crucial to her in this search for selfhood outside of Ireland. As always, Kate O'Brien asserts the primacy of European civilisation, travel, education and language. Fanny's eventual escape to France is vital to her survival. In *The Flower of May*, Kate portrays the Irish bourgeoisie as a narrow, deceitful and selfish class, strongly contrasting with the freedom offered by Europe. However, there are still moments in the novel when she champions the superiority and elegance of the Irish middle class, especially over foreign claimants.

At one point in the novel, Fanny's beautiful older sister Lillian manages to intimidate the young Belgian aristocrat, Lucille, simply by the fact of her beauty and poise.

> It is perhaps curious that a young woman of formidable and powerful beauty, rich and brought up in that world where beauty can indulge itself in exaggeratedly careful cultivation, should have felt the shock of cold power from a beautiful Irish girl whom she had despised at school, whom now she despised, and whose sophistication could only be of the skin-deep kind, put on in three or four months' marriage to a rich, infatuated but necessarily naive young Irish auctioneer.

The beautiful Lillian, however impressive, is also the villain of the novel, selfish and treacherous, and, like Hannah Kernahan in *The Last of Summer*, she is implicated in the narrow-mindedness of her country and her class. *The Flower of May* looks away from Ireland and towards Europe. At the end of the novel, Fanny is released from her Mespil Road world into a more expansive European selfhood, with the prospect of education, employment and even the possibility of artistic achievement.

There is a new imaginative element presented within *The Flower of May*. Up to this point, Kate had created fictions that contrasted the wealthy, conventional world of the Mellick bourgeoisie with the expansiveness of European Catholicism in Spain and France. In this novel, another Irish class, the Catholic landed gentry, is introduced. She locates this new strain of Irishness at Glassala, the home of Fanny's mother in County Clare. Glassala is the ancestral home of the Delahunts and this family provides an alternative to the bourgeois Morrows of Dublin. Glassala is a version of Kate's own home in Roundstone. Eleanor Delahunt, Fanny's aunt and the owner of Glassala, is a version of Kate herself, or Kate as she imagined herself to be in the setting of Connemara. (However, as Kate presents it, the Delahunts were in the West of Ireland for generations, rather than for four years!)

Eleanor Delahunt is in her early fifties, like Kate at this time, and is a natural aristocrat, severe, handsome, ascetic and a landowner. She runs Glassala as Ana de Mendoza ruled Pastrana: 'incapable of fuss.... But she had authority and Glassala responded always to the crack of her whip.' Eleanor is another 'holy' woman, like Agatha Conlon, Helen Archer and Ana de Mendoza, a woman whose natural austerity enables her to be a secular figure of female power. When her niece Fanny sees Eleanor's private room, referred to by Eleanor as her 'cell', she exclaims: 'I know what this room is like, Aunt Eleanor, it's like Mère Generale's study.' The source of Eleanor's determination and strength is her affinity with the religious life and, at the end of the novel, she plans to leave Glassala to Fanny and retire to Brussels to live in the convent where she was educated – a *religieuse manquée*.

This is Kate O'Brien's only novel where a house, Glassala, lives in the imagination of her characters in an almost sensual way. Julia Delahunt, living in exile from Glassala, dreams her way back home to Connemara in the midst of her daily life in Dublin:

> The tide was out at home. She knew that because, from where she stood above the artichoke bed, she could not hear the last small suck of it below the Golden Rocks.... For her home, swept indeed by sounds of sea and wind and bird, was yet a silent place, silent as she so awkwardly was herself, and as her father was and her dear sister Eleanor. And silently now, salvaging her from loneliness, the place, the faithful place encompassed her.

The plot of the novel turns on the subversion of the male control of property and presents instead an alternative system of female inheritance, from aunt to niece, similar to Virginia Woolf's *Orlando*.[37] Glassala is symbolic both of an inherent generosity and of an aristocratic way of life in Ireland, both of which are lacking in the middle class. Glassala also represents a tradition of female support and inheritance.

After the publication of *The Flower of May*, Kate's delight in having her own home was beginning to fade. Money troubles, the isolation of Connemara, pressures of work and an intensification of her habitual heavy drinking all contributed to her sense of disillusion with Roundstone. At this point in her life, Kate's drinking had become problematic and her alcoholism was now clear. As Lorna Reynolds, a frequent visitor to The Fort, writes:

> Life in Connemara was not turning out to be the ideal it had seemed at first. The place was too isolated, offering too few engagements for the active intellect. It was easy to fall into a routine of good fellowship which involved the too frequent and too long continuing lifting of the elbow. Financial problems grew threatening.... Vittoria [a character in Kate's last novel, *As Music and Splendour*] was not the only artist who dissolved the problem in the anodyne of alcohol.[38]

This sense of Kate's gradual disintegration was also noted by another visitor, Paul Smith:

> Kate saw this world for what it was, and turned to it only during drinking bouts, turning sharply away when they were over. She was out of place in Roundstone. Knowingly or unknowingly, she had stepped too early into solitude and the drinking made uninteresting people matter less and late at night, not matter at all.[39]

Her drinking must have contributed to her difficulties with money. Interestingly, one of her friends, the novelist Antonia White, a literary contact from London in the 1930s, saw this dependence on alcohol as a legacy of Kate's troubled relationship with Catholicism. As she wrote in her diary: 'The lapsed Catholics who interest me most are all "cradle Catholics" – Enid Starkie and Kate O'Brien – exceptionally attractive characters and of great honesty and integrity. Enid and Kate are very gay but obviously not happy – they are both alcoholics.'[40]

By the mid-1950s, Kate's letters were filled with money worries. In a letter to the Royal Society of Literature in May 1954, she painted a very bleak picture of her finances, complaining that her overdraft meant that the bank actually owned her house and that all cheques and payments from her account had been stopped.[41] She often wrote letters of profound despair with regard to money, portraying herself as on the brink of ruin, especially to those who wanted money from her. In a letter to her American publisher, Cass Cassfield, she predicted that she would have to finish writing her new novel in jail![42] The lack of a fixed income contributed to her state of financial insecurity, but she also perfected the art of crisis letter-writing when asking for an advance or dealing with a demand for money.

With all these pressures, she decided to spend some time in Italy in 1954, to research for her next novel, *As Music and Splendour*. This decision was made partly because she could let The Fort to a tenant while she was away. In addition, her American publishers allowed her an advance of £4,000, despite the fact that her previous novel had earned little more than that. (This was a large sum of money for 1954, half the sum she had spent on buying The Fort, and an indication of the extent of her financial responsibilities.) She moved to Rome, her first time in the Italian capital, at the beginning of March 1954, travelling down from Paris by train[43] and joining Lorna Reynolds, who was already there on study leave from her university teaching. While in Rome, Kate lived in an apartment on the Via di Ripetta, an address that she would give to her fictional Irish heroines in *As Music and Splendour*. Her friends in Rome included the novelist Ignazio Silone and Jenny Nicholson, Robert Graves's daughter. Kate used this time to gather all the necessary background material for her novel, which was set in the world of Italian opera.

It is clear from a talk she gave on Rome when she returned to Ireland[44] that Kate read widely from the vast corpus of travel writing on Rome and on Roman Church history. She spent some of her time wandering around the city, forming opinions and impressions on its churches, gardens and squares and picking up a great deal of knowledge of the everyday workings of the city. Soon after her arrival, she set off on a research trip on Italian opera that took in Naples, Milan and then Ferrara and Ravenna. From Ferrara in April, she wrote the first instalment of a travel journal, which was published in the literary journal *Irish Writing* as part of a series called

'Andantino'. In it, she recorded her love of Naples, her admiration for Rome and her indifference to Ferrara. Her next instalment, entitled 'Rome: June', records her sufferings in the middle of the Roman summer – 'Rome engulfs, defeats, overwhelms'[45] – and her attempts to escape the 'heat-maddened tiger'[46] by taking bus journeys out of Rome. She spent much of that summer in the hills outside Rome, in Tivoli, under the cool shades around Hadrian's Villa, and from this time comes a short story called 'A bus from Tivoli',[47] published in 1957. In this story, a middle-aged Irish writer called Marian who is spending the summer in Rome finds herself in a café near Hadrian's Villa late one evening while waiting for a bus back into Rome: 'Marian was in her fifties and a heavy woman, one easily tired and who found life in Rome somewhat a physical ordeal.'[48] In this café, a young Italian waiter serves her:

> He was a large and powerfully built young man, handsome in the Roman fashion, he looked to be twenty-four or five.... 'He's curiously like me', she thought. 'He could be my son'. For she had, as she knew with dislike, a heavy Roman look. In youth she had been normally slender and beautiful of face; but middle age had taken the beauty away, and left her fleshy and Roman-looking.... Marian did not at all admire the Roman physical type, and very much disliked her own undeniable relation to it.[49]

(Marian is clearly a physical representation of Kate herself, who disliked her own looks in middle age.) To Marian's horror, the young man takes an instant liking to her and insists that she stay with him, even inveigling his young sister into pleading with Marian. She refuses him and leaves the café in a panic, appalled at the incongruity of this young man paying court to her. On her return to Rome, she is careful not to tell the story to the Italians of her acquaintances, 'sure that no Italian would believe her, and would gently dismiss her as another dreaming old lady from the queer, northern lands'.[50] Later in the summer, Marian returns to Hadrian's Villa with her friends Elizabeth, 'an English painter, a woman much younger than herself'[51] – clearly Mary O'Neill, who did visit Kate in Rome at that time. When Marian and her friend find themselves in the same café, the young man and his sister instantly renew their pleas for Marian to stay and, again with some difficulty, Marian escapes.

'A bus from Tivoli' is an unpleasant story, with much detail to suggest that it may have been based on a real incident, and it gives an impression of incongruous sexual attraction with a hint of incest (at one point Marian even compares the young man to Nero, thus casting herself as Agrippina). She submitted 'A bus from Tivoli' to BBC Radio for possible broadcasting, but, not surprisingly, it was turned down because the subject matter was considered to be 'depressing and subjective in an embarrassing way'.[52]

Throughout this time in Italy, Kate was gathering material for her novel. A crucial metaphor in this new novel was to be Gluck's opera *Orfeo ed Euridice*. She and Lorna Reynolds heard Maria Callas sing the opera in Milan around this time and the myth of Orpheus and Eurydice also provided Lorna Reynolds with her own creative inspiration, a poem called 'Euridyce': 'Cowslip-sweet the breath/ Blown down the dazzling south-facing shaft,/As we climbed and wound from dusty underground,/Up far on the way, you leading me,/You Orpheus, me Euridyce.'[53] Kate returned to Ireland in September 1954 and continued to work, albeit slowly, on her new novel. In fact, it would take her six years to finish, one of the longest periods of composition for any of her novels.

In November 1955, Kate gave a talk on Italy to the Italian Society in Limerick. When she returned to Roundstone, her journalism and her lecturing work on other writers continued, with a long talk on Turgenev delivered to the Graduates Society of University College, Dublin, in 1955 and then published in the *University Review* in 1957. In this lecture she traces the influence of Maria Edgeworth and compares Turgenev favourably with Tolstoy and Dostoevsky, seeing him as 'content to love what he saw'.[54] As with her other critical work, Kate's view of Turgenev is very much her own. She did not care for *Fathers and Sons*, which is usually considered to be his masterpiece, arguing that his young women protagonists were better examples of his craft. She identified his central achievement as his lyricism: 'his lyricism is inexplicable, because he hardly seems to use it'.[55]

Side by side with this incisive critical commentary, Kate was still producing commercially viable but 'soft' pieces, like 'Father's Christmas' for *The Spectator* in 1955. In 1957, for the *Evening Standard*'s 'Did it happen' series, she wrote quaint, whimsical pieces like 'Sister Lucy's remedy'[56] and other similar titles. Despite this work, her finances were still in crisis and she wrote to Cass Cassfield, asking for another advance of £250 on *As Music and Splendour*. In May 1957, she was granted permission to return to Spain and so she rented out The Fort again and travelled to Madrid, revisiting a country she had last seen more than twenty years before. All through 1957 and into 1958 she struggled to finish the novel, as well as preparing a lecture on 'The Brontës and Haworth' in February 1958 for the National University of Ireland graduates in University College, Dublin. In addition, she was invited to be the featured novelist for 'Tea with an author' at Harrods in London on 3 April, another indication of her popularity as a novelist with the reading public.

Kate O'Brien's last novel, *As Music and Splendour*, was published in April 1958. Originally the novel was to be called 'My redeemer liveth', after the aria from Handel's *Messiah*. The phrase 'as music and splendour' comes from a poem by Percy Bysshe Shelley, 'When the lamp is shattered', where the poet laments the loss of love and the constancy of the abandoned lover. Kate's last completed novel was to prove one of her best, despite her difficulties while writing it. The quality of the novel comes, in part, from the sustained imagining of the life of European bohemianism and artistic fulfilment for her two Irish protagonists, Rose Lehane and Clare Halvey. *As Music and Splendour* is the novel that Kate had been working towards throughout her writing life. From *Without My Cloak* onwards, she had been attempting to express, through her fiction, the possibility for an Irish woman to live through art, independent of Mellick and all its constraints. This final novel realises her imaginative ambition.

The novel is set in the 1880s and traces the fortunes of two young Irish girls as they are trained into independence and success through their talents as singers. Rose and Clare emerge from rural poverty in Ireland and move towards fame and wealth in the opera houses of Europe and North America, all by dint of their talent and artistry. Kate's research in Italy paid off in the writing of *As Music and Splendour*. Her representation of the world of opera is convincing and full of absorbing detail, to such a degree that the music critic, Fanny Feehan, commented: 'Kate O'Brien knows music and musicians inside out... someone on the inside must have told Kate about the procedure at La Scala... it all rings as true as Waterford glass.'[57] Kate O'Brien had other sources of information for her portrayal of the world of opera. Micheál Mac Liammóir had introduced her to the Irish diva Margaret Burke Sheridan,[58] a former operatic star of La Scala and Covent Garden, who had lived in Dublin throughout the 1950s.

Kate's last novel also charts Rose and Clare's growth into selfhood and autonomy, and away from Ireland and family. At the height of her brilliant career, Rose comes to realise that 'Italy and music had educated her temperament as well as her talent.... She was in short, given to life and acceptance of its stresses.' The independence that Caroline Considine had sought in vain in *Without My Cloak*, the independence glimpsed by Mary Lavelle and anticipated by Fanny Morrow, is now fully realised by Rose Lehane and Clare Halvey. Kate departs from her usual class representation by presenting two Irish girls of peasant stock. This was due, in part, to the time she had spent in Connemara and her idealisation of the natural 'aristocrats' of the west of Ireland. Art gentrifies these primitive country girls, transforming them into ladies. Moreover, for the first time in her fiction, she presents two young Irish women with successful careers.

One of the consequences of this freedom is that they can control their own adult sexual lives, for good or ill. As the narrative unfolds, this independence brings its own limitations and disillusions. Both women assert their autonomy in sexual terms, Rose with male lovers and Clare with other women. As a writer, she found a way of negotiating her own imaginative difficulty by conflating love with music. The arias that Rose and Clare sing, from Mozart, Gluck and Verdi, all come to represent, metaphorically at least, their various loves. As in her earlier novels, Kate O'Brien uses music to represent the erotic and, more than this, she validates these 'forbidden' loves by investing them with the mythic quality of their art. So, when Kate finally presents two women as lovers, they sing together on stage: 'the music they both loved had carried them far tonight, together and above themselves'. Music elevates their love, placing them above the merely physical, and sexual identity is thus performed and ritualised.

It was a risk for Kate to portray a lesbian character, especially now that she was living in Ireland, but it is one of the most radical elements in the novel and is skilfully integrated into the narrative. Clare and Luisa sing together in Gluck's opera *Orfeo ed Euridice*, where the two women can legitimately play the part of lovers in public since these roles were originally written for female soprano and male castrato. The myth of the opera gives permission to their subversive love affair: 'Still Orpheus and Eurydice, their brilliantly made up eyes swept for each the other's faces, as if to insist that this disguise of myth in which they stood was their mutual reality, their one true dress, wherein they recognised each other.' Music makes safe the dangerous potential of their sexuality. Their teacher, watching them sing, muses that 'they are good for each other in music'. The directness and clarity of Clare's love for Luisa draws attack from the men who surround them, one sneering at the androgynous quality of Clare's 'castrato' voice, another calling her 'beast! You pale, self-loving ass! You – you stinking lily, you.'

Despite the clarity of sexual expression in Kate O'Brien's writing in this novel, there is still a great deal of Catholic unease around the unconventional loves that Rose and Clare pursue. As Clare expresses it: 'Certainly I am a sinner in the argument of my church. But so would I be if I were your lover. So is Rose a sinner.... We are so well instructed that we can decide for ourselves. There's no vagueness in Catholic instruction.' In no sense is *As Music and Splendour* an idealised view of love between women and there is no illusion about the transient nature of passion. In the end, Clare and Luisa part when Clare discovers that Luisa has other lovers, male and female. Clare returns a chain that Luisa had given her at the beginning of their affair: 'I couldn't wear it now. Would you want me to, you free, cool customer you – in common honesty?... Don't hand it out too often or too carelessly, will you, love?' The novel ends on an open note, with the future of the two girls still to be realised and the freedom of an artistic life in Europe still available to them.

After the book was published, Kate moaned to John Jordan about the bad press *As Music and Splendour* had received and declared that she had been badly wounded and beaten by critics this time. Yet most of the reviews of the novel were respectful, even positive and, unlike *Mary Lavelle* and *The Land of Spices*, it was never banned. *As Music and Splendour* has received positive criticism from modern critics and admiration for the directness of her representation of same-sex love. Emma Donoghue writes that the novel is 'more celebratory in its account of a relationship between two women. Instead of playing a supporting role, the lesbian is one of the two heroines, whose stories are presented equally and in parallel. Set at a safe distance in place (Paris and Rome) and time (the 1880s), *As Music and Splendour* nevertheless manages to create a modern Irish lesbian and give her a startling voice.'[59] This is ironic, considering that Kate was writing at a time when there was little or no Irish lesbian culture or community in Ireland, thus providing in fiction what was absent in reality. Another critic, Anne Fogarty, argues that, 'for the first time in O'Brien's œuvre, lesbian love is moved literally and metaphorically centre stage'.[60]

In September 1958 Kate returned to Spain and made straight for Madrid, where she could observe for herself the changes in that country after twenty years of Franco's rule. Although her books had never been banned in Spain, access there seems to have been a problem for her. With permission to return, Spain now came to represent an escape from her increasingly desperate finances in Ireland, somewhere cheaper to live and to travel, and she produced a series of travel articles for *The Observer*, published in 1959, on topics like 'Writing in Spain', 'A quick look around Madrid' and 'Castile at a gallop'.[61] It was becoming more and more difficult for her to maintain her house in Roundstone and, with Spain open to her again, in 1960 she made the decision to sell. She decided to move to Avila, in an attempt to stabilise her finances by living cheaply. Her sister Nance had been widowed in 1959 and Kate had spent some time with her, but there was no prospect of a long-term home for her in Limerick and Kate left Ireland for good in 1960. Returning to Ireland had stimulated her imagination and inspired her creativity. However, in the long term, life in Lotus Land had proved untenable.

7

Long distance: 1960–74

The last fourteen years of Kate O'Brien's life were lonely and difficult. Her professional and financial vulnerability as a freelance woman writer, without private income, husband or comfortable public sinecure, left her isolated and poor. She failed to complete any more novels, was dependent on her wealthy sister Nance O'Mara for her home and on freelance journalism for income. In a sense, she was living on her former reputation, reviewing and broadcasting on 'soft' journalistic topics. Her dream of recreating Boru House in Connemara had cost her dearly, yet she continued to travel, to work, to write and to entertain her friends, and her instinct for survival sustained her. She sold her house in Roundstone early in 1960 and, with her continuing financial struggles, spent the next three years homeless, staying either with her widowed sister, Nance, in Limerick, with Lorna Reynolds in Dublin or with Mary O'Neill in London. In between, she travelled to Rome or Spain for work purposes and continued with her usual heavy load of writing. Now in her middle sixties, her health began to give her some cause for concern, when she developed angina pectoris, and this left her depressed and anxious: 'For me, also there have been many dark hours and I find myself now with little taste at all for life but none for death.'[1] Her circumstances continued to be unstable for the rest of her life and Enid Starkie noted that Kate was in 'very low water financially'.[2] (Until her own death in 1970, Enid did her best to assist Kate financially.) Allied to this financial worry was Kate's disappointed sense of herself as a writer outside her time. She was working on a new novel called 'Constancy', but she never completed it. Effectively, she stopped writing fiction and, instead, turned to her own life for creative interest.

For the last fourteen years of her life, she wrote continuously about Limerick, about her family, her education at Laurel Hill and her life as a university student, though always with a selective eye. As with her fiction, her memoirs were shaped by her need to create sustaining images of herself and of her class, idealised images resistant to the conflicts and insecurities of her earlier life and to her current straitened circumstances. Her imagination was now focused on writing these memories and, as she put it, 'The past blows up when it will, and cannot be commanded; but the tonic sharpness of its accidental visitations is a gift, a restitution to age for which no one would know how to pray but which must not go unthanked.'[3] She wrote extensively of her family during this period of her life and her essay 'Aunt Mary in the parlour'[4] was expanded into a memoir of all her aunts, published as *Presentation Parlour*. This autobiographical writing was idealised, selective and even elusive but, throughout, compellingly readable.[5] In old age, Kate had an ambivalent attitude towards her past self and her early life. In these autobiographical writings, she presents acceptable versions of her earlier self – or selves – and is careful to stay away from any difficult episodes in her past, like her marriage. However, as Mademoiselle Davide, a character in her unfinished novel 'Constancy', says:

> When you are my great age, you will see a whole series of persons of your name ranging out behind you...but if my experience is any guide – you won't like anyone of them especially – and what is really amusing – you won't feel much about them. Yet, they have all been you, at one time or another.[6]

In this last, unfinished novel, Kate was able to be honest about her uneasy relationship with her past self.

With the effective end of her novel writing, Kate believed that she had outlived her readership and was now redundant. As she ruefully admitted in a late radio broadcast: 'Of course, one goes out of fashion and my kind of book isn't as much liked as it used to be, but that is inevitable. All writers have to go through that and I don't think that my rather quiet analytical young Catholic ladies' love affairs are of great interest to the vast majority of the world now.'[7] However, she continued to lead a full and engaged writing life as a journalist during the last years of her life. All through the 1960s and right up to her death in 1974, she was still giving lectures, travelling, writing articles and broadcasting. The publication and broadcasting of her memoirs attest to this. Her fiction was also still of interest to the public, as three long newspaper interviews in the late 1960s prove, and some of her novels remained in print up to her death. Indeed, at her death, six of her books were still available. However, her royalties from these books for the first half of 1974 amounted to only about £22.[8] She was still successful enough as a novelist to make a limited amount of money but not successful enough to retire.

Kate went to Kilkenny in February 1960 to give the inaugural lecture to the newly founded Kilkenny Literary and Bibliographical Society. One of the members of the society left a description of the event:

> That was Kate, planted in an easy chair, a strong jaw thrust upwards as her head rested against the back of the chair. Her eyes were lost in the bland, plump flesh, no eyebrows, pale fat hands like Oscar Wilde's, with a small square emerald on her middle finger. For the lecture she was dressed as the quintessential lady writer, in black with a kind of stole affixed to the back of her garment, ornamenting her shoulders like a professor's toga, a monocle strung on a gold chain. All the while she read, she polished the monocle between thumb and finger and not once called it into play. After a few stiff whiskies, Kate sat back and demanded if someone could give a song in a nice fluting tenor.... 'Can no one even recite a poem he wrote himself? This is proving a hopeless evening... You don't understand what I'm trying to say. Something is required to give this evening an accent and there has been nothing'.... The maudlin disappointed expression on her face almost made me burst into tears... Kate lit another cigarette and immediately pitched it into the fire. The host took Kate firmly by the arm. She bade us a very tired Good Night and her sandaled feet found their way unsteadily downstairs and up the steps of the Club House to bed. We put on our overcoats.... resembling nothing so much as a group attending a wake.[9]

In a way, it was a wake. Kate's time as an Irish writer living among her people was at an end.

However, Kate continued to write about Ireland. In 1961, she wrote a short introduction for a book of photographs of Dublin and Cork,[10] where she makes a number of astute observations about contemporary Irish architecture and goes on to praise the 'time-lag', the slowness of urban building in Ireland, which preserves the older buildings. Around the same time, her travel book *My Ireland* was published. This book marked a return home to Limerick and to her own beginnings: 'But the scenes of early childhood are those that shine the clearest and best refresh the middle-aged, the ageing mind'. She dedicated the book to Limerick – 'With warmest love, as my father, Tom O'Brien would have thought proper, I humbly dedicate this little book to Limerick, my dear native place.' This was the first time she had dedicated a book of hers for nearly thirty years. About Limerick, she wrote: 'It is really all you know about yourself – that life began, that you became involved, that you asked all your leading questions there, in Avila or in Limerick.' In *My Ireland*, Kate loyally aligns herself to Limerick and honours her imaginative debt to her birthplace, but this belies the difficult relationship between Kate and her 'dear native place'. Although she often returned to visit her brother Gerry and her sister Nance in Limerick, there was some unease in people's reaction to this banned writer with an unconventional personal appearance and a distinctly unIrish mode of speech. As Jim Kemmy, the Limerick Labour politician, wrote:

> At a time when Limerick was sensitive and even hostile to self-analysis of any form, criticism from Kate O'Brien would not have been welcome. Perhaps because of this factor and in consideration of her relatives still living in Limerick, she displayed in public an uncritical attitude towards the city and its people. This relationship was never an unguarded or a comfortable one. For instance, even in the last decade of her life, when her creative writing had almost dried up and she was largely dependent on casual journalism for her writing, she was not given the Freedom of Limerick, despite intensive lobbying by her friend and champion, Mrs Mary Hanly. Three mayors of the city were directly approached to seek their help in this campaign but to no avail. The three main political parties were faint-hearted about the proposal and Kate O'Brien was to die in 1974, largely unhonoured in her native city, except by a small group of her admirers.[11]

Reflecting her own writing career, *My Ireland* begins and ends in Limerick, travelling outwards through Connemara, Belfast, Dublin and back again via Munster. The impressions that Kate gives of Ireland are highly personal and always lively: 'I feel the desire to assemble in some sort the scattered impressions which Ireland has made on me over the years. No autobiography, need I say?' The text is accompanied by clichéd images of Ireland (donkeys, children, Connemara), but Kate's written version of Ireland is original and very personal. In writing about her own country, she strikes some notes that are already familiar from her fiction. For example, the landscape around Limerick is figured as austere – 'Austerity? A kind of cold restraint, an underflow of silence, a bony, throwaway grace' – echoing her description of the landscape around Avila, the childhood home of St Teresa. In Kate's writing, there is always an unconscious identification between herself and the reformer she so much admired.

In her fiction, Kate had a complex attitude towards sexuality, and this led her to make generalisations about the young Irish women of 1962:

> The Irish girl is still by habit chaste...the young Irishwomen I have in mind...are chaste in their lives not just innocently or out of shrinking fear but consciously and by choice. It is their business and they mind it....I do not think that I am wrong.

My Ireland proved popular and the reviewers liked it. It was read on Radio Éireann by the novelist John Broderick, and John Jordan reviewed it in the *University Review*, calling it 'most valuable as a gloss to her more important work'.[12]

Without a permanent home base, Kate went to live in Spain for six months at the end of 1961 and into 1962. She spent her sixty-fourth birthday alone, staying at the Hotel Jardin in Avila and keeping her living expenses to a minimum. Kate was in daily contact by letter with her eldest sister, May. This time in Spain also produced a short story, which was published in 1962 under the title 'A view from Toledo'.[13] The story centres on Anna, a middle-aged Irish novelist travelling to Madrid on a research trip for her writing. Unlike her Roman story, 'A bus from Tivoli', where the protagonist, Marian, is a clear version of Kate herself, this Spanish story has a female protagonist more akin to a middle-aged Mary Lavelle. Anna is a widow, the mother of an adult daughter and with a baby grandson, a fair-haired beauty who has kept her looks into middle age. On the train for Madrid, she shares her dining car with a handsome middle-aged Spaniard who turns out to be a former lover, a young man she had made love to, despite being married, and then abruptly abandoned. In a sense, 'A view from Toledo' is a reprise of *Mary Lavelle*, even down to an episode of furtive love-making in the countryside. The story deals with sexual desire and guilt and Anna's memory of her one act of infidelity assails her as she remembers her flight from her Spanish lover with shame. However, her lover, now grown middle-aged, forgives the injury of her flight and the story ends with the possibility of a renewed relationship. In her last writings, Kate approached romantic love with greater pragmatism and a lessened sense of tragedy.

On her return from Spain, her work as a professional writer was recognised when she was invited to travel to Rome in November 1962 as a delegate for the Comunita Europea Degli Scrittori, COMES. (Her visit was recorded in an article for *The Spectator* called 'Rome Relaxed'.)[14] This work with COMES invigorated her and led to further trips to Europe and a sense of engagement with other writers.

In 1962, she was invited to participate in a Radio Telefís Éireann (RTE) television series, *Self Portrait*, where Irish writers and artists were given a chance to talk directly to the camera – without interruption – about their lives and their art. This is the only sustained visual record that Kate left and in it she looks relaxed and confident as she speaks for twenty minutes about her work (the sole evidence of any nervousness is the lighted cigarette she holds but fails to smoke). As she herself had written, middle age had left her with a heavy handsomeness and the agreeable quality of her voice, which was deep and resonant, and her lively wit made her a good subject for television. She began by justifying the confessional nature of her talk and made the point that:

> A writer is someone who throws himself or herself at the head of the public and asks to be listened to. We confront you with our conceptions of human life and our recreations and inventions from life as we see it. And if those inventions and recreations please you or interest you at all, it is natural for us to talk to you about how we arrive at our strange profession.[15]

In her recounting of the course of her own life, Kate sounded familiar autobiographical notes, evoking her father's wealth, the comfort of Boru House, her time in Laurel Hill. Not surprisingly, her marriage was not mentioned but then neither was her time spent in Washington working for Stephen O'Mara nor the experience of having her books banned. Recounting the failures of some of her plays with a certain rueful good humour, Kate observes that she had only herself to blame for these failures and went on to say:

That puzzling reflection sums up one's career as a writer. Whatever you do, good or bad, you have only yourself to blame....From life, from outside, I have received as a writer an enormous amount of help. The trouble is that one feels that one has put so very little back into life for what one has got out of it. But after all, what could one give back that would be noticeable?[16]

Despite the self-deprecation of these final words, Kate was in fact very confident about her own worth as a writer.

Her most important work of memory, *Presentation Parlour*, was published in 1963 and centred on her recollections of her five aunts, the sisters of her mother and her father. In presenting her memories, she made the disclaimer that:

...my recollections are not pure. Time and myself have worked upon my aunts for me and the portraits I have sketched are perhaps not portraits even in the freest, most expressionist sense, for anyone but me. And even for me, they are not representational or within sight of being photographic. The time is too long; I peer through half-shut eyes from very far away, and the knowingness of adult life cannot help but throw in accents and shadows which the child who knew these women could not have perceived.

Presentation Parlour was Kate's most striking recreation of self within the context of her family and her upbringing, central to her portrayal of her aunts. Therefore, it was not exactly a work of memory, but rather a recreation of her family, her parental home, her father and Limerick itself in the light of her imaginative needs. As she puts it: 'No one but I will care about their "short and simple annals". Yet it has rested with me to set them down, and to try to find in their modest lives the essence of them....And for all my searching back, for all my will to reach them, I have not found the very heart of anyone of them.' In this family history, Kate presented her family in an idealised way, just as she idealised her characters.

The memoir was structured around the imaginative touchstones of her fiction: the transforming power of music, the austere authority of nuns, the secure civility of the Irish bourgeoisie. The figure of her father, Tom O'Brien, dominates her memories of home but, interestingly, always in terms which belie the description of him as being loving and benign. *Presentation Parlour* is her most sustained and arresting record of autobiography, but one that is more like a blueprint for her fiction rather than any real attempt to explore her past.

As part of her work with COMES, the European Community of Writers, Kate went to the Soviet Union – to Leningrad and Moscow – in August 1963 for ten days, at the invitation of the Soviet Writers' Union. During her short stay, she visited various literary sites, such as Tolstoy's country estate and Chekhov's home, and she recalled all this in a radio talk called 'Moscow unforeseen'. While in Russia, Kate struck up a friendship with her interpreter, a young woman called Freida Lurie, and corresponded with her for some time afterwards, sending her copies of her books and preserving her letters.

After three years of displacement, Kate finally settled in Kent in Christmas 1963. Her sister, Nance O'Mara, bought Kate a house in a small village called Boughton, near Canterbury. This house cost Nance £1,000, a seventh of what The Fort had cost Kate twelve years previously, and Kate, who had already made her will leaving everything to Mary O'Neill and her sister May, now added a codicil, willing this house back to Nance. The small village of Boughton is close to the historic Kentish towns of Canterbury and Faversham and Kate's house there, at 17 The Street, was to be her home for the last ten years of her life. In many ways, it was an isolated place for her to end her life. In an interview she described the house:

> ...a very small weatherboarding, early 19th-century, two-storey cottage, standing just back from the village street. And the village is very near Canterbury and very near Faversham, two lovely old English towns. It's a Jane Austenish sort of house – not grand Jane Austen but the sort of little house that some of the very minor characters might have lived in. It drops down into cherry orchards; in fact there's nothing behind me except the cherry orchards of Kent.[17]

Kate had very little interest in establishing a domestic life within her house, apart from entertaining visitors from Ireland and from London – and she soon found herself a circle of amenable friends and acquaintances. In a Radio Éireann interview, she described her life there in somewhat dismissive terms:

> I like the villagers, they are very very ordinary, the villagers there, not at all interesting like the Connemara ones were, but they are very pleasant people, very kind...but I don't count them as society. I have

numbers of friends, actors and painters and people, who live in the neighbourhood and I'm very near the Kent and Canterbury University. A great many friends in the University, some Irish people, Leland Lyons of Trinity, people like that are friends.... I have a garden but I don't garden. I see that it is gardened, such as it is. I often think, with amusement, that when I'm not asleep, I'm either reading or writing or talking.[18]

Always able to fit in socially and make herself agreeable, Kate struck up a connection with a fellow countryman called George Semple, who was the vicar of the nearby village of Dunkirk. Other friends in Boughton included a young woman, Sylvia Hitchcock, whose husband, much to Kate's delight, was an English bullfighter, and an academic couple at the University of Kent, Jim and Kate Hughes, who were newly married and living in Boughton. A close friendship grew up between Kate and the Hughes, with regular trips to the cinema or to Kate's favourite pub, The Shakespeare, in Canterbury, which was run by an Irish man, Ignatius Dempsey. Kate Hughes remembered telling her mother about her new friend and discovering to her amazement that she was a celebrated novelist and that her mother, an admirer, had a collection of her work on her shelves.[19] Kate's fiction was now unknown to young women of Kate Hughes's generation. She also remembered her references to 'a husband I once had' or 'dear Gustaaf, now in his grave' (Gustaaf Renier died in 1962, the year before Kate moved to Boughton). In addition, Kate had visitors who came to Boughton regularly: Mary O'Neill, Stephie and her daughter Ruth and her family, Lorna Reynolds and her O'Brien nephews, John and Donough, and this helped in some degree to stave off her loneliness.

From her new home, she began to write a regular column for the *Irish Times* in 1967 called 'Long distance', which was to continue until the early 1970s. There was no specific theme to her writing for this column, just a general airing of her opinions and her preoccupations. Although the *Irish Times* was not the most widely read newspaper in Ireland, it was much respected for its intellectual and literary interests. Her reviews tended to be of European literature: Russian and Italian novels, memoirs and travel books. As always, she was a shrewd and distinctive critic. The 'Long distance' column was important in presenting Kate as a significant figure in Irish cultural life during this period of her life and her face in the accompanying photograph – stern, bespectacled, slightly grizzled – fixed her as a distinguished writer. She wrote as a formidable woman of letters, always strongly opinionated, even irritable, and sometimes touchingly elegiac and melancholic, like much of her writing in these years. On New Year's Eve in 1969, she wrote, 'I consoled myself for the wounded and self-wounding world with this paradox... private life remains and cannot be taken away, except by death'.[20] From her home in Kent she could comment on Ireland long distance, as she had often done in her fiction: 'I for my part cannot write of Ireland without a great effort of exile, spiritual detachment.'[21]

In her column, she interested herself in Irish public life, calling it 'talking back to Ireland'.[22] She celebrated the building of a National Concert Hall in Dublin and praised Charles Haughey for lifting taxes from writers. Often she railed against the ravages of the mid-twentieth century, lamenting the building of Stansted Airport in 1967[23] in the Essex countryside near to Ashurst Bank, where she had written *Without My Cloak* forty years previously.

With old age came the death of many of her friends and she recorded these too. When Enid Starkie died in April 1970, Kate wrote at length about the 'forever aflame scholar and truth seeker'.[24] Then, in October of the same year, she paid tribute to John Gosworth, her friend from her days in Great James Street, describing him as 'a friend in his generous time'.[25] When Teresa of Avila was made a Doctor of the Church in Avila in 1970, Kate planned to travel there to observe the ceremony, but a 'really Hellish flu' kept her in Boughton and she recorded her chagrin in her column.[26] She was aware that she often sounded angry and pessimistic in her column: 'Friends have been telling me that I wail and groan too much in these communications. Well, I'm open to correction and I beat around this time for cheerfulness.'[27]

From Boughton, Kate managed to maintain a busy working life, travelling up to London to lecture – as she did in October 1964 to speak at the PEN club with the writer L.P. Hartley – or going back to Ireland to give various talks. Despite her age and increasing physical infirmity, her appetite for socialising was as strong as ever. On a visit to Dublin to speak on Spain at the Royal Dublin Society in January 1965, her packed schedule included lunching with Lorna Reynolds, Paul Smith and John Jordan, meeting Micheál Mac Liammóir and then going on to a party for the Dublin working-class playwright Brendan Behan. All this literary activity may have helped in her application for a British civil list pension, which was granted to her in March 1967. This pension was for £250 per annum and was increased to £350 in February 1968; it was much needed at this time because she was in overdraft to her bank.

Her literary activities brought her back into contact with her fellow novelist Antonia White. (White's best-known work, *Frost in May*, resembles *The Land of Spices*, but White's novel reads like a subversion of Kate's.) In 1965, Antonia White's *The Falcon and the Hound* was published and Kate wrote to her that she was 'tremendously justified under the heads of intelligence, vision, modesty, tolerance and human warmth'.[28] This reopened the friendship between the two writers. In fact, Antonia White was due to stay with her in Boughton in 1968 when she fell and broke her arm. The Arts Council of Great Britain awarded White a grant of £1,200 in November 1968 and she immediately sent Kate a cheque so that she could share in her good fortune, much to Kate's delight (among Kate's papers after her death was another uncashed cheque from Antonia White).

COMES business took Kate to Rome with Lorna Reynolds in May and June 1968 and, in 1969, to her great pleasure, *Without My Cloak* was broadcast on BBC Radio (Kate wrote to the BBC to say how much she liked the production). She was still in demand as a speaker and a broadcaster, talking on 'Yeats' country' on BBC Radio 2 in September 1969 and delivering a lecture on Joyce in October of the same year at the Canterbury School of Art. She was also in demand as a guest speaker in Ireland, and recorded a series of talks on Teresa of Avila for the early morning RTÉ programme 'Thought for the Day' in November 1969. RTÉ also invited her to take part in a television programme celebrating Micheál Mac Liammóir's seventieth birthday in November 1970.

Throughout these years in Boughton, Kate struggled with 'Constancy', but she completed only the first few chapters. She worked on this final novel for nearly ten years and, in 1970, a young Irish novelist, Kevin Casey, invited Kate to his home for dinner to discuss the work. He wanted to publish a section from 'Constancy' in a collection of Irish short stories called *Winter Tales*.[29] Kevin Casey's wife, the poet Eavan Boland, remembered this visit:

> Kate O'Brien was then in her early seventies but frail and not far from death.... I hardly knew how to take this woman with her cropped hair and deep voice, and a way of slicing through a conversation.... She

was a graceful guest but with a keen ear for evasion and rhetoric. When I reflexively defended one or two people on the grounds they had a good sense of humour, she made a half-turn and fixed her eye on me. I was too young to appreciate the deft combination of mirth and menace in her tone. 'I am entirely against,' she said, 'the promotion of a sense of humour as a philosophy of life.'[30]

As a result of this visit, a portion of 'Constancy' was published in 1972. In the sections that have survived, it is a confident, readable novel, progressing from the imaginative concerns of *As Music and Splendour*. It is a familiar O'Brien narrative: the young Irish girl seeking independence and selfhood in a European society. The novel is set in 1929 in Grenoble in France and has an Irish girl as protagonist, Catherine Doherty from Galway. Catherine arrives in Grenoble to learn French in a summer language course and becomes part of a cosmopolitan group of young students from Spain, America, Mexico and Australia (while at UCD, Kate had been sent as a language student to Grenoble in the summer of 1919). Catherine Doherty is as beautiful as other O'Brien heroines and the daughter of a prosperous Galway doctor.

Elements of Kate's own family life are evident in her representation of Catherine's world: the widowed father, the married, stay-at-home sister, the charming younger brothers. The bohemian lifestyle of this group of young people is Kate's primary interest in the chapters that survive. There is a new tone of sexual directness in this novel, a tone already apparent in *As Music and Splendour*. In one episode, a handsome young Australian student, a tennis champion, confidently declares his love for a fellow male student, who accepts the declaration with quiet pleasure. In this context, references to the poems of Rimbaud and Baudelaire figure in the conversations of the young students, and the protagonist, Catherine, finds herself disturbed yet fascinated by these poets and the 'decadent' sexuality they explore. An older woman, Mademoiselle Davide, a version of Kate herself, presents Catherine with a volume of Rimbaud's poetry. (This gift has a personal significance for Kate because Enid Starkie had presented Kate with her own study of Rimbaud, and Kate had also given Mary O'Neill a volume of Rimbaud's poems in 1940.)

Indeed, 'Constancy' is filled with insider references to Kate's own life. At one point in the novel, Catherine goes to see Micheál Mac Liammóir performing in a theatre in Galway, where much is made of Micheál's youthful good looks and the brilliance of Hilton

Edwards's directing. At another point, the village of Roundstone is visited by some of the characters and, again, there are many insider references to the local pubs and shops. Overall, 'Constancy' reads well, with a confident pace established early on in the narrative.

Kate had her own perspective on the tradition of Irish writing and this emerges with clarity and authority in her critical writing during this period of her life. It is evident in her lecture on Joyce at the Canterbury Art School, her Tuairim Lecture on the Irish novel in Limerick and her radio talk on her contemporaries in Anglo-Irish poetry.[31] It is clear that her own imagination was influenced by a sense of racial defensiveness and protectiveness towards Irish writing. Her fiction was, in many ways, the angry riposte of the colonised writer. (In this context, Kate repeated a comment made to her by a 'distinguished don of Oxbridge': 'Considering how expert and indeed famous you Irish are in words, it is odd to observe how little literature you have produced up to now.')[32] Most importantly, her writing on Irish literature revealed much of her own sense of the function of the novel. As most writers do, she tended to evaluate other novelists in the light of her own imaginative interests. Her 1969 lecture on Joyce and the 'lonely violence'[33] of his writing was one of her finest pieces of critical writing and revealed much of her own aesthetic on fiction. In reading Joyce's life, Kate declared that the business of being an artist was to take the surrounding reality and 'illuminate and translate it', not accepting everyday life but 'enlarging it in terms of your free imagination'. She rejected Joyce's ringing challenge in *A Portrait of the Artist as a Young Man*, where he declared that the conscience of his race of Ireland was 'uncreated'. Rather, she believed that, 'without any help from the exile in Zurich, Ireland had created its own conscience. Or rather re-created it, I would say.'[34] In a radio talk called 'My Kind of Poetry' on 6 January 1972, she delivered an insightful, decisive view of Irish poetry in the twentieth century. She considered the influence of Gaelic poetry and language on Yeats's poems and called her old lecturer, Austin Clarke, 'troubled and richly endowed for service to poetry...a lutanist and a medievalist'. She dubbed her friend Patrick Kavanagh 'a born singer and strong, the hard celebrator of life. He was in all he wrote quite clearly great and isolated.' She approved of the impatience of contemporary young Irish poets, of their need to 'fling the old-fashioned away...to bring their own wild news to life', and saw much to look forward to in these coming generations of writers.

Although the quality of her critical and journalistic work was undiminished, the early 1970s was a time of fatigue and sadness for Kate, with the death of her sisters Clare and May (necessitating a change in her will), and her own increasing bad health and feebleness. Despite this, she accepted an invitation to lecture in Spain during December 1971 and spoke on 'The writing of imaginative prose' at the University of Vallidolid on 6 December. As one of the audience, a young Irish man called Brendan Flynn, recalled:

> Despite her enthusiasm to get things done, she looked tired and proceeded to give her lecture in Spanish. This was a great disappointment to those who had wanted to hear her soft-spoken English and frustrating to the Spaniards present as she had not been able to keep up accent and delivery for an hour and a quarter in a language she hadn't spoken for years.[35]

(By her own account, Spanish was a language she had never really spoken at all.) The Irish reading public continued to have an interest in Kate O'Brien and in her career, as evidenced by the lengthy profile called 'Kate O'Brien: First Lady of Irish letters', written by John Jordan in May 1973 for the Irish journal *Hibernia*. He recounted the now familiar facts of her life and referred to the fact that Kate was writing her memoirs. He ends his account of her life by complaining that 'neither of our universities had chosen to honour Kate O'Brien. Her offence may have been that she wrote at least two best sellers. It would be fitting to recognise her when "Constancy" is published.'[36] This lack of official recognition and honour was consistent throughout her final years. It may have been as much owing to the perception that her fiction was populist and not literary as to a problem with her sexuality and her self-presentation.

There is a clear sense of loneliness throughout the accounts of Kate's last years. Unusually for her, who had no interest in popular music, she had a favourite pop song at this time, 'Those Were the Days' sung by Mary Hopkin. Kate liked the song because it was a plangent lament for a lost time, for the company of long-dead drinking companions and for the vigour and anger of youth.[37] On an RTÉ Radio programme broadcast on 29 September 1973, she admitted the isolation of her life and confessed: 'Sometimes it would be nice to have somebody else to put on the kettle. Still I like being alone.'

Her nephew John O'Brien recalled how, around this time, she had had a meeting with Hugh Hunt, the artistic director of the Abbey

Theatre in Dublin, in the hope of interesting him in an adaptation of one of her novels: 'Hunt cut her short. She should forget about raking over old coals, he said, and write something original for them. She was silent for several minutes and then said wistfully: "If only I could".'[38] Paul Smith visited her around this time and left a melancholy account:

> I was there on and off for most of those years, but in 1972 I didn't want to see the drinking any more. We saw each other of course but the generation difference between us seemed shorter as I grew older and I was irritable now with people who drank too much and I found that Kate's drinking made her dull and repetitive, and she made me sad. I last saw Kate in her house in Boughton in September 1973. The present was grim, the future uncertain. She was a sad lonely woman and she gave me my first concern about age because she talked about the horrors of growing old. She lived alone with her cat and her books and with no visible means of support.[39]

As Paul Smith mentioned, her drinking was now a part of her daily life and the Irish novelist, John McGahern, remembers meeting her in the Royal Hibernian Hotel, in Dublin sometime in the late 1960s. He was in company with her friends John Jordan and John Broderick when they telephoned Kate, inviting her to join them for a drink. She arrived, cross and very drunk, complaining that they had interrupted her, like Flaubert, in the middle of writing a sentence. The Irish poet James Liddy, a distant relation, remembers her telling the story that she would ask the barman of a pub on Baggot Street in Dublin that if her sister Nance phoned looking for her at one o' clock sharp for lunch, as prearranged, he was to answer, 'The National Library of Ireland', her supposed place of research.[40]

Despite ill health, she braved the elements and travelled to Canada in March 1973 to give an impressively knowledgable talk at McGill University in Montreal on the tradition of Anglo-Irish prose. This was to be her last foreign speaking engagement. Her capacity for work and for writing was finally exhausted. The rest of 1973 saw no more writing and there are few entries in her surviving appointment book. Her working and social life was finally winding down and, as Paul Smith had foreseen, the future was bleak. Her health now took a turn for the worse and her death was to be as lonely and desolate as her final years in Kent.

By the summer of 1974, Kate's health had declined to such an extent that she was admitted to the Kent and Canterbury hospital suffering from pneumonia. She grew steadily worse and had to undergo the horror of having her left leg amputated because of the danger of gangrene from blood clots. At seventy-six, this operation proved too much for her and she died on the afternoon of 13 August 1974, four months short of her seventy-seventh birthday, away from Ireland, from family and from close friends. (Kate's death certificate states that she died of bronchi-pneumonia and peryshal vascular disease and also mentions the 'above the knee amputation' on the left leg.)

Although her family was in Ireland and friends like the faithful Mary O'Neill were in London, Kate was not actually alone at the time of her death. Mrs Jennifer Lyons, the wife of the historian F.S.L. Lyons, happened to call in to see her in the hospital. (Mrs Lyons was more of an acquaintance than a close friend and she was paying this visit out of courtesy.) She and Kate were talking quietly about the news that F.S.L. Lyons had just been appointed Provost of Trinity College in Dublin when Kate asked for a drink of water. The nurse was called and, before Mrs Lyons had realised what had happened, Kate died.[41] Immediately, Mary O'Neill was contacted and her Limerick nephews John and Donough O'Brien and Peter O'Mara travelled from Ireland to organise her funeral. Her sister Nance was the last of her sisters to survive, but she was too ill to attend. Nance died a year later, in 1975.

A decision had to be made about where Kate should be buried. Once, in *My Ireland*, she had written:

> On a little hill of Gurteen Beach at an angle before it curves into Dog's Bay, there is a graveyard where the Roundstone people are buried; and I used to say that one reason why I lived in Roundstone was to have the pleasure of being buried there. This will not happen now, for where the tree falls, let it lie, in Heaven's name.

The tree had fallen in Kent and so it was decided to hold the funeral there. With Mary O'Neill, her nephews John and Donough O'Brien, Nance's son Peter and her friends from Boughton, Jim and Kate Hughes, all in attendance, she was buried in the graveyard in Faversham. Her occupation, 'Irish Novelist', was inscribed on her gravestone and the visitor to her grave is asked to 'Pray for the wanderer'. There are few visitors to this neat Faversham cemetery and Kate's grave is as isolated as her last years in Kent.

After her affairs had been settled, Kate left the sum of £187.28, to be divided between Mary O'Neill and her O'Brien nephews. Her papers and the literary executorship she also entrusted to Mary O'Neill, with half of her future royalties. Mary, who lived until 1988, was faithful in these duties, taking care of Kate's books, writing up the entry for Kate's life in the *Dictionary of Biography* and assisting in the republication of Kate's books by the Irish feminist publishers Arlen House. The house in Boughton had been given to Kate by her sister Nance, and so it was sold in Nance's favour. Kate's funeral was also paid for by Nance's son, Peter O'Mara.[42] A lengthy and respectful obituary in *The Times* paid tribute to Kate's writing: 'Her taste was impeccable and she had subtlety, beauty and imagination at her command.'[43]

The most moving personal tribute came from her friend John Jordan in his poem, 'Without Her Cloak': 'so in walled Avila of unspeakable Teresa/I recalled you to the manager of the Hotel Jardin.../When I told him you were dead/(Dead, though you walk beside me, cloaked, ribald, vulnerable)/His dark mild eyes crinkled.'[44]

Though Kate was largely neglected as a writer at the time of her death, her literary reputation was to revive in time. She is now considered one of Ireland's most important writers of the twentieth century. This revival of interest came about in 1980, when Arlen House reissued her novels. This coincided with a television adaptation of *The Last of Summer* by RTÉ television. In 1984, the British publisher Virago republished seven of her novels. Virago's interest meant a whole new readership for Kate's work and greater accessibility also meant renewed critical interest. These novels remain in print to date (with the exception of *Pray for the Wanderer*), some of them selling more than 10,000 copies overall.[45] Louise C. Callaghan was responsible for a seminar on Kate's fiction that was held in Limerick in 1984 to commemorate the tenth anniversary of her death and celebrate her writing. As a result of this seminar, the annual Kate O'Brien Weekend was instituted and continues to be held to this day, attracting speakers on themes like 'Kate O'Brien and feminism', 'Ireland and Spain' and 'The embrace of love', and with audiences of over 150 for lectures and recitals.

A selection of the lectures from the Kate O'Brien Weekend was published in 1994 under the title *With Warmest Love*. This collection is one of a series of critical studies on her fiction, starting with an undated edition of the Limerick literary journal *The Stony Thursday*, which is dedicated to her work and edited by John Jordan and John Liddy. Lorna Reynolds, then the Professor of English at University College, Galway, published *Kate O'Brien: A Literary Portrait* in 1987, and this was followed by Adele Dalsimer's *Kate O'Brien: A Critical Study* in 1990. My own edited collection, *Ordinary People Dancing: Essays on Kate O'Brien*, appeared in 1993 . Kate O'Brien's fiction is now taught at secondary and third level in Ireland, the United States and the UK, and she has been the subject of postgraduate study and doctoral research. In 1997, on the centenary of her birth, a commemorative stamp was issued in Ireland and a series of radio lectures in her honour was broadcast. Continuing this revival, *Mary Lavelle* became the second of Kate's novels to be made into a film when it was released under the title *Talk of Angels* in 1995, with a script by the Irish dramatist Frank McGuinness. Kate O'Brien is now recognised as one of the pivotal figures of twentieth-century Irish fiction.[46] Her novels continue to attract a loyal readership and her importance in terms of women's writing in Ireland is central to this revival.

Towards the end of her life, Kate O'Brien was asked what she would do if she could live her life over again: 'I would hope to go through things very differently. I made every mistake known to man and I wouldn't want to make all those idiotic and cross mistakes again. I wouldn't mind having some of my time back again if I could use it better.'[47] Despite her misgivings, her writing life was a successful one. Over fifty years she produced a significant body of creative and critical writing and assembled a fully realised imaginative world. In her novels, she found expression for her belief in independence, her fascination with Europe, her attraction towards Catholicism as an aesthetic and her need to idealise her own class. As a writer, she inhabited her fictive world completely and, as a critic, she had force, authority and wit. Her working life as a writer was a busy and a demanding one, although it gave her little financial security, a punishing work schedule and little in the way of honours or recognition. Her sense of self was an unhappy and tormented one and her private life was, at times, lonely, turbulent and chaotic. However, in her writing, she lived completely and her writing sustained and satisfied her. For this reason, her fiction will endure.

Notes

1 LIMERICK 1897–1916

1 Kate O'Brien to Stephen O'Mara (7 December 1936). My thanks to Clare Hannigan, Stephen O'Mara's granddaughter, for this letter.
2 Kate O'Brien, 'Memories of a Catholic education', *Sunday Press* (2 January 1977).
3 *Kate O'Brien: A self-portrait*, RTÉ Television (1962).
4 Terence McQueen, 'Meet Kate O'Brien', *The Word* (September 1966).
5 Frank O'Connor, *The Midnight Court* (Maurice Friberg, 1946).
6 Kate O'Brien, 'Recollections of childhood', unpublished memoir, Kate O'Brien Papers, Special collection (Northwestern University Library).
7 *Self-portrait.*
8 Kate O'Brien, 'Recollections of childhood'.
9 John Logan, 'Family and fortune in Kate O'Brien's Limerick', in J. Logan (ed.), *With Warmest Love* (Limerick: Mellick Press, 1994).
10 Declan Kiberd, *Irish Classics* (London: Granta Books, 2000), p. 558.
11 *Self-portrait.*
12 Kate O'Brien, *Older and Wiser*, RTÉ Radio programme (29 September 1973).
13 Kate O'Brien, 'Memories of a Catholic education'.
14 Terence McQueen, 'Meet Kate O'Brien'.
15 Kate O'Brien, 'Father's Christmas', *The Spectator* (23 November 1956), p. 722.
16 p. 724.
17 Kate O'Brien, 'Recollections of childhood'.
18 Lorna Reynolds, *Kate O'Brien: A Literary Portrait* (Gerrards Cross: Colin Smythe, 1987), p. 31.
19 Interview with Mother. Patrick O'Brien, FCJ a schoolfriend of Kate O'Brien's by Michael O'Toole at Laurel Hill, Limerick. 21 September 1975.
20 Kate O'Brien, *Musical Evening* (Northwestern collection).
21 p. 2.
22 Kate O'Brien, 'Manna' (Northwestern collection, 1962).
23 Ibid., p. 4.
24 Ibid., p. 5.
25 For a history of Laurel Hill Convent, see 'Laurel Hill: a French foundation', *Limerick Journal*, 25 (Summer 1989).
26 Logan, 'Family and fortune in Kate O'Brien's Limerick'.
27 *Self-portrait.*
28 *Self-portrait.*
29 *Self-portrait.*

30 *Self-portrait.*
31 Kiberd, *Irish Classics*, p. 571.
32 Frank O'Connor, *Leinster, Munster and Connaught* (1949), quoted in Jim Kemmy (ed.), *The Limerick Anthology* (Dublin: Gill and Macmillan, 1996), p. 17.
33 See Dermot Keogh, *Jews in Twentieth-Century Ireland* (Cork: Cork University Press, 1998).
34 Frank O'Connor, *Leinster, Munster and Connaught*, p. 17.
35 Kate O'Brien, 'Memories of a Catholic education'.
36 Ibid., p. 11.
37 Ibid., p. 12.
38 Northwestern collection (undated). Other school memories include 'Holy Week and Easter when I was at school' and 'St Michael's Day'.
39 Cork Tostal, author's exhibition (Northwestern collection, 23 May 1957).
40 Cork Tostal, author's exhibition (Northwestern collection, 23 May 1957).
41 Cork Tostal, author's exhibition (Northwestern collection, 23 May 1957).
42 Mother M. Patrick O'Brien interview (21 September 1975).
43 Kate O'Brien, 'Memories of a Catholic education'.
44 Kate O'Brien, 'James Joyce and Ulysses' (Canterbury: Canterbury School of Art, 1969).

2 EARNING A LIVING 1916–26

1 University Calendar, 1916–1919.
2 Interview with Mother M. Patrick O'Brien (21 September 1975).
3 *Self-portrait.*
4 Kate O'Brien, 'UCD as I forget It', *University Review*, 3, 2 (1962).
5 *Self-portrait.*
6 Kate O'Brien, 'Autumn term', undated radio talk (Reading BBC Archives).
7 Ibid.
8 Kate O'Brien, 'As to university life', *University Review*, 1, 6 (1955), p. 7.
9 Ibid., p. 3.
10 *Self-portrait.*
11 W.H. Mills, *The Manchester Guardian* (London: Chatto and Windus 1921), p. 129.
12 John Jordan, 'Kate O'Brien: First Lady of Irish letters', *Hibernia* (May 1973).
13 *Self-portrait.*
14 *Self-portrait.*
15 See interview with Kate O'Brien, *Manchester Guardian* (14 July 1926).
16 John Jordan, 'Kate O'Brien: First Lady of Irish letters'.
17 Terence McQueen, 'Meet Kate O'Brien'.
18 Now in the possession of Orlaith Kelly, Cambridge.
19 See Dorothy Macardle, *The Irish Republic* (London: Corgi, reprinted 1968), p. 201, and J.J. Lee (ed.), *Remembering Limerick* (Limerick: Limerick Civic Trust, 1997), pp. 268–73.
20 For a full account of James O'Mara's career and his decision to resign, see Patricia Lavelle's *James O'Mara* (London: Burns and Oates, 1961).
21 John Jordan, 'Kate O'Brien: First Lady of Irish Letters', *Hibernia.*
22 Ibid.
23 Dermot Keogh, *Twentieth-century Ireland* (Dublin: Gill and Macmillan, 1994), p. 202.

24 David Fitzpatrick, *Harry Boland's Irish Revolution* (Cork: Cork University Press, 2003), p. 251.

25 David Fitzpatrick, *Harry Boland's Irish Revolution*, p. 305.

26 John Jordan, 'Kate O'Brien: First Lady of Irish Letters'.

27 Kate O'Brien, 'My Spain' (Northwestern collection, n.d.).

28 Kate O'Brien, 'Friends, Ladies, Irish Countrywomen', a talk given to the Claremorris Irish Countrywomen's Association (Northwestern collection, 1957).

29 José María Areilza, 'Kate O'Brien: a personal literary portrait', in J. Logan (ed.), *With Warmest Love*.

30 Ibid., p. 34.

31 Kate O'Brien, 'Friends, ladies, Irish countrywomen'.

32 I am very grateful to Aintzane Legarrreta Mentxaka for all her help with this research on the Areilza family in Bilbao. I also want to thank her for translating José María Areilza's 1937 speech from Inaki Egana. *Guerra Civil en Euskal Herria*. (Volumen vi – *La Ofensiva de Mola: Defensa y Caida de Bizkaia*) (Andoain: Aralar Liburuak, 1999), (pp. 218–19). See Aintzane Legarreta Mentxaka. 'Girl meets politics "The 'Don Pablo" chapter in Kate O'Brien's *Mary Lavelle*' (Dublin PaGes Publication of the Faculty of Arts, UCD, December 2005). See also Paul Preston's *Franco* (London: HarperCollins, 1993) p. 540.

33 José María Areilza, 'Kate O'Brien: a personal literary portrait', p. 38.

34 Ibid., p. 39.

35 Ibid., p. 36.

36 Interview with Mary O'Neill by M. O'Toole (Hampstead, September 1976).

37 Ibid.

38 See Olive Renier, *Before the Bonfire* (Warwick: Drinkwater, 1984).

39 Reynolds, *Kate O'Brien: A Literary Portrait*, p. 38.

40 Ibid., p. 38.

41 Paul Smith, 'A personal memoir', in J. Logan (ed.), *With Warmest Love*.

42 Olive Renier, *Before the Bonfire*, pp. 71–2.

43 Gustaaf Renier, *Oscar Wilde* (London: Peter Davies, 1933).

44 Gustaaf Renier, *The English, Are They Human?* (London: Williams and Norgate, 1931).

45 Gustaaf Renier, *He Came to England* (London: Peter Davies, 1933).

46 Review in *The Times* (24 November 1933).

47 Gustaaf Renier, *He Came to England*, p. 9.

48 Ibid., p. 25.

49 Ibid., p. 91.

50 Ibid., p. 166.

51 Olive Renier, *Before the Bonfire*, p. 79.

52 Gustaaf Renier, *Oscar Wilde*, p. 89.

53 Gustaaf Renier, *Oscar Wilde*, p. 93.

54 Compton McKenzie, *Daily Mail* (23 March 1933).

55 Robert Sherard, *André Gide's Wicked Lies about the Late Oscar Wilde* (Corsica: Vindex, 1933).

56. Ibid., p. 3.

57 I am grateful to Clare Hannigan, Peter O'Mara's daughter, for her help with this question of her father's parentage.

58 'Aims of the Sunlight League', in *The Sunlight League* (London: British Library, 14 May 1924).

59 *Self-portrait*.

60 *Evening Standard* (10 July 1926).

61 *Evening Standard* (13 July 1926).
62 *Evening News* (13 July 1926).
63 *Evening Standard* (13 July 1926).
64 *Sunday Times* (18 July 1926).
65 *Sunday Pictorial* (18 July 1926).
66 *The Observer* (18 July 1926).
67 *The Observer* (27 July 1926).
68 *Daily Telegraph* (14 July 1926).

3 WRITING MELLICK 1926–34

1 Theodora Bosanquet and Kate O'Brien, 'Susannah and the Elders' (1931, manuscript in the Northwestern collection).
2 Kate O'Brien, 'Gloria Gish' (probably written between 1926 and 1931, manuscript in the National Library of Ireland) Acc. 4941. I am grateful to Dr Fiorenzo Fantaccini for alerting me to the existence of this play and to Elizabeth Kirwan of the National Library of Ireland for her help in locating the manuscript.
3 Terence McQueen, 'Meet Kate O'Brien'.
4 *Self-portrait.*
5 Kate O'Brien, 'The Art of Writing', *University Review*, 3, 4 (1963) pp. 6–14.
6 Terence McQueen, 'Meet Kate O'Brien'.
7 I am indebted to Stephie's daughter, Ruth Whitehead, and her granddaughter, Caroline Whitehead, for this information about her life and for access to family photos and letters.
8 Emma Donoghue, 'Kate O'Brien's lesbian fictions', in Eibhear Walshe (ed.), *Ordinary People Dancing* (Cork: Cork University Press, 1993), p. 48.
9 Lillian Faderman, *Surpassing the Love of Men* (London: The Women's Press, 1981), p. l8.
10 Violet Powell, *The Life of a Provincial Lady* (London: Heinemann, 1988), p. 98.
11 From Eibhear Walshe (ed.), *Ordinary People Dancing*, Essays on Kate O'Brien (Cork: Cork University Press, 1993), p. 4.
12 Lilian Faderman, *Surpassing the Love of Men* (London: The Women's Press, 1981), p. 16.
13 Ibid., p. 20.
14 Letter to author (9 June 1997).
15 I am grateful to Professor Pat Coughlan for this inherited memory.
16 Letter to author (13 May 1997).
17 E.O. Somerville and Martin Ross, *Irish Memories* (New York: Longman Green and Company, 1917), p. 326.
18 Mrs Elizabeth (O'Neill) Hall in conversation (London, November 1995).
19 Mrs Elizabeth (O'Neill) Hall in conversation (London, November 1995).
20 Micheál Mac Liammóir to Mary O'Neill (14 October 1966).
21 Emma Donoghue, 'Kate O'Brien's lesbian fictions', in Eibhear Walshe (ed.), *Ordinary People Dancing*, p. 36.
22 Sally Cline, *Radclyffe Hall: A Woman called John* (London: John Murray, 1997), p. 82. See also Joanne Glasgow, 'What's a nice lesbian like you doing in the Church of Torquemada?', in Joanne Glasgow and Karla Jay (eds), *Lesbian Texts and Contexts* (London: Only Women Press, 1992).
23 See Ellis Hanson, *Decadence and Catholicism* (London: Harvard University

Press, 1997).

24 Brian Fallon, *An Age of Innocence* (Dublin: Gill and Macmillan, 1999), p. 192.

25 See *John O'London Weekly* (19 December 1931), p. 491.

26 See John St John, *A Century of Publishing* (London: Heinemann, 1990).

27 Ibid., p. 267.

28 Kate O'Brien. Undated research notebook (Northwestern collection).

29 Ibid.

30 *Book Society News* (December 1931), p. 1.

31 Author's note for the manuscript of *Without My Cloak* (Northwestern collection).

32 Sylvia Norman (ed.), *Contemporary Essays* (London: Elkin Mathews and Marrot, 1933).

33 Ibid., p. 26.

34 '33, Great James St', BBC Radio (Reading: BBC Archives, 29 June 1962).

35 For an account of Anna Wickham's life and poetry, see James Hepburn (ed.), *The Writings of Anna Wickham, Free Woman and Poet* (London: Virago, 1984).

36 Mary Steward, personal interview (London, 15 September 1992).

37 Anna Wickham to Kate O'Brien (23 June 1938), University of Limerick.

38 Kate O'Brien, 'Golden lady', in Helen Gosse (ed.), *The First Class Omnibus* (London: Hodder and Stoughton, 1934), pp. 457–95.

39 For two excellent critical essays on *The Ante-Room*, see John Cronin's *The Anglo-Irish Novel*, Vol. 2 (Belfast: Appletree Press, 1990), p. 138, and Anthony Roche's 'The Ante Room as drama', in Eibhear Walshe (ed.), *Ordinary People Dancing*.

40 Patricia Coughlan, 'Kate O'Brien: feminine beauty, feminist writing and sexual role', in Eibhear Walshe (ed.), *Ordinary People Dancing*, p. 59.

41 Letter to John Jordan (National Library of Ireland, 10 November 1954).

42 John Jordan, 'Kate O'Brien: A note on her themes', *The Bell*, 19 (January 1954), pp. 55–9.

43 Vivian Mercier, *Irish Writing*, Vol .1 (1946), pp. 86–100.

44 *Self-portrait*.

45 Denys Blakelock, *Around the Next Corner* (London: Camelot Press, 1967), pp. 95–6.

4 BANNED 1934–41

1 Kate O'Brien, 'Imaginative prose by the Irish, 1820–1970', in J. Ronsley (ed.), *Myth and Reality in Irish Literature* (Ontario: Wilfrid Laurier University Press, 1977), pp. 305–16.

2 Benedict Kiely, introduction to Eibhear Walshe (ed.), *Ordinary People Dancing*, p. 3.

3 Among her own books, Kate had a copy of Rupert Hart-Davis's *The Letters of Oscar Wilde* that bore the inscription: '6/3/63 Thirty Year Friendship'.

4 Lorna Reynolds, *Kate O'Brien: A Literary Portrait*.

5 *The Bystander* (November 1934).

6 Kate O'Brien, 'Overheard', in *Time and Tide* (2 March 1935), pp. 307–8.

7 I am indebted to Dr Anne Walsh and Professor Terry O' Reilly at University College Cork for their insightful comments on Kate O'Brien's reading of Spanish literature.

8 Emma Donoghue, 'Kate O'Brien's lesbian fictions', in Eibhear Walshe (ed.), *Ordinary People Dancing*, p. 42.

9 Ibid.

10 See Michael Adams, *Censorship: The Irish Experience* (Dublin: Scepter, 1968), p. 242.

11 Censorship of Publications Act 1929, Part 2, Section 6 (Dublin: Stationery Office, 1929).

12 Julia Carlson, *Banned in Ireland* (London: Routledge, 1990), p. 4.

13 See Terence Brown, *Ireland: A Social and Cultural History 1922–1970* (London: Fontana, 1981).

14 Donal O'Driscoll, *Censorship in Ireland* (Cork: Cork University Press, 1996), p. 2.

15 From Nicole O'Connor (Producer), 'Kate O'Brien: Une femme maîtresse', University College Cork Campus Radio (February 1997).

16 Stephen O'Mara to Kate O'Brien (Dublin: O'Mara family papers, 28 November 1936).

17 Stephen O'Mara to Kate O'Brien (Dublin: O'Mara family papers, 28 November 1936).

18 Stephen O'Mara to Kate O'Brien (Dublin: O'Mara family papers, 28 November 1936).

19 Stephen O'Mara to Kate O'Brien (Dublin: O'Mara family papers, 5 November 1936).

20 Kate O'Brien to Stephen O'Mara (Dublin: O'Mara family papers, 7 December 1936).

21 Ibid.

22 Margaret Ward, *Hanna Sheehy Skeffington* (Dublin: Attic Press, 1990), p. 324.

23 Her first *Spectator* review appeared on 24 September 1937. See full list of her *Spectator* reviews below.

24 For an excellent account of the Spanish Civil War, see Raymond Carr's *Modern Spain* (Oxford: Oxford University Press, 1980).

25 Kate O'Brien, 'Thought for the Day' (RTÉ Radio, 22–8 November 1969).

26 'Crumbling Castle in Spain', *The Spectator* (27 August 1937), p. 357.

27 Ibid.

28 Paul Preston, *Franco* (London: HarperCollins, 1993), pp. 219–20.

29 Jordan, 'Kate O'Brien, First Lady of Irish letters'.

30 University of Limerick collection.

31 Dated 12 July 1946, from the archives of Archivo Central de la Administración, Alcala de Henares.

32 Ibid. I am greatly indebted to Sheila Quinn for her research in Madrid and in Alcala de Henares.

33 Kate O'Brien, 'Friends, ladies, Irish countrywomen' (University of Limerick papers).

34 For a brief mention of Spain in the writings of Kate O'Brien, see the essay 'Each other's country: some twentieth-century Irish and Spanish writers', in John Logan (ed.), *With Warmest Love*, p. 15, by the translator of *Mary Lavelle* (Edhassa: Madrid, 1991), Maria Isabel Butler de Foley. Kate's own travel writings on Spain include this series of five articles for the *The Observer* in 1959, a talk to the Claremorris Irish Countrywomen's Association in the mid-1950s, an article for *The Guardian* on Madrid in the 1960s and an address to the Spanish Society in University College Dublin in the 1960s.

35 For a discussion on the pejorative characterisation of the Irish Catholic middle class in the fiction of Somerville and Ross, see Roz Cowman's essay, 'Lost time: the smell and taste of Castle T', in Eibhear Walshe (ed.), *Sex, Nation and Dissent* (Cork: Cork University Press, 1997).

36 See Gerardine Meaney's essay, 'Decadence, degeneration and revolting aesthetics: the fiction of Emily Lawless and Katherine Cecil Thurston', *Colby Quarterly*, 36, 2 (June 2000).

37 John Broderick, *Irish Independent* (17 April 1987).

38 Vivian Mercier, 'Kate O'Brien: a note on her themes'.

39 Vivian Mercier, 'Kate O'Brien', *Irish Writing*, 1 (1946), pp. 94–5.

40 Evelyn Waugh, 'The Irish bourgeoisie', *The Spectator* (29 April 1938), p. 768.

41 Kate O'Brien to Barbara Gosworth (Harry Ransom Center Collection, 6 September 1939).

42 Kate O'Brien to Barbara Gosworth (Harry Ransom Center Collection, 20 November 1940).

43 'Moving back into village life', Radio Éireann (University of Limerick collection, 13 September 1964).

44 Joanna Richardson, *Enid Starkie* (London: John Murray, 1973), p. 124.

45 Ibid., pp. 133–4.

46 Lorna Reynolds, *Kate O'Brien: A Literary Portrait*, pp. 68–9.

47 Enid Starkie, *A Lady's Child* (London: Faber and Faber, 1941), p. 20.

48 Lorna Reynolds, *Kate O'Brien: A Literary Portrait*, pp. 68–9.

49 Kate O'Brien, 'Long Distance', *Irish Times*, 28 April 1970.

50 Kate O'Brien to Nance O'Mara (O'Mara family papers, 3 April 1941).

51 I am indebted to Nicole O'Connor for her research on O'Brien and the female artist. See '"Facing the Muse": Female Artists in Kate O'Brien', MA thesis, NUI Cork, 1998.

52 Austin Clarke, *The Bell* (1941), pp. 93–4.

53 Ibid., p. 95.

54 Kate O'Brien, 'A masterpiece spoiled', *Irish Independent* (11 March 1941).

55 Séan O'Faoláin, *The Bell*, 2, 3 (June 1941), p. 7.

56 See *The Bell* (November 1941), pp. 140–9; (January 1945), pp. 313–22; (February 1945), pp. 395–409.

57 Seanad Debate (November 1942), Vol. 27, Cols 16–55, pp. 24–5.

58 Terence Brown, *Ireland: A Social and Cultural History*, p. 197.

59 From 'Kate O'Brien: une femme maîtresse', University College Cork Campus Radio (February 1997).

60 Benedict Kiely, interviewed in Julia Carlson (ed.), *Banned in Ireland* (London: Routledge, 1990).

5 RESISTANCE WRITING 1941–50

1 Letter from Kate O'Brien to John Gosworth (Harry Ransom Center Collection, July 1942).

2 O'Brien Papers (15 June 1942, University of Limerick).

3 Anne Fogarty, 'The business of attachment: romance and desire in the novels of Kate O'Brien', in Eibhear Walshe (ed.), *Ordinary People Dancing*, p. 177.

4 Ibid., p. 114.

5 William Whitebait, review in *New Statesman and Nation* (17 June 1944).

6 Ibid.

7 Herbert Farjeon, review in *Time and Tide* (June/July 1944), p. 530.

8 The manuscript for this is dated 23 February; it was published by Collins in London in 1943.

9 Kate O'Brien papers (University of Limerick collection).

10 Kate O'Brien, 'E.M. Delafield as I Knew Her', a radio talk for the BBC's Home Service (19 March 1945). Later published in the *Literary Digest* in 1947.
11 Violet Powell, *The Life of a Provincial Lady* (London: Heinemann, 1988), p. 181.
12 Letter from Kate O'Brien to Barbara Gosworth (Harry Ransom Center Collection, 27 June 1943).
13 Kate O'Brien to Gosworth (Harry Ransom Center Collection, 8 February 1944).
14 Kate O'Brien, 'E.M. Delafield as I Knew Her'.
15 Violet Powell, *The Life of a Provincial Lady*, p. 98.
16 Violet Powell, *The Life of a Provincial Lady*, p. 179.
17 Letter to author (4 July 1997).
18 E.M. Delafield, *Late and Soon* (London: Macmilllan and Co., 1943), p. 35.
19 Ibid., p. 51.
20 Violet Powell, *The Life of a Provincial Lady*, p. 179.
21 Letter to author (4 July 1997).
22 Letter to author (9 June 1997).
23 E.M. Delafield, *The Provincial Lady* (London: Macmillan, 1947).
24 Kate O'Brien, 'The art of writing', *University Review*, 3, 4, pp. 6–14.
25 G. Muro, *Vida de la Princesa de Eboli* (Madrid, 1877).
26 Terence McQueen, 'Meet Kate O'Brien'.
27 Kate O'Brien, 'Introduction' to *That Lady: A Romantic Drama* (New York: Harper and Brothers, 1949).
28 Kate O'Brien, 'Foreword' to *That Lady*.
29 See Gregorio Maranon's *Antonio Perez 'Spanish Traitor'* (London: Hollis and Carter, 1954), for a profoundly hostile portrayal of Ana de Mendoza.
30 M. Mignet, *Antonio Perez et Phillipe II* (Paris, 1854).
31 C. De Muth, 'That Lady', *Catholic Mirror* (1945).
32 Harold C. Gardiner, *Catholic Book Club Newsletter*, 1945, quoted in the *Irish Bookman* in January 1947.
33 Letter from Kate O'Brien to Joanna Scott Moncrieff (Reading: BBC Archives, 1956).
34 Letter to Denys Blakelock, (Northwestern Collection, 8 February 1954).
35 Ibid.
36 Quoted in Vivian Mercier, 'Kate O'Brien', *Irish Writing*.
37 Paul Smith, 'A personal memoir', Logan. p. 101.
38 Kate O'Brien, 'The lady was a problem child', Introduction to *That Lady* (New York: Harper and Brothers,1949), p. viii.
39 Letter to Kate O'Brien from Denys Blakelock (Harry Ransom Center Collection, 8 February 1954).
40 McQueen, 'Meet Kate O'Brien'.
41 Kate O'Brien, *Anglo-Irish Writing since 1945*, radio talk (Northwestern Collection, 1960s).
42 I am indebted to W.F. Richardson and Mary Leland for this information.
43 For a lively account of Mac Liammóir's life, see Christopher Fitzsimons, *The Boys* (Dublin: Gill and Macmillan, 1994).
44 Lorna Reynolds, *Kate O'Brien: A Literary Portrait*, p. 83.
45 Paul Smith, 'A personal memoir' from J. Logan (ed.), *With Warmest Love*, p. 100.
46 Ibid., p. 100.
47 Ibid., p. 103.
48 Ibid.
49 Ibid.

50 Ibid., p. 101.
51 Lorna Reynolds, *Kate O'Brien: A Literary Portrait*, p. 83.

6 LOTUS LAND 1950–60

1 Kate O'Brien, *Older and Wiser*, RTÉ Radio programme (29 September 1973).
2 Letter to the Royal Society of Literature (24 May 1955).
3 See *That Was Then, This is Now: Changes in Ireland 1949–1999*, Central Statistics Office: Dublin, 2000.
4 Michael Wishart, *High Diver* (London: Blond and Briggs, 1977), p. 71.
5 John Jordan, 'Kate O'Brien: First Lady of Irish letters'.
6 Letter to John Jordan (21 August 1952), National Library of Ireland.
7 Terence McQueen, 'Meet Kate O'Brien'.
8 James MacIntyre, *Three Men on an Island* (Belfast: Blackstaff, 1996), pp. 31–2.
9 Val Mulkerns, 'Kate O'Brien: A memoir', *The Stony Thursday Book*, 7 (Limerick undated), p. 50.
10 Ibid.
11 Ibid., p. 51.
12 Ibid.
13 Paul Smith, 'A personal memoir', in, J. Logan (ed.), *With Warmest Love*, p. 100.
14 Lorna Reynolds, *Kate O'Brien: A Literary Portrait*, p. 85.
15 Kate O'Brien, 'Clifden pony show', radio talk for Radio Éireann (Northwestern collection).
16 Kate O'Brien, 'Connemara', *The Spectator* (16 November 1951), p. 631.
17 Kate O'Brien, 'Clifden pony show'.
18 'Between ourselves', Radio Éireann (Northwestern collection, 12 April 1956), p. 2.
19 Kate O'Brien, 'Chrissie's First Confession' (Northwestern collection undated).
20 Kate O'Brien, 'Writers of letters', *Essays and Studies*, 9 (1956), pp. 7–20.
21 Kate O'Brien, 'George Eliot: a moralizing fabulist', in G.R. Hamilton (ed.), *Transactions of the Royal Society of Literature*, 27 (London, 1955), p. 40.
22 Ibid.
23 Kate O'Brien, *Teresa of Avila* (London: Max Parrish, 1951), p. 10.
24 Teresa Deevy, review in *Irish Writing* (March 1952).
25 Clare Boothe Luce (ed.), *Saints for Now* (London and New York: Sheed and Ward, 1952).
26 Ibid., p. 161.
27 Kate O'Brien, 'Why don't they emigrate to our smaller cities?', *Irish Digest* (1959).
28 Northwestern collection.
29 Jordan went on to lecture at University College Dublin in the 1960s and to run *Poetry Ireland*. He died in 1988.
30 Letter to John Jordan, National Library of Ireland, Acc. 4594.
31 Letter to John Jordan (National Library of Ireland, 10 November 1954).
32 John Jordan, *Collected Poems* (Dublin: Dedalus, 1991), p. 114.
33 John Jordan, 'First draft', in Jordan, *Collected Stories* (Dublin: Poolbeg, 1991), p. 243.
34 Kate O'Brien, 'The divine Garbo', *Woman and Beauty* (October 1952), pp. 28–29.
35 Personal interview with Mary Steward (London, February 1998).

36 Letter to John Jordan, 5 August 1959.
37 I am indebted to Nicole O'Connor for her work on *The Flower of May* in her MA thesis, University College Cork, 1998.
38 Lorna Reynolds, *Kate O'Brien: A Literary Portrait*, pp. 93–4.
39 Paul Smith, 'A personal memoir', in J. Logan (ed.), *With Warmest Love*.
40 Antonia White, *Diaries 1958–1979* (London: Constable, 1992), p. 203.
41 Letter to the Royal Society of Literature (24 May 1955), Archives of the Royal Society of Literature.
42 Letter to Cass Cassfield (Harry Ransom Center Collection, February 1957).
43 For an account of that train journey, see Kate O'Brien, 'The leaning tower' (Northwestern Collection, undated).
44 Kate O'Brien, 'Italy', a lecture given to the Italian Society of Limerick (Northwestern collection, November 1955).
45 Kate O'Brien, 'Andantino', *Irish Writing*, 28 (September 1954), pp. 46–50.
46 Ibid.
47 Kate O'Brien, 'A bus from Tivoli', *Threshold* (Summer 1957), pp. 6–11.
48 Ibid., p. 7.
49 Ibid., p. 8.
50 Ibid., p. 9.
51 Ibid.
52 Kate O'Brien File (Reading: BBC Archives, 25 October 1956).
53 Lorna Reynolds, 'Euridyce' (written in 1963), in A.A. Kelly (ed.), *Pillars of the House* (Dublin: Wolfhound, 1987), p. 104.
54 Kate O'Brien, 'Ivan Turgenev', *University Review*, 1, 3 (1957), p. 21.
55 Ibid., p. 22.
56 Northwestern collection.
57 Fanny Feehan, 'Kate O'Brien and the Splendour of Music', in Eibhear Walshe (ed.), *Sex, Nation and Dissent* (Cork: Cork University Press, 1997), pp. 41–3.
58 See Anne Chambers, *La Sheridan* (Dublin: Wolfhound, 1989).
59 Emma Donoghue, 'Kate O'Brien's lesbian fictions', in Eibhear Walshe (ed.), *Ordinary People Dancing*, p. 50.
60 Anne Fogarty, 'The Ear of the Other', in Eibhear Walshe (ed.), *Sex, Nation and Dissent*, p. 175.
61 Drafts of these 1959 *Observer* articles are in the Northwestern collection.

7 LONG DISTANCE 1960–74

1 Letter to Denys Blakelock (Northwestern collection, 10 September 1963).
2 Enid Starkie to John Jordan (National Library of Ireland, 29 January 1967).
3 Kate O'Brien, 'UCD as I forget it', p. 7.
4 'Aunt Mary in the Parlour', *University Review*, 3, 3, pp. 3–10.
5 Other autobiographical works include a 1962 television programme for RTÉ called *A Self-portrait*, 'UCD as I forget it' for the *University Review*, 3, 2 (1962), p. 7, and 'Memories of a Catholic Education', *Sunday Press* (January 1977).
6 Kate O'Brien, 'Constancy', unpublished novel, University of Limerick, p. 15.
7 'Une femme maîtresse', University College Cork Campus Radio, 1997.
8 University of Limerick collection.
9 From 'The Diary of Frank McEvoy', in Melosina Lennox-Conyngham (ed.), *Ireland* (Dublin: Lilliput, 1998), pp. 263–4.

10 R.S. McGowan, *Dublin and Cork* (London: Spring Books, 1961).
11 Jim Kemmy, 'Kate O'Brien's Limerick', *Old Limerick Journal*, 17 (1984), pp. 36–9.
12 John Jordan, review of *My Ireland* in *University Review*, 2 (1962), p. 72.
13 'A view from Toledo', *Argosy* (1962).
14 'Rome Relaxed', *The Spectator*, 16 August 1963.
15 *Self-portrait*.
16 Ibid.
17 McQueen, 'Meet Kate O'Brien'.
18 Kate O'Brien, *Older and Wiser*.
19 Personal Interview with Jim and Kate Hughes, Canterbury (4 July 1992).
20 *Irish Times* (6 January 1969).
21 *Irish Times* (8 August 1967).
22 *Irish Times* (2 October 1967).
23 *Irish Times* (7 August 1967).
24 *Irish Times* (28 April 1970).
25 *Irish Times* (6 October 1970).
26 Ibid.
27 *Irish Times* (3 March 1969).
28 Jane Dunn, *Antonia White* (London: Jonathan Cape, 1998), p. 263.
29 Kevin Casey, *Winter's Tales from Ireland* (London: Macmillan, 1972).
30 Eavan Boland, 'Continuing the encounter', in Eibhear Walshe (ed.), *Ordinary People Dancing*, p. 16.
31 Other lectures on Irish writing included 'Ireland and avant-gardisme' (Dublin: UCD, 1966) and 'Imaginative prose of the Irish' 1977.
32 'Imaginative prose of the Irish', p. 305.
33 1 October 1969, Northwestern collection.
34 Ibid., p. 8.
35 Brendan Flynn, 'A meeting with Kate', *The Stony Thursday Book*, undated p. 43.
36 John Jordan, 'Kate O'Brien: First Lady of Irish letters'.
37 I am grateful to Mary Steward for this information.
38 Michael O'Toole, 'The art of writing: Kate O'Brien's journalism', in Eibhear Walshe (ed.), *Ordinary People Dancing*, p. 128.
39 Paul Smith, 'A personal memoir', J. Logan, *With Warmest Love*, p. 103.
40 I am indebted to John McGahern and to James Liddy for these memories of Kate O'Brien.
41 Mrs Jennifer Lyons, personal interview (11 May 1992).
42 This information is contained in Kate's private papers left by Mary O'Neill in the care of her nephew, Austin Hall.
43 *The Times* (14 August 1974).
44 John Jordan, *Collected Poems* (Dedalus: Dublin, 1991), p. 118.
45 I am indebted to Ania Corless for these details.
46 There has been recent interest in tracing the influence of earlier Irish middle-class women writers on Kate's fiction. See Anne Fogarty (ed.), *Colby Quarterly* (June 2000), particularly the work by Gerardine Meaney, Margaret Kelleher and Tina O'Toole.
47 *The Late Late Show* (RTE 26 October 1969).

Bibliography

The important archive sources for Kate O'Brien include her literary papers at the McCormack Special Collections Library of Northwestern University, Evanston, Illinois, the Kate O'Brien papers at the University of Limerick, Ireland, various letters to her in the Harry Ransom Center for the Humanities at the University of Texas at Austin, USA, the BBC Archives in Reading, England, and the John Jordan letters at the National Library of Ireland.

NOVELS, PLAYS, DIARIES

Distinguished Villa (London: Ernest Benn Ltd, 1926).

Without My Cloak (London: Heinemann, 1931). Reprinted by Virago, London, 1986.

The Ante-Room (London: Heinemann, 1934). Reprinted by Arlen House, Dublin, 1980.

Mary Lavelle (London: Heinemann, 1936). Reprinted by Virago, London, 1984.

Farewell Spain (London: Heinemann, 1937).

Pray for the Wanderer (London: Heinemann, 1938).

The Land of Spices (London: Heinemann, 1941). Reprinted by Virago, London, 1988.

The Last of Summer (London: Heinemann, 1943). Reprinted by Arlen House, Dublin, 1982.

That Lady (London: Heinemann, 1946). Reprinted by Virago, London, 1985.

That Lady: A Romantic Drama (New York: Harper and Brothers, 1949).

Teresa of Avila (London: Max Parrish, 1951).

The Flower of May (London: Heinemann, 1953).

As Music and Splendour (London: Heinemann, 1958, reprinted by Penguin Ireland, 2005).

Dublin and Cork (photographs by R.S. McGowan and text by Kate O'Brien) (London: Spring Books, 1961).

My Ireland (London: Batsford, 1962).

Presentation Parlour (London: Heinemann, 1963, reprinted by Poolbeg Press, 1994).

'Constancy', in Kevin Casey (ed.), *Winter's Tales from Ireland* (Dublin: Gill and Macmillan, 1972).

UNPUBLISHED FULL-LENGTH WORKS

'Gloria Gish', late 1920s, unperformed, National Library of Ireland.

'Susannah and the Elders', 1931, unperformed, Northwestern collection.

'A Broken Song', film scenario for *That Lady*, Northwestern collection.

'Mary Magdalen', screenplay, Northwestern collection.

'The Bridge', performed play (London: The Arts Club, 1 May 1927). No manuscript.

'The Silver Roan'. 1926–27, unperformed play. No manuscript.

TRAVEL WRITING

'Why don't they emigrate to our smaller cities?', condensed from an article in *Hibernia*.

'Madrid', *The Guardian* (Northwestern collection, undated).

'Travel by train', *Evening Press*.

'Changing Ireland', *The Spectator* (May 1931).

'Ireland', Cork Tostal Exhibition (Northwestern collection, 23 May 1951).

'Connemara', *The Spectator* (November 1951).

'Andantino', *Irish Writing* (September 1954).

'Italy', a lecture given to the Italian Society of Limerick (November 1955).

'West Clare', *Ireland of the Welcomes* (September–October 1959).

'Castile at a gallop', *The Observer* (1959).

'A quick look around Madrid', *The Observer* (1959).

'Spain' 1, *The Observer* (1959).
'Spain' 2, *The Observer* (1959).
'Writing in Spain', *The Observer* (1959).
'Remembering Russia', September 1963, unpublished.

SHORT FICTION

'Aunt Johnny' (Northwestern collection, undated).
'Recollections of childhood' (Northwestern collection, undated).
'Dinner at Miss Upton's' (Northwestern collection, 1921).
'Golden lady', in Helen Gosse (ed.), *The First Class Omnibus* (London: Hodder and Stoughton, 1934).
'Singapore has fallen', *The Spectator* (27 February 1942).
'English diaries and journals' (London: Collins, 1943).
'On Ballycotton Strand' (Northwestern collection, September 1945).
'A fit of laughing', *The Bell*, 18, 4 (1952).
'Old Balls MacSweeny' (Northwestern collection, April 1956).
'Boney Fide' (Northwestern collection, April 1956).
'A bus from Tivoli', *Threshold*, 1, 2 (Summer 1957).
'Sister Lucy's remedy', *Evening Standard* 'Did it happen?' series (July 1957).
'A view of Toledo', *Argosy* (1962).
'Manna' (Northwestern Collection, unpublished 1962).
'Chrissi's first confession' (Northwestern Collection, undated).
'Overheard', *Time and Tide* (2 March 1935).
'Memories of a Catholic Childhood', *The Tablet* (4 December 1976).
'Return to Boston', 'Miss Finucane', 'Autumn term', 'Snakes and Ladders', 'Village Life in London' (Northwestern collection undated).

TELEVISION/RADIO PROGRAMMES

Between Ourselves, Radio Éireann (all in Northwestern collection):
Speranza – Lady Wilde (1964); *Maria Edgeworth* (n.d.); *Lady Gregory* (1956); *A Tribute to Evie Hone and Mainie Jellett – Book Review* (n.d.); *Alice Milligan* (n.d.); *The Beautiful Gunnings* (n.d.); *A Highbrow Cat* (n.d.); *The Irish in London* (n.d.); *Motor Cars* (n.d.); *The Leaning Tower* (n.d.); *The*

Autumn Term (n.d.); *The Nelson Classics* (n.d.); *Musical Evenings* (n.d.); *Christmas* (n.d.); *Up Jenkins* (n.d.); *The Bathing at Kilkee* (n.d.); *Holy Week* (n.d.); *Corpus Christi* (n.d.); *Fourteenth July in France* (n.d.); *Clifden Pony Show* (n.d.); *St Michael's Day* (n.d.); *St Francis Xavier's Day* (n.d.); *Out of Stone* (n.d.); *Living with Cats* (n.d.); *Christmas and New Year* (n.d.); *Moving Back into Village Life* (n.d.); *Poetry as I First Read It* (n.d.).

Poetry in Adult Life RTÉ Radio, undated, Northwestern collection.

E.M. Delafield as I Knew Her, BBC Home Service, March 1945.

At Féili Luimni, RTÉ Radio, 9 March 1958.

Kate O'Brien: A Self-Portrait, RTÉ Television, 1962.

My Home Town, RTÉ Television, 1963.

Personal Choice, RTÉ Radio, 5 March 1966.

Hometown, RTÉ Radio, 5 May 1969.

Thought for the Day, RTÉ Radio, 22–28 November 1969.

My Kind of Poetry, RTÉ Radio, 7 October 1971.

Older and Wiser, RTÉ Radio, September 1973.

Moments from a Life, RTÉ Radio, 5 March 1991.

LECTURES/ESSAYS

'Return in winter', *Contemporary Essays* (1933).

'Writers of letters', *Essays and Studies*, 9 (1956).

'Friends, Ladies, Irish Countrywomen', talk given to the Claremorris Irish Countrywomen's Association, 1957. Northwestern collection.

'Irish writers and Europe', *Hibernia* (March 1965).

'George Eliot: a moralizing fabulist', read to Royal Society of Literature (London 31 October 1951). Published in G. Rostrevor Hamilton (ed.), *Transactions of the Royal Society of Literature* (London: Oxford University Press, 1955).

'Ivan Turgenev', lecture given to the Ramsgate Arts Society (14 November 1967). Published in *University Review*, 1, 6 (1957).

'The Brontës and Haworth', lecture given to the women graduates of UCD (Northwestern collection February 1958, unpublished).

'James Joyce and Ulysses', lecture given to Canterbury College of Art (Northwestern collection 1 October 1969, unpublished).

'James Joyce the spoilt priest', lecture at University of Sussex

(University of Limerick collection 1 February 1968, unpublished).

'Spain', lecture given to the Association of Professional and Business Women, Canterbury (Northwestern collection, 10 March 1972).

'Imaginative prose by the Irish 1820–1970', in J. Ronsley (ed.), *Myth and Reality in Irish Literature* (Ontario: Wilfrid Laurier University Press, Waterloo, 1977).

'St Francis Xavier (1506–1552)', collected in Clare Boothe Luce (ed.), *Saints for Now* (London and New York: Sheed and Ward, 1952).

'The Empress Eugenie' (Northwestern collection, unpublished).

'An address on Irish theatre' (Northwestern collection, unpublished).

'As to university life', *University Review*, 1, 6 (1955).

'Lennox Robinson', *University Review*, 1, 5 (1958).

'Lady Gregory', *Kilkenny Magazine*, 2 (1960).

'UCD as I forget it', *University Review*, 3, 2 (1962).

'Aunt Mary in the parlour', *University Review*, 3, 4 (1963).

'The art of writing', *University Review*, 3, 4 (1963).

'Anglo-Irish writing since 1945' (Northwestern collection, unpublished).

'Ireland and avantgardism' (Northwestern collection, unpublished).

MISCELLANEOUS JOURNALISM

'Days in the sun: the story of Ken Wood', *Sunlight League* (December 1924).

'Sunlight activities: the story of a year's work', *Sunlight League* (December 1925).

'A year's study of sunlight', *Sunlight League* (December 1926).

'The task of the patient author', *The Author* (Autumn 1930).

'Overheard', *Time and Tide* (2 March 1935).

'Why the rage for French films?', *Star* (February 1938).

'Conversation in a country lodging', *The Spectator* (21 June 1940).

'From one generation', *The Spectator* (8 October 1943).

'Yeats comes home', *The Spectator* (24 September 1948).

'Father's Christmas', *The Spectator* (23 November 1956).

'A window for Christmas', *Creation* (December 1957).

'Divorce', *Creation* (1960s).

'Tribute to Marion Reeves', *The Times* (1 September 1961).

'Religion now and then', *Creation* (November 1967).

'The Grand Canal', *Creation* (January 1968).
'De Gaulle', *Creation* (June 1969).
Women and Beauty, 1952/53: 'The divine Garbo', 'Marie Curie: her immortal genius', 'George Eliot the woman', 'The Recamier legend', 'George Sand', 'Bernhardt: angels on her side'.
'Have music halls been killed?', *Daily Mirror* (7 July 1928).

SPECTATOR REVIEWS

24 September 1937
Antonia Yuri Herman; *Starting Point* C. Day Lewis; *Sacred Edifice* John Gloag; *Remembering Laughter* Wallace Stegner; *Daphne's Fishing* George A. Birmingham.
8 October 1937
Coming from the Fair Norah Hoult; *To Have and Have Not* Ernest Hemingway; *Closed Frontiers* Bruno Frank; *Katrina* Sally Salminen; *Europa in Limbo* Robert Briffault.
22 October 1937
The First Lover Kay Boyle; *Lonely White Sail* Valentine Kataev; *The Mortal Storm* Phyllis Bottome; *The Antagonists* Paul Hervey Fox; *The Man Who Started Clean* T.O. Beachcroft.
5 November 1937
Sally Bowles Christopher Isherwood; *College Square* Susan Goodyear; *The Sword and the Rose* A.W. Smith; *Sparrow Farm* Hans Fallada; *The Education of Hyman Kaplan* Leonard Q. Ross.
19 November 1937
Father Coldstream Julian Duguid; *Imperial City* Elmer Rice; *Bloody Murder* S.C. Mason; *A Stranger and a Sojourner* Nora K. Smith.
3 December 1937
Men of Good Will Jules Romains; *The Pasquier Chronicles* Georges Duhamel; *Children of Strangers* Lyle Saxon; *They are Transformed* Seton Peacey; *Brother Klaus* Maria Dutli-Rutishauser.
10 December 1937
The Golden Century of Spain R. Trevor Davies.
24 December 1937
Half an Eye James Hanley; *World's End* Pamela Hansford Johnson.
31 December 1937

The Silver Land J.M. Scott; *Treasure in Heaven* Rosalind Wade; *Emma* Louis Paul; *Journey on the Way* Frank Vernon.

14 January 1938

Over the Frontier Stevie Smith; *The Stroke of Eight* J.L. Hardy; *Northwest Passage* Kenneth Roberts; *A Giant in Chains* Marjorie Bowen; *Two for Joy* E. Morchard Bishop.

28 January 1938

Castle Corner Joyce Cary; *I'm not Complaining* Ruth Adam; *I Can Get it for You Wholesale*; Jerome Weidman *The Property of a Gentleman* Richard Ullman; *Strangers* Claude Houghton.

11 February 1938

The Charmed Life Jack B. Yeats; *The Mother* Sholem Asch; *The Rains Came* Louis Bromfield; *William's Wife* G.E. Trevelyan; *The Strikers* Goetze Jeter.

18 February 1938

My House in Malaga Peter C. Mitchell.

25 February 1938

Bidden to the Feast Jack Jones; *The House in the Dunes* Mayence Van Der Meersch; *Lena* Roger Vercel; *Lord Samarkand* Horace Annesley Vachell.

11 March 1938

What Hath a Man? Sarah Gertrude Millin; *Promised Land* Cedric Belfrage; *O Absalom!* Howard Spring; *Sleep in Peace* Phyllis Bentley; *Swiss Sonata* Gwethalyn Graham.

25 March 1938

Murphy Samuel Beckett; *The Mountains and the Stars* Valentin Tikhanov; *The Time of Wild Roses* Doreen Wallace; *The Larches* John Hampson and L.A. Pavey; *Kanthapura* Rajo Rao.

8 April 1938

A Traveller Came Sally Carson; *Characters in Order of Appearance* Romilly Cavan; *Pictures on the Pavement* G.S. Marlowe; *No Middle Way* Jeffrey Marston; *Winter in April* Robert Nathan.

22 April 1938

Courthouse Square Hamilton Basso; *Serenade* James M. Cain; *My Wife's the Least of It* William Gerhardi; *Miss Bendix* Naomi Royde Smith.

8 May 1938

Between Sleeping and Waking Dorothy Charques; *Nightingale Wood* Stella Gibbons; *Bird Under Glass* Robert Fraser; *Oh Say, Can You See!* Lewis Browne; *Minimum Man* Andrew Marvell.

20 May 1938

The Unvanquished William Faulkner; *The Houses in Between* Yvonne Cloud; *The Scapegoat Dances* Mark Benney; *Pomfret Towers* Angela Thirkall; *Pathetic Symphony* Klaus Mann.

3 June 1938

Shadows Around the Lake Guy de Pourtales; *Cancel All Vows* Lilo Linke; *They Drive by Night* James Curtis; *Crippled Splendour* Evan John.

17 June 1938

The Crowning of a King Arnold Zweig; *The Blackbird* Basil Creighton; *Julie* Francis Stuart; *Colonel Pontcarral* Alberic Cahuet; *Nya* Stephen Haggard.

1 July 1938

I See a Wondrous Land Gudmunder Kamban; *Late Harvest* George Blake; *Love Within Limits* Paul Frischauer; *The Gentle Phoenix* Dorothy Wright.

15 July 1938

Acquittal Graeme and Sarah Lorimer; *You Know You Can Trust Me* Charles Curran; *Young Man with a Horn* Dorothy Baker; *The Orange Lagoon* Kenneth Champion Thomas.

29 July 1938

Ruined City Neville Shute; *The Doomsday Men* J.B. Priestley; *Promenade* G.B. Lancaster; *The Traveller's Return* E.F. Bozman.

12 August 1938

Out of This Nettle Norah Lofts; *Long Haul* A.T. Bezzerides; *The Thought-Reading Machine* André Maurois; *Rebecca* Daphne du Maurier; *The Soul of Cezar Azan* Alun Llewellyn.

26 August 1938

William and Dorothy Helen Ashton; *Asleep in the Afternoon* E.C. Large; *Men Are Not Stars* C.A. Millspaugh; *A Child in Her Arms* Louise Redfield Peattie.

9 September 1938

Testament R.C. Hutchinson; *Dr Bradley Remembers* Francis Brett Young; *The Negroes Begin at Calais* Frederick Howard.

23 September 1938

A Day of Battle Vincent Sheean; *Bread* Alexi Tolstoi; *Crooked Eclipse* Edward Fitzgerald; *Jacobson's Ladder* John Pudney.

4 November 1938

The Professor Rex Warner; *The Bridegroom Cometh* Waldo Frank; *Already Walks Tomorrow* A.G. Street; *Caspar Hauser* Jacob

Wassermann.

2 December 1938

Death on the Instalment Plan Louis-Ferdinand Celine; *Story of a Lake* Negley Farson; *Margareta* Alec Brown; *Last Port of Call* Heinrich Hauser.

16 December 1938

Nine Years is a Long Time Norah Hoult; *People Are Curious* James Hanley; *Last Stories* Mary Butts; *French for Funny* Robert Westerby; *Something Wrong* James Stern.

20 January 1939

The Young Cosima Henry Handel Richardson; *There Needs No Ghost* Ruth Adam; *Cossack Commander* Arkady Perventsev; *Rabble in Arms* Kenneth Roberts; *The Adventures of Christopher Columin* Sylvia Thompson.

3 February 1939

The Daughter Bessie Breuer; *Wait Until Spring, Bandini* John Fante; *Be a Gent, Little Woman, Be a Gent,* Eileen Winncroft; *What's Become of Waring?* Anthony Powell; *The Happy Island* Dawn Powell; *This Nettle, Danger* Philip Gibbs.

17 February 1939

The School of Dictators Ignazio Silone; *Happy Valley* Patrick White; *Hawk among the Sparrows* Desmond Hawkins; *A Handful of Silver* Doreen Wallace.

3 March 1939

Goodbye to Berlin Christopher Isherwood; *Impromptu in Moribundia* Patrick Hamilton; *Kind Relations* Robert Liddell; *The Perplexed Heart* Angela du Maurier.

14 March 1939

Grandma Called it Carnal Berthe Damon; *The Wild Palms* William Faulkner; *At Swim-Two-Birds* Flann O'Brien; *O.B. Detroit.* Wessel Smitter.

28 April 1939

The Village Mulk Raj Anand; *A Good Home with Nice People* Josephine Lawrence; *Harlequin House* Margery Sharp; *The Rise of Ann Parnet* Michael Foster; *Spider's Silk* Mary Lutyens.

12 May 1939

Beware of Pity Stefan Zweig; *Passport for a Girl* Mary Borden; *The Open Sky* L.A.G. Strong; *Blind Man's Ditch* Walter Allen.

26 May 1939

The Heroes Millen Brand; *The World Owes Me a Living* John

Llewellyn Rhys; *The Shepherd's Fann* Adrian Bell; *Call The Tune*
Barbara Goolden; *Personal Effects* Barbara Willard; *Big Show*
Charles Cooke.

16 June 1939

The Duchess of Popocatapetl W.J. Turner; *Good Morning, Midnight*
Jean Rhys; *My Cousin Justin* Margaret Barrington; *Holiday
Adventure* George Woden.

7 July 1939

Nina Lessing Edward Crankshaw; *After the Death of Don Juan*
Sylvia Townsend Warner; *Entanglement* George Buchanan;
Nobody's in Town Edna Ferber; *Lowtown* Edward Hibbitt.

21 July 1939

The Bride Margaret Irwin; *The Last Days of Henri Quatre* Heinrich
Mann; *Coming up for Air* George Orwell; *Girdle of Venus*
Pamela Hansford Johnson.

4 August 1939

Jonathan North J.L. Hodson; *Pink Danube* Arthur Pumphrey;
Learn to Love First Amabel Williams-Ellis; *Family Ties*
Marguerite Steen; *Their Chimneys into Spires* Kathleen Wallace.

1 September 1939

Rogue Male Geoffrey Household; *Hudson Rejoins the Herd* Claude
Houghton; *Portrait of a Patriot* R.W. Thompson; *Luke* Noel
Streatfield; *The Elephant Is White* Caryl Brahms and S.J. Simon.

15 September 1939

The Grapes of Wrath John Steinbeck; *This is the Schoolroom*
Nicholas Monserrat; *Gentleman of Stratford* John Brophy;
Trance By Appointment G.E. Trevelyan.

3 November 1939

Grey Birds Arthur van Schendel; *The Green Tree and the Dry*
Morchard Bishop; *Sanda Mala* Maurice Collis.

17 November 1939

Lightning Flash Margaret O'Leary; *John Arnison* Edward
Thompson; *Urchin Moor* Naomi Royde Smith.

1 December 1939

What's in It for Me? Jerome Weidman; *The Hollow Mountain* Alec
Brown; *John Innocent at Oxford* Richard Buckle.

5 January 1940

Men of Good Will – Books XV and XVI: Verdun Jules Romains;
Nobody Ordered Wolves Jeffrey Dell; *Angels in Ealing* Eileen
Winncroft.

19 January 1940

War and Soldier Ashihei Hino; *Take Courage* Phyllis Bentley; *The Boon Companions* Hugh McGraw; *Idle Apprentice* Joanna Cannan; *Citizen of Westminster* Joan Morgan.

2 February 1940

Maid No More Helen Simpson; *Julie* Ethel Mannin; *Mr Skeffington* by 'Elizabeth'; *Philip* Joseph O'Neill.

16 February 1940

Four Women Grow Up Norah Hoult; *Summer's Lease* E. Arnot Robertson; *So Frail a Thing* Helen Beauclerk; *One Fight More* Susan Ertz.

1 March 1940

Our Time Is Gone James Hanley; *Kitty Foyle* Christopher Morley; *The Morning is Near Us* Susan Glaspell.

15 March 1940

The House in Haarlem Arthur van Schende; *The Power and the Glory* Graham Greene; *Other Gods* Pearl S. Buck.

29 March 1940

The Crazy Hunter Kay Boyle; *Sam* John Selby; *Peace, It's Wonderful* William Saroyan.

12 April 1940

Sun on The Water L.A.G. Strong; *Sons and Fathers* Maurice Hindus; *Mr Moonlight's Island* Robert Dean Frisbie; *The Man Who Dared* Nikilai Gubsky.

26 April 1940

The Witch in the Wood T.H. White; *The West Wind of Love* Compton Mackenzie; *The Way to Santiago* Arthur Calder Marshall; *Our Lady of the Earthquakes* Peter Brooke.

10 May 1940

The Backward Son Stephen Spender; *Charley Is My Darling* Joyce Cary; *Gypsy Gypsy* Rumer Godden; *Harvest* Jean Giono.

24 May 1940

Fanny Gaslight Michael Sadleir; *Still Glides the Stream* B. Dew Roberts; *Pigeon Pie* Nancy Mitford; *Iron Gustav* Hans Fallada.

7 June 1940

The Mixture As Before W. Somerset Maugham; *Mrs Oliver Cromwell* Margaret Irwin; *I Fell for a Sailor* Fred Urquhart; *Best Stories of Theodora Benson* Theodora Benson.

21 June 1940

And No Man's Wit Rose Macauley; *Nuns in Jeopardy* Martin Boyd; *Priest Island* E.L. Grant Watson; *The Rich Uncle* Jack Single.

5 July 1940

The Pool of Vishnu L.H. Myers; *Fame Is the Spur* Howard Spring; *Hester Roon* Norah Lofts.

19 July 1940

Cockcrow Oliver Onions; *Fairweather Faith* Rosalind Wade; *These, Our Strangers* Adrian Alington; *Lady With Jade* Margaret Mackay.

2 August 1940

High Sierra W.R. Burnett; *Living Space* Walter Allen; *The Room Within* Richard Church.

16 August 1940

Moment in Peking Lin Yutang; *Trouble in July* Erskine Caldwell; *A Footman for the Peacock* Rachel Ferguson.

30 August 1940

Hamlet had an Uncle Branch Cabell; *The Lights Go Down* Erika Mann; *Framed in Hardwood* Eric Lowe.

20 September 1940

Death of a Common Man Desmond Holdridge; *Loss of Eden* Douglas Brown and Christopher Serpell; *Jacaranda* Kathleen Bellamy.

4 October 1940

Under the Rose Rhys Davies; *Time's Harvest* Dorothy Charques; *Cheerfulness Breaks In* Angela Thirkell; *Bewildering Cares* Winifred Peck; *The Wonderful Journey* Frank Tilsey.

18 October 1940

The Don Flows Home to the Sea Mikhail Sholokhov; *Youth, Love and Adventure* Piotr Choynowski; *Mr Bunting* Robert Greenwood.

1 November 1940

Babes in the Darkling Wood H.G. Wells; *Lighter Than Day* Desmond Hawkins; *Basilissa* John Masefield.

15 November 1940

Ask Me Tomorrow James Gould Cozzens; *Angels on Horseback* C.K. Jaeger; *Elephant* Ruth Manning-Sanders.

29 November 1940

Turn Away No More Sarah Campion; *Those Sinning Girls* Catherine Gayton; *Antimacassar City* Guy McCrone; *Captain Cerise*

Dorothy Mackinder; *Quietly My Captain Waits* Evelyn Eaton.

13 December 1940

Cousin Honore Storm Jameson; *September to September* Jacobine Menzies-Wilson; *The Ghost and the Maiden* R.H. Mottram; *Heart of a Child* Phyllis Bottome.

27 December 1940

The Beauty of the Dead H.E. Bates; *The Parents Left Alone* T.O. Beachcroft; *Simplicity Jones* Martin Armstrong; *Christmas at Cold Comfort Farm* Stella Gibbons.

24 January 1941

Look at All Those Roses Elizabeth Bowen; *Summer 1914* Roger Martin du Gard; *The Red Tapeworm* Compton Mackenzie.

21 February 1941

Anno Domini 32 Paul Hervey Fox; *A House of Children* Joyce Cary.

7 March 1941

Three Days Reckoning Hans Otto Storm; *Troubled Waters* Roger Vercel; *Adventures of Gilead Skaggs* James E. Baum; *Delilah Upside Down* Bruce Marshall.

21 March 1941

The Defenders Franz Hoellering; *Crown of Life* Barbara Goolden; *Tadpole Hall* Helen Ashton.

4 April 1941

The Man of the Mountain Zora Thurston; *The Warrior* Thomas Ryan; *For Our Vines Have Tender Grapes* George V. Martin; *Peonies and Ponies* Harold Acton.

18 April 1941

The Herr Witch Doctor Sarah Gertrude Millin; *Nebraska Coast* Clyde Davis; *Reap the Wild Wind* Thelma Strabel; *Tom Tiddler's Ground* Ursula Orange.

2 May 1941

The Fields of Paradise Ralph Bates; *Fingal's Box* Harley Williams.

16 May 1941

Up at the Villa W. Somerset Maugham; *Light in Italy* Jack Lindsay; *The Lie Triumphant* Reyner Barton.

27 June 1941

The Cheat Karel Capek; *Salutation Inn* Richard Gray; *The Beehive* Winfred Williams.

11 July 1941

No One Now Will Know E.M. Delafield; *The Living and the Dead*

Patrick White; *Shadows on the Wall* Helen Beauclerk.

25 July 1941
Far from the Madding War Lord Berners; *Walk into My Parlour* Margaret Lane; *To Sea in a Bowl* Edward S. Hyams.
10 August 1941
This Little Hand Pamela Kellino; *Sapphira and the Slave Girl* Willa Cather.
22 August 1941
The Transposed Heads Thomas Mann; *Ramping Cat* Christian Mawson.
5 September 1941
The Gulls Fly Inland Sylvia Thomson; *To Make Us Glad* J.A. Cole; *Martin Croft* Josephine Bell.
19 September 1941
The Search for Susie George A. Birmingham; *Northbridge Rectory* Angela Thirkell; *The Quiet Place* D.M. Large; *Frenchman's Greek* Daphne du Maurier; *The Blind Man's House* Hugh Walpole.
3 October 1941
The Sun is my Undoing Marguerite Steen; *Handsome Johnnie* Frances Lobb; *Cholly Clover* Reginald Pound.
17 October 1941
To Sing With the Angels Maurice Hindus; *Sophia* St John Ervine; *Conquer* John Masefield.
31 October 1941
A Garden Enclosed Winifred Peck; *Delayed Action* Hugh McCraw; *The Best Laid Schemes* Barbara Goolden; *Love Story* by Ernest Borneman.
14 November 1941
The Empty Room Charles Morgan; *Faro's Daughter* Georgette Heyer; *The Man in Grey* Lady Eleanor Smith; *Beckoning Ridge* Emerson Waldman.
21 November 1941
A Lady's Child Enid Starkie.
28 November 1941
Percy Wallingford and Mr Pidger Lord Berners; *Two Days in Aragon* M.J. Farrell; *June to September* Frances Harris; *Dagger of the Mind* Kenneth Fearing.
12 December 1941

A Man's Place Ramon J. Sender; *Mo Burdekin* Sarah Campion; *The Rich House* Stella Gibbons.

26 December 1941

The Vulgar Streak Wyndham Lewis; *Count Omega* Lord Berners; *London Pride* Phyllis Bottome.

9 January 1942

English Story Woodrow and Susan Wyatt (eds); *Boo* Peter de Polnay; *Blind Messenger* Joanna Cannan; *You Can't Be Too Careful* H.G. Wells.

23 January 1942

Seven Tempest Vaughan Wilkins; *A Common Enemy* J.D. Beresford; *I Ordered a Table for Six* Noel Streatfield; *Singing Tree* Kathleen Wallace.

6 February 1942

The Black Milestone Catherine Gavin; *A Different Drummer* Margot Arnold; *Inexperience* Edward Knoblock.

20 February 1942

H.M. Pulham Esquire John P. Marquand; *And One Was Beautiful* Alice Duer Miller; *Under New Management* Naomi Jacob.

6 March 1942

Lost Fields Michael McLaverty; *Period Piece* Frances Gray; *A Story to Tell* Peter Fleming.

20 March 1942

A Stricken Field Martha Gellhorn; *The Sword and the Net* Warren Stuart; *Ake and His World* Bertil Malmberg.

3 April 1942

Put Out More Flags Evelyn Waugh; *Saratoga Trunk* Edna Ferber; *Wakefield's Course* Mazo de la Roche.

17 April 1942

The Sword and the Sickle Mulk Raj Anand; *Musk and Amber* A.E.W. Mason; *Laugh at Polonius* Jack Hilton.

24 April 1942

Never No More Maura Laverty.

1 May 1942

Dragon Seed Pearl S. Buck; *Singapore River* Robert Payne; *Sunset Over France* Stephen Lister.

15 May 1942

Tiger, Tiger Max White; *The Family Pattern* Pamela Hansford Johnson; *So They Were Married* Mabel Constanduros; *Penny Lace* Hilda Lewis.

29 May 1942

A Leaf in the Storm Lin Yutang; *Bird of the Wilderness* Vincent Sheehan; *The Cage* Kathleen Bellamy; *God's Warrior* Patry Williams.

12 June 1942

The Brittle Glass Norah Lofts; *Distinguished Visitors* Lenore Glen Offord; *Mrs Appleyard's Year* Louise Andrews Kent.

26 June 1942

Growing Up and Other Stories Edward Gaitens; *Mr Buckby is Not at Home* John Gloag; *Miss England* Emmeline Morrison; *I Am the World* Peter Vansittart.

3 July 1942

Bowen's Court Elizabeth Bowen.

10 July 1942

The Moon is Down John Steinbeck; *Requiem for Robert* Mary Fitt; *Mrs Frensham Describes a Circle* Richmal Crompton.

24 July 1942

But We Are Exiles Elisabeth Kyle; *Scarlet Petticoat* Nard Jones; *Over the Border* George A. Birmingham; *The Nine Lives of Bill Nelson* Gerald Kersh.

7 August 1942

Financial Times Ronald Fraser; *Mrs Morel* M.H. Tiltman; *Our Little Town* Adelaide Phillpotts.

21 August 1942

Black-out in Gretley J.B. Priestley; *The Day Will Come* Lion Feuchtwanger; *Augusta Steps Out* Norah Hoult.

4 September 1942

Return Journey Beatrice Kean Seymour; *Enter Three Witches* D.L. Murray; *I Live Again* Warwick Deeping.

18 September 1942

A Finger in Every Pie Rhys Davies; *Anna* Norman Collins; *The Fighting Littles* Booth Tarkington; *The Killer and the Slain* Hugh Walpole.

2 October 1942

Lyndley Waters George R. Preedy; *The Siege of Malta* S. Fowler Wright; *Marling Hall* Angela Thirkell.

16 October 1942

The Greatest People in the World 'Flying Officer X'; *Not Me Sir* J.T.C. Pember; *The House of Mrs Caroline* C.M. Franzero; *A Time for Silence* André Maurois.

30 October 1942

Signed with Their Honour James Aldridge; *Bring Me My Bow* Maurice Moiseiwitsch; *Go Down, Moses* William Faulkner.

13 November 1942

To Be a Pilgrim Joyce Cary; *Grand Canyon* Vita Sackville West; *The Song of Bernadette* Franz Werfel; *Sweet Chariot* Frank Baker.

27 November 1942

Was There Love Once? Ernest Raymond; *Housebound* Winifred Peck; *Darkness Falls from the Air* Nigel Balchin.

11 December 1942

Ellen Rogers James T. Farrell; *Cross Creek* Marjorie Kinnan Rawlings; *The Green Curve Omnibus* Ernest Swinton; *Best Sporting Stories* J. Wentworth Day (ed.).

25 December 1942

The Fall of Paris Ilya Ehrenburg.

22 January 1943

We Shall Return Jack Lindsay; *Ding Doll Dell* Joan Morgan; *And Now Tomorrow* Rachel Field; *How Can We Sing?* Alexandra Dick; *The Cloven Pine* Frank Clare.

5 February 1943

The Edge of the Sword Vladimir Pozner; *Wife to Mr Milton* Robert Graves; *Daughter of Time* Nelia Gardner White.

5 March 1943

Mildensee Naomi Royde Smith; *Ticky* Stella Gibbons; *The Dead Look On* Gerald Kersch; *A Place in the Sun* Frank Fenton; *The Quick Brown Fox* W.R. Burnett; *Rabboni* Susan Miles.

19 March 1943

Long Division Hester Chapman; *The Day Must Dawn* Agnes Sligh Turnbull; *Polonaise* Doris Leslie.

2 April 1943

The Heart is a Lonely Hunter Carson McCullers; *A Time to Be Born* Dawn Powell; *This is the Road* Kathleen Wallace.

16 April 1943

The Just and the Unjust James G. Cozzens; *The Devil and King John* Philip Lindsay; *Somebody at the Door* Raymond Postgate.

30 April 1943

Frossia E.M. Almedingen; *Send Me Down* Henry Steig.

14 May 1943

Perelandra C.S. Lewis; *If Ever I Cease to Love* Frances P. Keyes; *Still as a Stranger* Marjorie Villiers.

28 May 1943

The Ministry of Fear Graham Greene; *The Ship* C.S. Forester, *Escape into the Past* George Slocombe.

11 June 1943

Scene for Death Norah Hoult; *Upside Down* Denis Mackail; *A Matter of Duty* Edward Cranston.

25 June 1943

Daylight on Saturday J.B. Priestley; *The Serpent* Neil M. Gunn; *O Western Wind* Honor Croome.

9 July 1943

The River of Life Alexander Kuprin; *The Alphabet* Annabel Farjeon; *They Came to London* Paul Tabori; *Along These Streets* Struthers Burt.

23 July 1943

A Curtain of Green Eudora Welty; *The Signpost* E. Arnot Robertson; *Hell on the Way* James M. Fox.

6 August 1943

A Garland of Straw Sylvia T. Warner; *Daniel Cavour* E.S. Evans; *Rainbow* Wanda Wassilewska.

20 August 1943

The Returning Heart Dorothy Charques; *Green Hands* Barbara Whitton; *Mean Sensual Man* Stephen McKenna.

3 September 1943

Within the Cup Phyllis Bottome; *Pride of the Family* Rosalind Wade; *The Music goes Round* Margery Maitland Davison.

17 September 1943

Valiant Dust Margaret Mackprang Mackay; *Wolf on the Fold* Nellise Child; *So Near To Heaven* Mary Lutyens.

1 October 1943

None but the Lonely Heart Richard Llewellyn; *Alvina Foster* Josephine Bell; *Sunset Over Soho* Gladys Mitchell; *Aesop* A.D. Wintle.

15 October 1943

Cloudless May Storm Jameson; *The Human Comedy* William Saroyan; *The Darkening Hill* Helen Hull.

29 October 1943

Gideon Planish Sinclair Lewis; *The Time Between* Gale Wilhelm; *Sun Over the Palms* Paschoal Carlos Magno.

12 November 1943

The Mighty Years Iris Morley; *Alone We Embark* Maura Laverty.

26 November 1943

Arrival and Departure Arthur Koestler.
10 December 1943
Comedy in Chains Dennis Gray Stoll; *The Small Back Room* Nigel
   Balchin.
24 December 1943
The People Immortal Vassili Grossman; *The Barricades* Philip
   Toynbee.
7 January 1944
The White Mare Michael McLaverty; *Mildred Pierce* James M.
   Cain; *Grig in Retirement* H.B. Creswell.
21 January 1944
The Darkening Meridian Richard March; *Fables from Russia* Ivan
   Krilov; *The Magic Jacket and Other Stories* Walter de la Mare;
   Myra Carrol Noel Streatfield.
4 February 1944
A Family and a Fortune Ivy Compton-Burnett; *The Unbroken Heart*
   Robert Speaight; *No Star Is Lost* James T. Farrell; *The City Lies
   Foursquare* Edith Pargeter.
18 February 1944
Mad Grandeur Oliver St John Gogarty; *Ugly Anna and Other Tales*
   A.E. Coppard; *Green Afternoon* Margaret Duley.
3 March 1944
A Haunted House and Other Stories Virginia Woolf; *The Devil in
   Crystal* Louis Marlow; *News for Heaven* Jeffrey Dell; *Let Thy
   Moon Arise* Anna Sebastian.
17 March 1944
The Sea Eagle James Aldridge; *We Poor Shadows* Hermynia zur
   Muhlen; *The Educated Pin* Marjorie Mack.
31 March 1944
The Grand Design David Pilgrim; *Sydney Duck* Eric Baume; *On the
   Edge of the Sea* F.L. Green.
14 April 1944
Laura Vera Caspary; *Being Met Together* Vaughan Wilkins.
28 April 1944
The Heart of Jade Salvador de Madariaga; *People Apart* L.T.
   Shortell.
12 April 1944
Number One John Dos Passos; *99%* John Gloag; *Katherine
   Christian* Hugh Walpole.
26 May 1944

Crab Apple Jelly Frank O'Connor; *The Long Ago and Other Stories* Mary Lavin.

9 June 1944

The Trespassers Laura Z. Hobson; *The Hours and the Centuries* Peter de Mendelssohn; *Many Sided Mirror* Joan Morgan.

23 June 1944

Young Tom Forrest Reid; *The Barber's Trade Union and Other Stories* Mulk Raj Anand; *Sweet Is the Rose* Helen Douglas Irvine.

7 July 1944

Pity My Simplicity Chris Massie; *The Looking-Glass* William March; *Cluny Brown* Margery Sharp.

21 July 1944

The Razor's Edge W. Somerset Maugham; *So Linked Together* Michael Harrison; *This Marriage* Edith Roberts.

4 August 1944

Stephen Hero James Joyce; *The Musk Ox and Other Tales* N.S. Leskov; *Fidus Achates* George Baker.

18 August 1944

Where Helen Lies Margaret Lane; *The Wood and the Trees* Mary Mitchell; *Sunrise to Sunset* Adrian Bell.

1 September 1944

The Horse's Mouth Joyce Cary; *The Friendly Young Ladies* Mary Renault; *The Spinners of Silk* Hsiao Ch'ien.

15 September 1944

Yeoman's Hospital Helen Ashton; *The Devil Held the Aces* Patrick Doncaster; *The Close Game* Elizabeth Delehanty.

29 September 1944

The Power House Alex Comfort.

13 October 1944

The Black Venus Rhys Davies; *The Bachelor* Stella Gibbons.

27 October 1944

Simone Lion Feuchtwanger; *A Bomb and a Girl* Hugh Shearman; *Bombardier.* Stephen Gilbert.

24 November 1944

A Walk in the Sun Harry Brown; *There's No Story There* Inez Holden; *Fair Stood the Wind for France* H.E. Bates.

8 December 1944

Two Mirrors Peter de Polnay; *The Cup of Astonishment* Vera T. Mirsky; *Love on the Supertax* Marghanita Laski.

22 December 1944

Avalanche Kay Boyle; *No More Than Human* Maura Laverty.
19 January 1945
Dasha E.M. Almedingen; *The Journey Home* Robert Henriques; *The Water Music* Glyn Jones.
2 February 1945
Now I Lay Me Down to Sleep Ludwig Bemelmans; *The Transplanted* Frederick Niven; *St Felix '39* Jeanne Gosse.
16 February 1945
Home is the Hunter Gontran de Poncins; *Ladies May Now Leave Their Machines* Diana Murray Hill; *The Sighing of the Heart* Maritta Wolff.
2 March 1945
The Story of Ragged Robyn Oliver Onions; *My Days of Anger* James T. Farrell; *In Youth Is Pleasure* Denton Welch.
16 March 1945
The Forty Days Franz Werfel; *The Commodore* C.S. Forester.
30 March 1945
Time Must Have a Stop Aldous Huxley; *A Bell for Adano* John Hersey.
13 April 1945
Odd Man Out F.L. Green; *Descent from Nowhere* Reyner Barton; *The Steep Ascent* Anne Morrow Lindbergh.
27 April 1945
Chronicle of Dawn Ramon J. Sender; *Gone for a Burton* Arthur Gwynn-Browne; *Aunt Ailsa* Jean Ross.
11 May 1945
The Wide Net and Other Stories Eudora Welty; *The Lost Week-End* Charles Jackson.
25 January 1946
The Collected Stories of Katherine Mansfield.
1 March 1946
The Trip to London Rhys Davies; *What Farrer Saw* James Hanley; *One Fair Daughter* Bruno Frank.
15 March 1946
Three William Sansom; *Carp Country* Elizabeth Kyle; *Appassionata* C.M. Franzero.
29 March 1946
Yes, Farewell Michael Burn; *Titus Groan* Mervyn Peake; *Sally Park* Margaret Hassett.
12 April 1946
Cass Timberlane Sinclair Lewis; *We Are Besieged* Barbara Fitzgerald;

The King's General Daphne du Maurier; *False World, Goodnight* Mary Leigh.

26 April 1946

A Woman of the Pharisees François Mauriac; *The Gypsy's Baby and Other Stories* Rosamund Lehmann.

10 May 1946

Twelve Stories Steen Steensen Blicher; *Bottle's Path and Other Stories* T. F. Powys; *First One and Twenty* John Gloag.

24 May 1946

Auto-Da-Fé Elias Canetti; *Swing Low* Edwin A. Peeples; *Prodigal Giver* Susan Glaspell.

7 June 1946

The Moonlight Joyce Cary; *Sons of the Morning* Otto Schrag; *Selected Tales* A.E. Coppard.

21 June 1946

Land Liam O'Flaherty; *Bright Day* J.B. Priestley; *Country Beat* Louis Quinain.

5 July 1946

A Summer Day and Other Stories Kate Roberts; *The Devil in Woodford Wells* Harold Hobson; *Remember Me* Edward F. Meade.

19 July 1946

The Heretics Humphrey Slater; *They Grew in Beauty* Caroline Seaford; *Candles to the Dawn* Vian C. Smith.

2 August 1946

More Fellow-Countrymen J.T. Farrell; *A Winter in Geneva* Anne Goodwin Winslow; *Tomorrow's Another Day* W.R. Burnett; *Little Jo* Robert Bright.

16 August 1946

Aurelien Louis Aragon; *Dragon Harvest* Upton Sinclair; *On My Faithless Arm* John Kovack.

30 August 1946

Judgement in Suspense Gerald Bullett; *House Under Mars* Norah Hoult; *No Promise in Summer* Elizabeth Evelyn.

13 September 1946

Rogue Elephant Walter Allen; *Silver Fountain* Dorothy Mackinder; *The Jug* Barnaby Brook; *The Trouble With Yesterday* Maurice Levinson; *Thanks God! I'll Take It from Here* Jane Allen and M. Livingstone.

27 September 1946

Deborah Esther Kreitman; *Uninvited Guests* Parr Cooper.

11 October 1946
The Blue Danube Ludwig Bemelmans; *Palladian* Elizabeth Taylor; *Madame Benoit's Secret* Charles Lascelles.
25 October 1946
The Stormy Dawn Mark Freshfield; *Of Our Time* James Gordon; *Falcon* Clifford Hornby; *The River Road* Frances Parkinson Keyes.
8 November 1946
Children of Vienna Robert Neumann; *The Great Promise* Noel Houston; *Doctor Carmichael* Juliet Rhys-Williams; *Roger Sudden* Thomas H. Raddall.
29 November 1946
Thieves in the Night Arthur Koestler; *Back* Henry Green; *A Foolish Wind* Francis Askham.
13 December 1946
Suzanne and Joseph Pasquier Georges Duhamel; *A Stroll Before Sunset* Rachel Ferguson; *King Jesus* Robert Graves.
20 December 1946
All For Hecuba Micheál Mac Liammóir.
3 January 1947
Dangling Man Saul Bellow; *The Angel with the Trumpet* Ernst Lothar; *Three Colours of Time* Anatoli Vinogradov.
24 January 1947
The Flight and the Song S.M.C. and L.M. Anderson; *The Faithless Mirror* Honor Croome; *The Haunted Woman* Davis Lindsay.
21 March 1947
Children of Wrath Edmund Buchet; *Medusa* E.H. Visiak; *The Web and the Rock* Thomas Wolfe.
18 April 1947
Somewhat Angels David Cornel Dejong; *The Horizontal Man* Helen Eustis; *The Passion Left Behind* Lewis Masefield; *The Adventures of Wesley Jackson* William Saroyan.
2 May 1947
Sainte Colline Gabriel Chevallier; *Two Names upon the Shore* Susan Ertz; *Mally Lee* Elisabeth Kyle; *The Far Away Music* Arthur Meeker.
23 May 1947
Beautiful Friend Richard Collier; *Before the Crossing* Storm Jameson; *Peal of Ordnance* John Lodwick; *A Summer in Buenos*

Aires Isobel Strachey.

6 June 1947
Passengers of Destiny Louis Aragon; *The Bitter Box* Eleanor Clark; *Where Freedom Perished* Hilda Monte.
1 August 1947
The Song in the Green Thorn Tree James Barke; *The Song and the Silence* Morchard Bishop; *Eustace and Hilda* L.P. Hartley.
12 September 1947
Lord, I Was Afraid Nigel Balchin; *Georgia Boy* Erskine Caldwell; *Mrs Mike* Benedict and Nancy Friendman; *Silver Nutmeg* Norah Lofts.
7 November 1947
Square Pegs Constance Butler; *Letters to a Sister* Christopher Hollis; *The Sound of Years* Merriam Model; *Galanty Show* Douglas Reed; *You Can't Go Home Again* Thomas Wolfe.
18 January 1952
Joachim of Babylon Mannix Gijsen; *Sylvester* Edward Hyams; *The Day of the Locust* Nathanael West.
8 February 1952
Colette on Animals Colette.
22 February 1952
The Mill on the Po Riccardo Bacchelli.
25 April 1952
A Matter of Conscience Werner Bergengruen.

IRISH TIMES 'LONG DISTANCE' COLUMN

8 May 1967: 'Exile and detachment in Kentish pastures'
3 June 1968: 'Government by students'
21 April 1969: 'Long distance'
5 May 1969: 'Taking Ireland as a joke'
19 May 1969: 'Proud self-dismissal by De Gaulle'
2 June 1969: 'De Gaulle in land of magic'
7 July 1969: 'The Prince's questioning face under the coronet'
18 August 1969: 'Glasgow – city of misery'
1 September 1969: 'Thinking about Ulster'
15 September 1969: 'That Peace Line'
5 January 1970: 'That Peace Line, continued'
2 March 1970: 'The great BBC row'

16 March 1970: 'Long distance'
28 April 1970: 'Long distance'
She also wrote the 'Long distance' column on the following dates:
2 May 1970, 11 May 1970, 25 May 1970, 27 July 1970, 6 September
    1970, 19 October 1970, 2 November 1970, 12 November 1970,
    3 May 1971, 17 May 1971.

SELECT BIBLIOGRAPHY

Adams, Michael. *Censorship: The Irish Experience* (Dublin: Scepter Books, 1968).

Blakelock, Denys. *Around The Next Corner* (London: Camelot Press, 1967).

Brown, Terence. *Ireland: A Social and Cultural History 1922–2002* (London: Harper Perennial, 2004)

Carlson, Julia. *Banned In Ireland* (London: Routledge, 1990).

Carr, Raymond. *Modern Spain* (Oxford: Oxford University Press, 1980).

Cline, Sally. *Radclyffe Hall: A Woman Called John* (London: John Murray, 1997).

Cronin, John. *The Anglo-Irish Novel* (Belfast: Appletree Press, 1990).

Dalsimer, Adele. *Kate O'Brien: A Critical Study* (Dublin: Gill and Macmillan, 1990).

Delafield, E.M. *The Diary of A Provincial Lady* (London: Virago, 1984).

—. *Late and Soon* (London: Macmillan and Co., 1943).

Dunn, Jane. *Antonia White, A Life* (London: Jonathan Cape, 1998).

Faderman, Lilian. *Surpassing the Love of Men* (London: The Women's Press, 1981).

Fallon, Brian. *An Age of Innocence* (Dublin: Gill and Macmillan, 1999).

Fitzpatrick, David. *Harry Boland's Irish Revolution* (Cork: Cork University Press, 2003).

Fitzsimons, Christopher. *The Boys* (Dublin: Gill and Macmillan, 1994).

Hall, Radclyffe. *The Well of Loneliness* (London: Virago, 1982).

Hamilton, Sir George, *Essays by Divers Hands* (London: Oxford University Press, 1955).

Hanson, Ellis. *Decadence and Catholicism* (London: Harvard University Press, 1997).

Hartley, Jenny. *Millions Like Us* (London: Virago 1997).

Jordan, John. *Collected Poems* (Dublin: Dedalus, 1991).

—. *Collected Stories* (Dublin: Dedalus, 1991)

—. *The Stony Thursday Book* (Limerick, n.p., n.d.).

Kelly, A.A. (ed.) *Pillars of the House* (Dublin: Wolfhound, 1987).

Keogh, Dermot. *Twentieth-century Ireland* (Dublin: Gill and Macmillan, 1994).

—. *Jews In Twentieth-century Ireland* (Cork: Cork University Press, 1998).

Kiberd, Declan. *Inventing Ireland* (London: Jonathan Cape, 1995).

—. *Irish Classics* (London: Granta, 2000).

Lavelle, Patricia. *James O'Mara* (London: Burns and Oates, 1961).

Laverty, Maura. *No More Than Human* (London: Longmans, 1944).

Lennox-Conyngham, Melosina. *Diaries of Ireland* (Dublin: The Lilliput Press, 1998).

Logan, John (ed.) *With Warmest Love* (Limerick: Mellick Press, 1994).

Luce, Clare Boothe. *Saints For Now* (London and New York: Sheed and Ward, 1952).

McCormack.W.J. *Sheridan LeFanu and Victorian Ireland* (Dublin: Lilliput, 1991).

Macardle, Dorothy. *The Irish Republic* (London: Corgi, 1968).

MacIntyre, James. *Three Men on an Island* (Belfast: Blackstaff Press, 1996).

McCartney, Donal. *UCD, A National Idea* (Dublin: Gill and Macmillan, 1999).

Maranon, Gregorio. *Antonio Perez* (London: Hollis and Carter, 1954).

Mills, W.H. *The Manchester Guardian* (London: Chatto and Windus, 1921).

Norman, Sylvia. *Contemporary Essays* (London: Elkin Mathews and Marot, 1933).

Powell, Violet. *The Life of a Provincial Lady* (London: Heinemann, 1988).

Preston, Paul. *Franco* (London: HarperCollins, 1993).

Renier, Gustaaf. *The English, Are They Human?* (London: Williams and Norgate, 1931).

—. *He Came To England: A Self-portrait* (London: Peter Davies, 1933).

—. *Oscar Wilde* (London: Peter Davies, 1933).

Renier, Olive. *Before The Bonfire* (Warwick: Drinkwater, 1984).

Reynolds, Lorna. *Kate O'Brien, A Literary Portrait (*Gerrards Cross: Colin Smythe, 1987).

Richardson, Joanna. *Enid Starkie* (London: John Murray, 1973).

St John, John. *A Century of Publishing* (London: Heinemann, 1990).

Sherard, Robert. *André Gide's Wicked Lies About the Late Oscar Wilde (*Corsica: Vindex, 1933).

Starkie, Enid. A *Lady's Child (*London: Faber and Faber, 1941).

Walshe, Eibhear. (ed.). *Ordinary People Dancing, Essays on Kate O'Brien (*Cork: Cork University Press, 1993).

—. *Sex, Nation and Dissent* (Cork: Cork University Press, 1997).

Ward, Margaret. *Hanna Sheehy Skeffington* (Dublin: Attic Press, 1990).

White, Antonia. *Diaries, 1958–1979* (London: Constable, 1992).

Wickham, Anna. *The Writings of Anna Wickham* (London: Virago, 1984).

Wishart, Michael. *High Diver* (London: Blond and Briggs, 1977).

SELECTED ARTICLES/ESSAYS ON KATE O'BRIEN

R. Ahern, 'Laurel Hill, A French Foundation'. *Old Limerick Journal*, 25, (Summer 1989), p. 129.

Eavan Boland, 'Kate O'Brien', *The Irish Times* (24 August 1973).

—. 'That lady, A profile of Kate O'Brien', *The Critic*, 34 (February 1974).

—. 'Daughter of the middle-classes', *The Irish Times* (27 February 1987).

—. 'Kate O'Brien', *The Stony Thursday Book*, 7 [Limerick., n.p., n.d., pp. 46–8.

—. 'Preface' to The *Anteroom* (Dublin: Arlen House, 1980).

Mary Carr, 'Taking a fresh look at Kate O'Brien', *The Irish Times* (28 November 1988).

Adele M. Dalsimer, 'A not so simple saga, Kate O'Brien's *Without My Cloak*', *Eire Ireland* (21 March 1986), pp. 55–71.

Emma Donoghue, 'Noises from the woodshed', in S. Raitt (ed.), *Volcanoes and Pearl Divers* (London, Onlywomen Press, 1989).

Irish Times 'Obituary' (14 August 1974).

Joanne Glasgow, 'What's a nice lesbian like you doing in the church of Torquemada', in J. Glasgow (ed.), *Lesbian* Texts and Contexts (London: Onlywomen Press, 1992).

John Jordan, 'Kate O'Brien, A note on her themes', *The Bell* (19 February 1954).

—. 'Kate O'Brien, First Lady of Irish letters', *Hibernia* (11 May 1973).

—. 'A passionate talent', *Hibernia* (30 August 1974).

Jim Kemmy,' Kate O'Brien's Limerick', *Old Limerick Journal*, 17 (Winter 1984), p. 39.

Benedict Kiely, Preface to *The Last of Summer* (Dublin, Arlen House, 1981).

Aintzane Legarreta-Mentxaka, 'Girl meets politics – The "Don Pablo" chapter in Kate O'Brien's Mary Lavelle' (Dublin: PaGes Publication of the Faculty of Arts , UCD, December 2005).

Eamon Maher, 'Love and the loss of faith in the novels of Kate O'Brien.' *Crosscurrents and Confluences (*Dublin, Veritas 2000).

Vivian Mercier, 'Kate O'Brien', *Irish Writing*, 1 (1946).

Seamus O'Cinneide, 'Kate O'Brien's pride in Limerick achievements', *Limerick Leader* (24 August 1974).

Séan O'Faoláin, 'Standards and Taste', *The Bell*, 2, 3 (June 1941).

Terence McQueen, 'Meet Kate O'Brien' *The Word* (September 1966).

Rose Quiello, 'Disturbed desires: the hysteric in *Mary Lavelle*', *Eire Ireland*, 5 (1990).

Lorna Reynolds, 'The image of Spain in the novels of Kate O'Brien', in W. Zack and H. Kosok (eds), *National Images and Stereotypes*, (Tubingen: Gunter Narr, 1988).

Lorna Reynolds, 'Kate O'Brien and her "Dear Native Place"', *Ireland of the Welcomes* 39, 5 (September–October 1990), pp. 33–6.

Medb Ruane, 'Women's work is rarely done', *Sunday Times*. (23 February 1997).

Joan Ryan, 'Class and creed in the novels of Kate O'Brien', M. Harmon (ed.), *The Irish Writer and the City* (Gerrards Cross: Colin Smythe, 1984).

Liz Stanley, 'Does it matter if they did it?' *Women's History Review*, 1, 2 (1992), p. 197.

Caroline Walsh, 'In search of Kate O'Brien', *The Irish Times* (14 August 1981).

Eibhear Walshe, 'How soon is now?', *Graph*, No. 4 (1988).

Ann Weekes Owens, 'Kate O'Brien' *Irish Women Writers*, (Lexington, KY: University Press of Kentucky, 1990).

REVIEWS OF KATE O'BRIEN'S NOVELS/PLAYS

Michael Campbell, review of *As Music and Splendour*, *The Irish Times* (1 March 1958).

Austin Clarke, review of *The Land of Spices*, Vol. 2, April 1941 *The Bell* (vol. 2, no 1, April 1941), pp. 93–5.

Patricia Craig, review of *Mary Lavelle*, *Times Literary Supplement* (1 June 1984), p. 623.

—, review of *That Lady*, Times Literary Supplement (5 July 1985).

Teresa Deevy, review of *Teresa of Avila*, *Irish Writing* (March 1952).

The Dublin Magazine, review of *Without My Cloak* (October–December 1934), pp. 76–7.

Helen Fletcher, review of *The Ante-Room*, *Time and Tide* (25 August 1934), pp. 1056–7.

Robert J. Graf Jr., review of *As Music and Splendour*, *Chicago Tribune* (15 June 1958).

John Hampson, review of *The Last of Summer*, *The Spectator* (9 April 1943), pp. 344–6.

Robert C. Healey, review of *As Music and Splendour*, *New York Herald Tribune* (15 June 1958), Section 6, 1.

Irish Bookman, review of *That Lady* (January 1947), pp. 56–7.

John Jordan, review of *The Flower of May*, in 'Some books of the month', *The Bell*, 19, 2 (January 1954), pp. 53–9.

—, review of *My Ireland University Review*, 3, 2 (1962), pp. 72–4.

Maura Laverty, review of *The Ante-Room*, *The Irish Book Lover*, (September–October 1934), pp. 120–1.

Manchester Guardian, review of *Without My Cloak* (11 December 1931), p. 12.

Father and son. Review of *Without My Cloak* by Lilian Arnold. *John O'London Weekly* (19 December 1931), p. 491.

Sylvia Lynd, review of *Without My Cloak*, *The Book Society News* (December 1931), pp. 1–2.

John Marks, 'Crumbling castle in Spain', review of *Farewell Spain*, *The Spectator* (27 April 1937), p. 357.

Dorothy McArdle, review of *As Music and Splendour*, *Irish Times* (12 April 1958).

Eugene McCabe, review of *The Flower of May*, *Irish Writing* (25 December 1953), p. 64.

William Plomer, review of *The Ante-Room*, *The Spectator* (3 August 1934), p. 172.

Peter Quennell, review of *The Ante-Room, New Statesman and Nation* (4 August 1934), p. 155.

Lorna Reynolds, review of *That Lady, Dublin Magazine*, 21, 3, (July–September 1946), pp. 55–6.

Naomi Royde Smith, review of *That Lady, Time and Tide* (25 May 1946), pp. 494–6.

The Spectator, review of *The Land of Spices* (14 February 1941), p. 184.

The Tatler, review of *Without My Cloak*, 1731 (29 August 1934).

Time and Tide, review of *The Land of Spices* (22 February 1941).

The Times, review of *As Music and Splendour* (3 April 1958), p. 13.

The Times, review of television adaptation of *That Lady* (10 July 1961).

P.C.T., review of *Pray for the Wanderer, Irish Book Lover*, (November–December 1938), pp. 69–70.

Evelyn Waugh, review of *Pray for the Wanderer, The Spectator* (29 April 1938), p. 768.

William Whitebait, review of *The Last of Summer* by Kate O'Brien and John Perry, *New Statesman and Nation* (17 June 1944), p. 404.

Index

Agate, James 40
Annie (Smith) 111
Areilza, Dr. Enrique 29
Areilza, José Mariá 28, 29, 30–1
Arlen House 148
Ashurst Bank, Kent 42, 44, 141
Association of Professional and
  Business Women 75
At-Swim-Two-Birds (Flann
  O'Brien) 70
Aunt Annie (maternal aunt) 11,
  24, 28
Avila, Spain 72, 131, 136

Barnes, Djuna 49
Barney, Natalie 55
BBC 98, 100, 108, 117, 127, 142
Becket, Samuel 70
Beecham, Audrey 54
Before the Bonfire (Olive Renier)
  33
The Bell 1, 89, 119
Bernhardt, Sarah 121
Betjeman, John 96
Bilbao, Spain 28–30, 31, 72
Blackett, Anne 15, 16, 17–18, 19
Blakelock, Denys 59, 108
Boland, Eavan 142
Boland, Harry 27, 28
Boru House, Limerick 3, 6–7, 10,
  12, 20
Bosanquet, Theodora 41, 48–9
Boughton, Kent 139–40, 148
Bowen, Elizabeth 71, 96
Brideshead Revisited (Waugh) 50
Britain in Pictures (ed. Turner) 96
Broderick, John 76
Brontë, Emily 118
Brontë family 117, 118, 128
Buckingham Street, London 98
Burney, Fanny 97

Callaghan, Louise C. 148
Canada 146
Canterbury School of Art 142, 144
Casey, Kevin 142
Cassfield, Cass 125, 127
Castile, Spain 62, 72, 73, 103, 118
Catholicism
European Catholicism 15, 60, 77,
  86, 123
extremism 15
and homosexuality 49–50, 130
Irish Catholicism 15, 50, 60, 77,
  86
K.O'B.'s loss of belief 2, 14, 19,
  50, 106–7, 124
in novels of K.O'B. 14, 49, 50, 77,
  86, 106, 117–19, 130
views on K.O'B. 18, 68, 106, 118
Cecil, Lord David 97
Celtic Revival 16, 17, 71

Chauvire, Professor Roger 23
Chekhov, Anton 139
Clarke, Austin 23, 88, 144
The Collegians (Griffin) 76
COMES (European Community of
  Writers) 137, 139, 142
Connemara 112, 116–17, 123,
  124, 132, 135, 139 *see also*
  Roundstone
Connolly, Violet 23
Cork Tostal festival (1957) 119
Cornell, Katherine 59, 107
Croyle, Kentisbeare, Devon 99,
  100, 101
Curie, Marie 117, 121

Dalsimer, Adele 149
Dashwood, Paul (husband of E.M.
  Delafield) 99, 100
Dashwood, Rosamund (daughter
  of E.M. Delafield) 47, 100,
  101
de Valera, Eamon 21, 27, 28, 68,
  77
'The Dead' (Joyce) 77
Deevy, Teresa 118
Delafield, Elizabeth (E.M.) 46, 49,
  92, 98–100, 101, 102
The Diary of a Provincial Lady
  (Delafield) 99, 102
Donoghue, Emma 45, 49, 65, 130
Dostoevsky, Fyodor 127
du Maurier, Daphne 69

Easter Rising (1916) 17, 21, 22
Edgeworth, Maria 76, 119, 127
Edwards, Hilton 109–10, 120,
  143–4
El Escorial, Madrid 72, 76
El Greco 45
Eliot, George 117, 121
End Farm, Witney, Oxfordshire 81
Ervine, St. John 40
Esther's Altar (Smith) 111
European Community of Writers
  (COMES) 137, 139, 142
Evans, Charles 51
Evelyn, John 97
Evening Standard 127

The Falcon and the Hound (White)
  142
Fallon, Brian 50
Farjeon, Herbert 40, 96
Father and Sons (Turgenev) 127
Faversham Cemetery, Kent 147
Feehan, Fanny 128
Femina Vie Heureuse prize (1939)
  80
Ferrara, Italy 125, 126
'The First Class Omnibus' (ed.
  Gosse) 55

Flynn, Brendan 145
Fogarty, Anne 94, 130–1
For One Sweet Grape (That Lady)
  107
The Fort, Roundstone, Connemara
  113–14, 125
Francis Xavier, Saint 117, 118
Franco, General 71–2, 74–5
Frost in May (White) 142

Gadney, Margaret *see* Stephens,
  Margaret
Garbo, Greta 117, 121
Gardiner, Harold C. 106
'Generacion del 98' 29
Gibbon, Monk 89
Gielguid, John 95, 96
Gordon Square, Bloomsbury 45
Gosworth, Barbara 54, 80, 81, 99
Gosworth, John 54, 61, 92, 141
Great James Street, Bloomsbury
  37, 42, 54, 61, 77, 80, 81
Greene, Graham 70, 96
Grenfell, Joyce 115
Griffin, Gerald 76

Hall, Radclyffe 39, 47, 49
Hallett, David 34–5
Harcourt Cottage, Witney,
  Oxfordshire 81
Hart-Davis, Rupert 61
Haughey, Charles 141
Hawthornden prize (1932) 51
He Came to England (Renier)
  34–5, 36
Hemingway, Ernest 70
Hickey, Aunt (paternal aunt) 4,
  121
Hitchcock, Sylvia 140
homosexuality
and Catholicism 49–50, 130
in Ireland 109–10
K.O'B. on 35, 36, 45, 51, 88
Renier on 34, 35
see also lesbianism
Hopkin, Mary 145
Hughes, Jim and Kate 140, 147
Hunt, Hugh 145–6

Institute of the Blessed Virgin
  Mary, Hampstead 26
Irish Censorship Board 66, 67, 89,
  90
Irish Countrywomen's Association
  119
Irish Digest 119
Irish Times 1, 140–1
Irish Writing 119, 125–6
Italian Society, Limerick 127
Italy 111, 115, 125–6, 127, 137,
  142

James Tait Black prize (1932) 51
Jordan, John 21, 27
on birth of a child rumours 36
correspondence 58, 61, 120
and The Fort 114, 120
friendship with K.O'B. 109, 120–1
on K.O'B.'s lesbianism 46
on K.O'B.'s work 74–5, 106, 110,
    120, 145
literary career 120, 121
tributes to K.O'B. 148, 149
Joyce, James 19, 76, 77, 142, 144

Kate O'Brien: A Critical Study
    (Dalsimer) 149
Kate O'Brien: A Literary Portrait
    (Reynolds) 149
'Kate O'Brien: First Lady of Irish
    Letters' (Jordan) 145
Kate O'Brien Weekend 46, 148
Kavanagh, Patrick 144
Keane, Sir John 89–90
Kelly, Orlaith 49
Kemmy, Jim 135
Kiberd, Declan 7, 14
Kiely, Benedict 61, 90–1
Kilkenny Literary and
    Bibliographical Society 134
Kilkenny Magazine 119

Late and Soon (Delafield) 100–1
Laurel Hill convent school,
    Limerick 3, 8, 12–14, 15–18,
    19, 22
lesbianism
and Catholicism 49, 130
of K.O'B. 39, 41, 44, 45–7, 49
as romantic friendship 46–7
of Stephie 45
in works of K.O'B. 65–6, 129–31
see also homosexuality
Liddy, James 146
Liddy, John 149
Limerick 2–3, 6, 15, 134–5, 136
Limerick Pogrom (1904) 15
London 24, 26–7, 31, 37–8, 45,
    54, 61, 81
Lowndes, Marie Belloc 61
Lurie, Frieda 139
Lyons, Jennifer 147

MacIntyre, James 114–15
Mackenzie, Compton 35
Mac Liammoir, Mícheál 17, 48,
    109–10, 111, 120, 128, 143
MacSwiney, Terence 25, 29
Maginnis, Professor William 90
Manchester 25–6
Manchester Guardian 76
Manchester Guardian Weekly
    24–5, 26
Marks, John 73–4
McClintoc, Guthrie 59, 107
McDiarmid, Hugh 54
McGahern, John 146
McGill University, Montreal 146
McGuinness, Frank 66–7, 149
'Mellick' (Limerick) 12, 20
Mercier, Vivian 78, 107, 110

Moore, George 76
Mulkerns, Val 115

Naples, Italy 125, 126
National Concert Hall, Dublin 141
Nightwood (Barnes) 49

O'Brien, Clare (sister) 4, 9, 10, 12,
    24, 145
O'Brien, Donough (nephew) 11,
    140, 147, 148
O'Brien, Eric (brother) 4, 10–11
O'Brien, Flann (writer) 70
O'Brien, Gerry (brother) 4, 11, 24,
    135
O'Brien, Jack (brother) 4, 10, 24
O'Brien, John (nephew) 11, 140,
    145, 147, 148
O'Brien, Johnny (paternal uncle)
    93
O'Brien, Kate
banned in Ireland 2, 18, 66, 67–8,
    77, 78, 89–91
civil list pension 141–2
on Irish government 2, 77, 78,
    79–80, 86, 91
lesbianism of 39, 41, 44, 45–7, 49
money troubles 55, 80, 81, 98,
    112, 119, 124–5, 132
nomadic life 42, 81–2, 92, 132
not good at driving 115–16
popularity of her work 53–4,
    66–7, 95, 107, 128, 133–4,
    145, 148–9
public appearances 1, 128
radicalism 2, 49
rumoured to have had a child 36,
    37
writing methods 42–3, 77–8
during WWII 80, 81, 92–3, 94–5,
    96–8, 108
early life
anxiety about her father 3, 8–9
birth (3 December 1897) 2
Boru House 3, 6–7, 10, 12
death of her mother 3, 7, 8
hurt at being sent away 13
known as Katty (then Kitty) 2
at Laurel Hill convent school 3, 8,
    12–14, 15–18, 19, 22
learns Irish 17–18
loss of religious belief 2, 14, 19
family
background 2, 3–4, 5
relationships: with brothers 10,
    135; with father 3, 8–9, 13,
    138; with sisters 9–10, 27,
    132, 135, 139
personality and appearance 60–1
appearance: when young 23, 30,
    39, 61; in middle age 5, 102,
    115, 126, 134, 137; in old age
    142
detachment 14–15, 19, 22
imperious nature 115, 120
intelligence 23, 60–1
Irish accent 39, 98, 101, 110, 137
need for solitude 7, 20, 145
self-criticism 14, 15, 97

self-presentation 39, 59, 61, 133
social manner 60, 61, 113, 114,
    115, 142–3
style of dress 39, 47, 101–2, 134
career
assistant to Stephen O'Mara 27–8
early journalistic career 24–6
early writing career 37–8, 40, 41,
    42–3, 50–1, 54–5
governess in Bilbao 28–30, 31
secretary to Sunlight League 37, 42
teaching 26–7
university life 20, 21–4
end of her life
alcoholism 113, 124, 146
death and burial 147
ill-health 132, 144, 146–7
loneliness 145, 146
obituary 148
will 139, 148
relationships
Anna Wickham 54, 55
E.M. Delafield 46, 92, 98–102
Enid Starkie 82–4
Gustaaf Renier: marriage 31–2, 80,
    140; friendship 33, 36
Harry Boland 27, 28
John Jordan 61, 75, 109, 120–1
Laura Reynolds 109, 110–11;
    K.O.B. stays with 132; travels
    110–11, 125, 127, 142; visits
    K.O'B. 120, 124, 140
Mary O'Neill: letters 48; pet
    names for 48; relationship
    renewed 48; schooldays 26,
    27; travels 48–9, 62, 72, 73,
    126
Mícheál MacLiammoir 17, 109–10
Paul Smith 109, 111, 115
Stephie: K.O'B.'s fear of 45;
    K.O'B.'s first affair 44; travels
    44–5, 62, 72
plots and themes 43–4, 56–7, 60
art and transformation 43, 60, 64,
    128, 129, 138
beauty 5–6, 12, 42, 56–7, 63
Castile and austerity 62, 73, 103,
    118, 136
Catholicism 14, 49, 50, 77, 86,
    106, 117–19, 130
cultural nationalism 17, 18, 29,
    77, 119
education 84, 86, 87
Europe as civilising influence 77,
    84–5, 86, 87, 122, 123
family life 11, 19, 51, 52, 55–6,
    87, 122
female creativity 88, 97
female support 88, 124
Ireland and the Irish 91, 93,
    119–20, 141, 144
Irish class system: the bourgeoisie
    (middle-class) 2, 40, 76–7, 80,
    95, 116, 122, 138; landed
    gentry 123; peasant class 51,
    129
literary references 85–6, 94, 143
music and opera 58, 125, 127,
    128, 129, 138

nuns and holy women 13, 14, 19, 66, 73, 117–18, 123, 138
search for independence 14, 43, 60, 63, 85, 91, 122, 128–9
sex and passion 11–12, 43–4, 45, 59, 64–5, 87–8, 105, 136–7
sexual identity: homosexuality 35, 36, 45, 51, 88; lesbianism 65–6, 129–31; sexual freedom 50, 136
letters: Anna Wickham 55; Antonia White 142; Barbara Gosworth 80, 81, 99; Denys Blakelock 108; Frieda Lurie 139; John Gosworth 61, 92; John Jordan 58, 61, 120; Laura Reynolds 110; Mary O'Neill 48; May O'Brien 61, 136; Stephen O'Mara 68–9; Vivian Mercier 107
television and radio programmes: 'Between Ourselves' 119; literary reviews 98; 'Moscow Unforeseen' 139; 'My Kind of Poetry' 144; plays 98; on Roundstone and Connemara 116–17; *Self Portrait* 137–8; talk on Teresa of Avila 73; 'Thought for the Day' 142; tribute to E.M.Delafield 100; *Woman's Hour* 98, 117; 'Yeats' Country' 142
works
biography: *St. Francis Xavier* 118–19; *Teresa of Avila* 73, 118
essays: 'Aunt Mary in the parlour' 133; *Contemporary Essays* 54; 'English Diaries and Journals 96–7; on George Eliot 117, 121; on George Sand 117, 121; on Greta Garbo 117, 121; on Madame Recamier 121; on Marie Curie 117, 121; 'Memories of a Catholic education' 3, 16; 'Return in Winter' 54; on Sarah Bernhardt 121; on St. Francis Xavier 118–19; on Teresa of Avila 117; 'Writers of Letters' 117
films: life of Mary Magdalen 108; *Talk of Angels (Mary Lavelle)* 66–7, 149; *That Lady* 75, 108, 121
journalism: 'Brilliant Women' *(Woman and Beauty)* 121; 'Castile at a gallop' *(Observer)* 131; on Connemara *(Spectator)* 116; on emigration *(Irish Digest)* 119; 'Father's Christmas' *(Spectator)* 8, 127; 'Long Distance' *(Irish Times)* 140–1; 'Rome Relaxed' *(Spectator)* 131; 'Sister Lucy's remedy' *(Evening Standard)* 127; on Spain *(Manchester Guardian)* 127; on Turgenev *(University Review)* 127;

'Writing in Spain' *(Observer)* 131
lectures/talks: 'The Brontës and Haworth' 128; on the Irish novel 144; on James Joyce 142, 144; on Spain 75, 119, 141; on Teresa of Avila 128; 'The writing of imaginative prose' 145; on the tradition of Anglo-Irish prose 146; on Turgenev 127
literary reviews 69, 77, 119, 140; *Annie* 111; *Bowen's Court* 71; *The Grapes of Wrath* 70; *To Have and Have Not* 70; *A Lady's Child* 70, 83; *Murphy* 70; *The Power and The Glory* 70
memoirs: *Presentation Parlour* 3, 4, 8–9, 14, 24, 93, 133, 138–9; 'Recollections of childhood' 6, 9
novels: 'Constancy' (unfinished) 39, 50, 55–9, 107, 132, 133, 142, 143–4; *The Flower of May* 7, 19, 121–4; *The Land of Spices* 13, 14–15, 16, 17, 19, 33, 36, 50, 81, 84–90, 92; *The Last of Summer* 92, 93–6; *Mary Lavelle* 2, 29, 31, 62–7, 68–9, 72, 77, 136; *As Music and Splendour* 11, 19, 22, 119, 124, 125, 127, 128–31; *Pray for the Wanderer* 43, 77, 78–80; *That Lady* 1, 5–6, 42, 43, 75, 92, 102–7; *Without My Cloak* 3, 11, 33, 44, 50–4, 107
plays: *The Ante-Room* 59; *The Bridge* 38, 41; *Distinguished Villa* 25–6, 38–40, 41; *The Last of Summer* 95, 148; *The Silver Roan* 41; *Susannah and the Elders* 41–2; *That Lady* 11, 59, 98, 107–8, 111–12; *Without My Cloak* 98, 142
poems: 'Jay's Hackles, Mallard's Wing and Pheasant's Tail' 109
short fiction: 'A bus from Tivoli' 126–7, 136; 'A view from Toledo' 136; 'Chrissie's First Confession' 117; *A Fit of Laughing* 119; 'Golden Lady' 55; 'Overheard' 62
travel books: 'Dublin and Cork' (text) 134
travel writing: 'Andantino' 125–6; *Farewell Spain* 29, 30, 44–5, 48, 71–2, 73–4, 75; on Italy 125–6; *My Ireland* 2, 11, 22, 23, 134–6, 147; on Spain 75–6, 131
unpublished: 'Gloria Gish' (play) 42; life of Mary Magdalen (film) 108; 'Manna' (short story) 11–12
characters: Ana de Mendoza *(That Lady)* 42, 92, 102, 106, 107; Angele Kernahan *(The Last of*

Summer) 7, 92; Anna Murphy *(Land of Spices)* 13, 14–15; Clare Halvey *(As Music and Splendour)* 7, 119; Helen Archer *(Land of Spices)* 7, 16, 17, 36, 92; Henry Archer *(Land of Spices)* 33, 36; Mary Lavelle *(Mary Lavelle)* 7, 136
O'Brien, Katty (mother, née Thornhill) 2, 4, 7
O'Brien, May (sister) 4
beauty 5
death of 145
goes to London for work 24
in K.O'B.'s will 139
letters from K.O'B. 61, 136
relationship with K.O'B. 9–10, 12
and Stephie 44
takes over *Sunlight* from K.O'B. 37
O'Brien, Michael (brother) 4, 11, 24
O'Brien, Mother Patrick 18
O'Brien, Nance (sister, later Mrs Stephen O'Mara) 4
adopts Peter 36–7
attends Laurel Hill 12
buys Boughton for K.O'B. 139, 148
death 147
edits *Without My Cloak* for Fan Thornhill 19
K.O'B. visits 131, 132, 135
in K.O'B.'s will 139, 148
living in Washington 27
marries Stephen 24
and Mary O'Neill 49
relationship with K.O'B. 9, 10, 27, 132, 135, 139
and Stephie 44
widowed 131
O'Brien, Thomas (paternal grandfather) 3–4, 6
O'Brien, Tom (brother) 4, 10
O'Brien, Tom (father) 2, 3, 4, 8–9, 10, 20, 138
The Observer 131
O'Casey, Sean 40, 89
O'Connor, Frank 6, 15, 119
O'Dwyer, Dr. (Bishop of Limerick) 21
O'Faolain, Sean 89, 90, 119–20
O'Mara, Peter (son of Nance and Stephen) 36–7, 147, 148
O'Mara, Stephen (brother-in-law)
adopts Peter 36–7
on K.O'B.'s work 10, 68–9
marries Nance 24
on *Mary Lavelle* 68–9
and Mary O'Neill 49
political career 24, 27, 68
relationship with K.O'B. 10, 68
and Stephie 44
in Washington 27
O'Neill, Austin (Mary's nephew) 48
O'Neill, Betty (Mary's sister) 48
O'Neill, Bill (Mary's brother) 48
O'Neill, Elizabeth (Mary's mother)

26, 48, 92
O'Neill, Mary
artistic career 48
beauty 48, 73
Catholicism 49
contact with Renier 33, 48
corresponds with K.O'B. 48
early affection for K.O'B. 26, 27
at funeral 147
at Great James Street 54
illustrates K.O'B.'s books 48
K.O'B. gives Rimbaud's poems 143
K.O'B. stays with 132
as K.O'B.'s literary executor 148
in K.O'B.'s will 139, 148
paints Ruth Stephens 48
pet names 48
pupil of K.O'B. 26, 48
stays with Nance 49
and Stephie 49
travels with K.O'B. 48–9, 62, 72, 73, 126
visits Boughton 140
during WWII 96
Ordinary People Dancing: Essays on Kate O'Brien (Walshe) 149
Oscar Wilde (Renier) 33, 35, 48

PEN club 41, 61, 141
Pepys, Samuel 97
Perry, John 95
Philip II of Spain 72, 76, 103
in *That Lady* 75, 104, 105, 106, 108
A Portrait of the Artist as a Young Man (Joyce) 76, 144
Powell, Violet 46, 100
Presentation Convent, Limerick 18

Radio Éirann 73, 98, 116, 119, 139
Radio Telefís Éireann (RTÉ) 137–8, 142, 145, 148
Recamier, Madame 121
Renier, Gustaaf Johannes 31–6, 49, 80, 87, 140
Renier, Olive 32, 33, 34–5, 36
Reynolds, Laura 107–8, 149
on Enid Starkie 83
friendship with K.O'B. 109, 110–11
K.O'B. stays with 132
on K.O'B.'s alcoholism 124
on K.O'B.'s family ties 10
on K.O'B.'s marriage 32
poetry of 127
travels with K.O'B. 110–11, 125, 127, 142
visits K.O'B. 120, 124, 140
Richardson, Frank 109
Rimbaud, Arthur 143
The Romance of English Literature (ed. K.O'B.) 97

Rome, Italy 125, 126, 137, 142
Ros, Amanda McKitterick 79
Roundstone, Connemara 83, 113–16, 131, 144, 147
Royal Dublin Society 141
Royal Literary Fund grant (1938) 80
Royal Society of Literature 109, 117, 125

Sand, George 117, 121
Sappho 118
Scott, C.P. 24
Semple, George 140
Shaw, George Bernard 89
Sheehy Skeffington, Hannah 69
Sheridan, Margaret Burke 128
Smith, Paul 32, 107, 108, 109, 111, 115, 124, 146
Society of Jesus 118
Somerville and Ross 76
Soviet Union 139
Spain
  bullfighting 63–4, 73
  in *Farewell Spain* 29, 30, 44–5, 48, 71–2, 73–4, 75
  as a governess in Bilbao 28–30, 31, 62
  invited to lecture 145
  and Ireland compared 60
  K.O'B. lives for 6 months 135
  on K.O'B.'s works 75
  in lectures/talks 75, 119, 141
  love of 30, 62, 71–2
  with Mary 48–9, 62, 72, 73
  in *Mary Lavelle* 29, 59, 60, 62–6, 72
  on the Moors 73–4
  permission to revisit (1957) 127–8
  refused entry (1947) 74–5
  on Spanish men 72–3
  on Spanish women 73
  with Stephie and Ruth 44–5, 62, 72
  in *That Lady* 75
  as a tourist 44–5, 48–9, 61–2
  in travel writing 75–6, 131
  see also Castile
Spanish Civil War (1936-1939) 62, 71–2, 74
The Spectator
  journalism 1, 8, 116, 127, 137
  literary reviews 69, 77, 83, 98
Stansted Airport, Essex 141
Starkie, Enid 120, 124, 132
  book review 70, 83
  death 83–4, 141
  friendship with K.O'B. 82–4
  gives K.O'B. Rimbaud's poems 143
  K.O'B. mocks 83
  unconventional dress 83
Steinbeck, John 70
Stephens, Margaret (Stephie)

background 44
contact with Renier 33
feared by K.O'B. 45
lesbianism 45
and Mary O'Neill 49
reviewed by K.O'B. 70
travels with K.O'B. 44–5, 62, 72
visits Boughton 140
Stephens, Ruth 44, 62, 140
The Stony Thursday (ed. Jordan) 149
Stravaganza! (Smith) 115
Sunlight 37
Sunlight League 37, 42

Teresa of Avila, Saint 73, 74, 117–18, 136, 141, 142
Thornhill, Fan (maternal aunt) 5, 18, 19
Thornhill, Mary (maternal aunt) 5, 18
Thornhill, Patrick (maternal grandfather) 4, 5
Thornhill family 4–5
'Those Were the Days' (Mary Hopkin) 145
Thurston, Katherine Cecil 76
Time and Tide magazine 99
The Times 148
Tolstoy, Leo 127, 139
Tuairim Lecture, Limerick 144
Turgenev, Ivan 127
Turleigh, Veronica 37–8, 44

Unamuno, Miguel de 29, 62
University College, Dublin 21, 22, 127
University of Vallidolid, Spain 145
University Review 119, 127

Valle de los Caidos, Madrid 76
Venice, Italy 111, 115
Vida de la Princesa de Eboli (1877) 102
Virago 148

War of Independence 17, 21–2, 77
Washington, USA 27–8
Waugh, Evelyn 50
The Well of Loneliness (Hall) 39, 45, 47
White, Antonia 49, 124, 142
Whitebait, William 95–6
Wickham, Anna 54, 55
Winter Tales 142, 143
Wishart, Michael and Anne 113
With Warmest Love 148–9
Woman and Beauty 121
Wordsworth, Dorothy 97
World War II 80, 81, 92–3, 94–5, 96, 98, 108